STORY REVOLUTIONS

Cultural Frames, Framing Culture

Robert Newman, Editor
Justin Neuman, Associate Editor

STORY REVOLUTIONS

Collective Narratives from the Enlightenment to the Digital Age

HELGA LENART-CHENG

University of Virginia Press
CHARLOTTESVILLE AND LONDON

University of Virginia Press
© 2022 by the Rector and Visitors of the University of Virginia
All rights reserved
Printed in the United States of America on acid-free paper

First published 2022

9 8 7 6 5 4 3 2 1

Library of Congress Cataloging-in-Publication Data
Names: Lenart-Cheng, Helga, author.
Title: Story revolutions : collective narratives from the Enlightenment to the digital age / Helga Lenart-Cheng.
Description: Charlottesville : University of Virginia Press, 2022. | Series: Cultural frames, framing culture | Includes bibliographical references and index.
Identifiers: LCCN 2022028837 (print) | LCCN 2022028838 (ebook) | ISBN 9780813948386 (hardcover ; acid-free paper) | ISBN 9780813948393 (paperback ; acid-free paper) | ISBN 9780813948409 (ebook)
Subjects: LCSH: Autobiography—Social aspects. | Autobiography—Political aspects. | Community life.
Classification: LCC CT25 .L426 2022 (print) | LCC CT25 (ebook) | DDC 920—dc23/eng/20220720
LC record available at https://lccn.loc.gov/2022028837
LC ebook record available at https://lccn.loc.gov/2022028838

Cover art: alsongel/martinlubpl/Shutterstock.com; Valeriia Sivkova/istock.com/

To Paul

CONTENTS

	Acknowledgments	ix
	Introduction	1
1	Toward Collective Intimacy	13
2	Early Story Collections: Setting the Stage	38
3	Libraries of Human Experience	55
4	To-Gather in Time	81
5	To-Gather in Space	103
6	Stories and Statistics	125
	Postscript: Toward Algorithmic Collectives	149
	Notes	163
	Bibliography	197
	Index	215

ACKNOWLEDGMENTS

Writing a book is like experiencing a pandemic: it makes you realize how much you depend on others. As I write these lines in Covid-19 isolation, it brings me special joy to remember and acknowledge all whose generosity and kindness contributed to this book. I started writing about stories because my father was such an inspiring storyteller. He enchanted me with tales about impossible worlds and about possible changes to our existing world. Later I learned to distrust storytellers, especially those reciting the official narratives of the totalitarian regime I grew up in. But I never lost my admiration for the endless creativity and resilience of those who know that the "universe is made of stories, not of atoms" (in the words of Muriel Rukeyser). Before the pandemic, when I used to sit in cafés writing this book, people would often walk up to me and ask what I was working on. When I said, "I write about people's personal stories," random strangers would pull up a chair and share their most intimate experiences and secrets. Some made me promise to include them in my book, which I do now, in this general way, by acknowledging that every life is extraordinary in some way and that every story shared is a chance to make someone feel less alone.

In preparing this book, I have been sustained by the companionship and generosity of many. My professors in Hungary and France, Olga Penke, Ilona Kovács, Géza Szász, and Philippe Lejeune, opened my eyes to the joys of scholarly life and the idea that I could make a career out of studying dusty diaries found in attics. At Harvard, professors Christie McDonald, Marc Shell, Susan Rubin Suleiman, Judith Ryan, János Kornai, and John Stauffer showed unflinching support, even as I had the crazy idea of having three children in four years while writing my dissertation. Grandmothers and babysitters are rarely acknowledged in academic books, even though they make the impossible possible. Had my mother and mother-in-law not pushed around the stroller while I was in the archives, this book would not exist. I also acknowledge the cheerful assistance of all who took care of our children over the years, including Bernadett Török, Anna Mudrák, Anna Fritz, Judit Nahaj, Zsuzsanna Prommer, Klára Széll, and Irén Bereknyei.

Financial support came from Harvard University, Collegium Budapest, the Fulbright Commission, and Saint Mary's College of California. This publication was subsidized in part by Harvard Studies in Comparative Literature. My current institution, Saint Mary's College of California, supported my project in myriad ways. I benefited from the support of my two deans, Stephen Woolpert and Sheila Hassell Hughes, and the leadership of my department chairs, Costanza Gislon Dopfel, Catherine Marachi, Lori Spicher, Frances Sweeney, and Claude-Rhéal Malary. Costanza and Catherine showed me that kindness in academia is not a lost virtue, while Claude keeps reminding me of the meaning of a well-lived academic life. I also express appreciation here for my departmental colleagues, Maria Grazia De Angelis, David Bird, Jane Dilworth, Renee Egan, Caralinda Lee, Br. Michael Murphy, Alvaro Ramirez, María Luisa Ruiz, Naoko Uehara, and Ana Ramirez, as well as for my lunch crowd.

I feel particularly indebted to those who reviewed and commented on parts of the manuscript. Their time and willingness meant more than they could ever know. Among these readers were Maureen Wesolowski, Joan Halperin, Meghan Sweeney, Viktor Lénárt, Chad Arnold, Mira Cheng, David Arndt, Molly Metherd, Joseph Albernaz, Edit Kincses, Aaron Sachowitz, Dan Leopard, Sunayani Bhattacharya, Lambert Lénárt, Elizabeth Hamm, Aeleah Soine, Ioana Luca, Paul Cheng, Cary Schmelzer, Lisa Manter, and Julie Cheng. I also thank my friends and colleagues at the International Auto/Biography Association, the American Hungarian Educators Association, the MLA, the RMMLA and the University of Bordeaux, whose cheerful company and common interests make academia so much homier. I have been particularly inspired by the scholarship of my colleagues John Zuern, Leigh Gilmore, Paul John Eakin, Julie Rak, Sidonie Smith, Julia Watson, Ricia Chansky, Louise Vasvari, Anna Poletti, and Gillian Whitlock. My students, Abigail Starkovich and Mathilde Fugère, contributed countless hours to ensuring the references are complete. I remain grateful to librarians at various institutions, including Swetta Abeyta, Elise Y. Wong, and Stephen Stonewell, for helping me hunt down obscure references. My anonymous peer reviewers made generous comments and valuable suggestions, which I tried to follow as best I could. I am also grateful to the superb editorial team at the University of Virginia Press, including Angie Hogan. I hope that this revised version demonstrates how much I have learned from all their insights and comments. Naturally, I remain responsible for any mistakes still present.

My large circle of family and friends keeps reminding me of the only things that matter. They are too numerous for me to name them all, but I thank for years of inspiration Bernadett and Jean-Charles Van Pée, Katalin and Rajiv Kapoor, Teréz Hamvas, Dezi Hamvas, Monika Mayer, Éva Priegl, Kamilla György, Szilvia Oszkó, Edina Szabó, Beáta Gurmai, Zsófia Falus, Zsuzsanna Hatosné Kriszten, Ágnes Benedict, and Éva Szekeres, as well as the Rizika, von Nagy, Maxim, Andrada, Mellin, Laszlo, Csoboth, Kozek, Pigniczky-Gero, Bihari, Kincses-Tóth, Wetherbee, Larson, Hamvas, Deák, and Dopfel families. My immediate family, Mária Hamvas, Zoltán Lénárt, Liang-Tsai Cheng and Chun-Yeu Cheng, Viktor, Réka, Lambert, Kata, Zoltán, Boglárka, Kati, Ábel, Julie, John, Jean, Eric, Bonnie, and all my nieces and nephews, accompany me on all of life's adventures. Paul, Mira, Loránd, and Olivér: thank you for showing me the fullness of life. You are all in this book, in one way or another. Growing up in communism, in poverty, in a tiny apartment with thousands of books, my parents modeled to us the virtues of lifelong learning. I only hope that I can pass on the intellectual courage I learned from them.

Chapter 4 is an expanded version of an article first published as "Concepts of Simultaneity and Community in the Crowd-Sourced Video Diary *Life in a Day*" in *Cultural Politics* 10, no. 1 (2014): 21–39 (© 2014 Duke University Press, all rights reserved, republished by permission of the publisher).

STORY REVOLUTIONS

INTRODUCTION

Every time I tell a story, I am putting out a call to community.
 —CHRISTOPHER MAIER

#metoo

At a youth camp in 1996, counselor Tarana Burke was listening to the story of a thirteen-year-old girl who had been sexually assaulted by her mother's boyfriend. Burke was shocked by the monstrosity of what she had heard and yet she turned the girl away: "I didn't have a response or a way to help her in that moment, and I couldn't even say 'me too.'"[1] According to Burke, that is when the Me Too movement was born. Haunted by that memory, ten years later she founded a nonprofit organization dedicated to survivors of sexual abuse. In 2006 she opened a MySpace site called Me Too, and the movement began to grow. A decade later, on October 15, 2017, actress Alyssa Milano reacted to the sexual misconduct allegations against Harvey Weinstein by inviting her followers to share their stories: "If you've been sexually harassed or assaulted write 'me too' as a reply to this tweet." The reactions were overwhelming. Within twenty-four hours, social media was flooded with a tsunami of #metoo tweets and comments. The hashtag was tweeted more than a million times in the first week, and there were more than twelve million Facebook posts within twenty-four hours.[2] Milano said that while she was not surprised that so many had #metoo stories, she was stunned by how many people were willing to share them.[3]

I begin with this example because #metoo is a powerful illustration of how telling personal stories and aggregating them in large numbers—in this case through a hashtag—can fuel a political movement by creating a heightened sense of community. Both organizers and participants have stressed the communal effects of sharing individual stories. Milano said she sent her original tweet to highlight the "magnitude of the problem."

In her later comments as well, she emphasized the collective aspects of the phenomenon: "the most beautiful thing from all of this is not only women standing up and using their voices but standing up for each other in solidarity"; "the collective pain we've felt has turned into a collective power;"[4] "one tweet has brought together 1.7 million voices from 85 countries. Standing side by side, together, our movement will only grow."[5] Likewise, Tarana Burke underscored the collective significance of sharing #metoo stories: "It's beyond a hashtag. It's the start of a larger conversation and a movement for radical community healing. Join us."[6]

The Storification of Culture

The #metoo movement, while unique in its scale and objectives, is not an isolated event. Two decades into the twenty-first century, the collective sharing of personal stories is on the rise. Social media companies, community groups, and for- as well as not-for-profit companies all encourage people to share their stories. The Moth, StoryCorps, and Humans of New York attract millions of users, and the popular "Stories" products recently introduced by Facebook, Instagram, Snapchat, and Twitter are used by more than a billion people daily, with the Stories format growing fifteen times faster than feeds are. According to analysts, "a multitude of indicators point to a surprising conclusion: Stories are quietly eating the social world, fundamentally changing how we share and consume content on social media."[7] "Stories creation and consumption is up 842 percent since early 2016," and "the repercussions of this medium shift are vast."[8] Observers have described this trend as the "storification" of culture. Live story-sharing events are also growing in popularity. The trend is further evidenced by a range of neologisms: the verb "storify" is now listed in dictionaries, along with job descriptions such as "story sherpa," "story architect," "story activist," and "story officer."

Many argue that we are on the cusp of a new communication era in which personal stories will play a central role, not only as entertainment but also as a key mode of social and political engagement. This book presents an overview of this storytelling revolution, as well as a historical and critical analysis of it. What exactly we mean by a "personal story" of course changes constantly, and our technological innovations keep diversifying both the forms of narratives we produce and the ways in which we share them.[9] Long-form narratives are being replaced by "small stories" and episodic modes of self-narratives, visual storytelling is becoming more dominant, and social media is making people more aware of the performative and fragmented nature of their stories. The most significant change, however, concerns not the form or content of these stories, but *why* we share them.[10]

Social media sharing has often been vilified for promoting narcissism. Indeed, the first phase of social media enabled people to share their stories with millions, which led to a drastic increase in output and oversharing. During the "memoir boom," everyone talked, but only a few listened. In the last few years, however, as social media has evolved, the motivation behind people's sharing is also beginning to change. The more interactive the internet becomes, the more people praise the collaborative and participatory spirit of story sharing. They increasingly evoke the common good and the value of community as a reason for sharing. The idea is that by sharing and assembling our personal stories we can become more aware of each other's daily joys and tribulations, and this sense of reciprocity can in turn improve our communities. Personal stories are said to help communities learn about their past and present, deepen relationships among members, disseminate knowledge to nonmembers, allow groups to gain public or legal recognition, and grow groups towards maturity.[11]

According to activists, personal story sharing can transform communities by making people more knowledgeable about their shared histories and more conscious of their shared values and objectives. Sometimes, sharing stories serves to promote specific goals. For example, development agencies rely on personal stories to better understand the needs of communities they seek to support, human rights groups archive refugee stories to trace migration, ecological groups use personal stories to map ecological disasters, and victims of sexual violence pin their stories onto world maps to create a better understanding of the global implications of sexual violence. At other times, the objectives are less specific and people share their stories simply to express their "shared humanity." As the founders of StoryCorps put it: "Our mission is to preserve and share humanity's stories in order to build connections between people and create a more just and compassionate world."[12] But what exactly is the connection between our personal stories and our sense of community? How do our most intimate, individual stories shape our understanding of communities? And what are the social and political implications of this emerging trend?

Assembling Stories

Ever since the dawn of civilization, people have been weaving their stories together, and story sharing has always created a powerful sense of belonging. Every culture has its forums for sharing personal stories, whether it is the communal fire, the kitchen table, the therapy room, or an online platform. Most people share their stories with a few others, whether acquaintances or strangers. Sometimes, however, societies come together in more organized ways to share their stories as a collective. They gather their stories into collections, hashtags, archives, or libraries, with the intention to reflect on their commonalities and their shared experiences. This book is about such story collections: not individual stories but projects that bring together the personal stories of many, such as live storytelling events, traditional anthologies of memoirs, crowdsourced diaries, memoir contests, oral histories, digital story maps, or selfie maps. Some of these story collections were initiated by a single person, others were crowdsourced from the get-go. Some only involve a dozen people, others millions. Some are contemporary, others centuries old. What is common to them all is that they celebrate, like #metoo, the collective power of assembled personal stories.

What I call "assembled stories" play a key role in the age of storification and aggregation, and as such, they raise urgent questions. In the second decade of the twenty-first century, collective story sharing has become a new means of social and political engagement, and analysts around the world celebrate its positive, transformative potential. The role of personal storytelling in participatory democracy is now a subject of substantial scholarly interest.[13] There exist ample studies of the social media mobilizations of the Arab Spring, the Occupy movements, and other upheavals. For one, activists value assembled stories for their potential to inform. They argue that from the collected voices of many we can gain a "deeper understanding of the motives, activities, and lessons learned."[14] Assembled stories are also said to increase cohesion in communities by making people more aware of their shared experiences.[15] Sharing stories is said to transform people from separate *I*'s into a *we*. Activists evoke ancient traditions of story sharing, like the Haitian "crick-crack," to explain the process:

> Every time I tell a story, I am putting out a call to community. A story presumes a community of listeners who will recognize some experience that they have lived or can imagine living in the narrative. It is a call and response (what in Haitian storytelling is known as a Crick—Crack) where the teller tosses out a community-gathering, a community-presuming device, in other words a story, in the hope that the group of listeners will respond by becoming "we." To the extent that a "we," responds, this means that there is

amongst the sea of "I"s sufficient shared assent to the virtual experience of the story that each relaxes the contraction of their I-ness to "we" themselves within the shared world of this story.[16]

According to activists, collective story sharing allows people to discover new connections between their personal stories and shared narratives of social action. It also plays a key role in participatory democracy, since it promises to replace abstract notions of democracy with a more personalized understanding of "my" democracy.

The potential of this new story-sharing mechanism is indeed tremendous. Story sharing can offer better knowledge about our communities (data-driven insights gained through aggregation, based on people's lived experience and experiential authority), as well as more bonding (more open, less segregated communities with more flexible boundaries and more mutual support based on shared experiences). The goal is to create *personalized* communities, in which people connect to others via their personal stories of shared experiences. The idea is that by sharing our individual stories we can discover connections between our own experiences and those of others, which in turn allows us to embrace shared narratives of social or political action. In this new form of story activism, the personal is seen as a means of deepening one's connection to others.

What I call here a "personalized community" is not the same as an "individualized society." A decade ago, sociologist Zygmunt Bauman cautioned about the increasing individualization of our societies. According to Bauman, the "me decades" at the turn of the millennium were filled with constant ego-chatter, which ended up colonizing the public space. As he put it, "The distinctive feature of the stories told in our times is that they articulate individual lives in a way that excludes or suppresses (prevents from articulation) the possibility of tracking down the links connecting individual fate to the ways and means by which society as a whole operates; more to the point, it precludes the questioning of such ways and means by relegating them to the unexamined background of individual life pursuits and casting them as 'brute facts' which the storytellers can neither challenge nor negotiate, whether singly, severally or collectively."[17] The problem, in Bauman's view, was that people could no longer connect their personal stories to larger, shared narratives.[18]

While some still lament the increasing individualization of societies, the "age of sharing" has given rise to a newfound optimism.[19] Our economic and communication systems have both been fundamentally transformed by new sharing technologies, which enable new types of connections. Bauman's hope was that people in the future would learn again to "translate back and forth between the languages of private concerns and public good,"[20] and that is exactly what is happening today. Bauman's dream is echoed almost verbatim in the mission statements of Mark Zuckerberg and other technocrats-turned-social visionaries. Their story-sharing platforms lure us with the promise of reconnecting the individual to the communal via the personal. Personalized communities, reimagined through personal story sharing, present a potential alternative to the age-old binary of individualism versus communitarianism. The challenge is to preserve this alternative from divisive definitions of "community."

On Community

The first thing that distinguishes this book is its focus on the collective aspects of personal storytelling. The collective role of personal stories has long been understudied, because for a long time, critics overidentified autobiographies with singularity and individuality. To correct this bias, scholars recently introduced the concept of "relationality," which stresses the implication of others in one's stories and narrative identity.[21] Indeed, there is no such thing as "my story only." We have no stable subjectivity, and the idea that we could create an independent and unified self through autobiographical storytelling is also just an illusion. Despite this consensus, in most contemporary studies the emphasis remains on individual stories and storytellers. For instance, critics may study the effects of social media on our understanding of identities, but their focus remains mostly on personal identity. To complement these studies, I propose to explore the collective aspects of personal storytelling, because how we collect and compile personal stories is symptomatic of how we view the relationship between individuals and communities.

In the first two decades of the twenty-first century, the rise of social networks, crowdsourcing, and collaborative forms of consumption has turned community into a hot commodity. It seems that after fascism and communism, it is the turn of capitalism to embrace community. Community is being celebrated everywhere today: in the sharing economy, in collaborative models of learning and healing, in big data analyses, in crowdsourcing, and in social and political activism. Nothing demonstrates better our renewed fascination with community than our vocabulary. In contemporary Western societies, we talk constantly about community. In terms of frequency, the word "community" belongs to the top 2 percent of our most commonly used words, along with some basic words such as "man," "woman," or "person."[22] The connected culture of the twenty-first century challenges us to think in new ways about community, and story collections play a fundamental role in how we imagine our togetherness.

I am of course fully aware of the dangers in engaging the concept of community in academia today. Community is a highly polarizing concept: while some see it as a cure for all our social ailments, others associate it with totalitarian regimes that sacrifice the individual on the altar of the masses. To some, community is "a metaphor for people's longing for a better life" and "an imaginary framework for political mobilization";[23] to others it is a utopian and dangerous notion.[24] Personally, I consider this ongoing discord about community a positive status quo. For as Jacques Derrida, Jean-Luc Nancy, and others warned, there is nothing more dangerous than making the discourse around community a taboo, because that will only enable its return under potentially more dangerous guises, such as the logic of fraternity, communion, or essence.[25] Etymology offers a useful lesson here, because the word "community" shares the same element, *munus* (duty), as the word "immune" (*in-munus*).[26] This should remind us that *com-munity* always carries the danger of the desire to be *im-mune* to all that is other. Or, to put it differently, community's inclusionary and exclusionary aspects are mutually dependent, meaning that I can never say "I belong" without excluding some.[27]

Throughout the book, I will keep this Janus-faced nature of community in mind as I explore various practices of story sharing. The question is: how do we make sure that our personalized communities, built on shared stories of shared experiences, do not degenerate into the same old tribalism of *us* versus *them*? This question is particularly urgent in the era of fake news and social influencers, when many exploit herd mentality to segregate people into communities of interest and action. I propose that the way to deal with the concept of community is not to ignore the utopian fantasies it evokes, but to admit that our sense of belonging is politically charged precisely because it develops from the many, conflictual ways of imagining our personal connections to it. I argue that assembled stories offer perfect case studies to examine our changing concepts of community, because by bringing together individual stories into larger collections, these archives model the many different ways in which we can think about togetherness. Collections of personal stories also raise exciting methodological questions for scholars in the digital humanities, for one of the most urgent challenges facing the humanities today is how to reconcile the "distant reading" practices occasioned by big data with our traditional "close reading" practices.[28] Studying collections of personal stories is highly relevant to this debate as well, because story collections model the many ways we can think about the relation between individual data and its aggregation into clusters.

A Historical Perspective

The second thing missing from our current analyses is a historical perspective. Literature and media have always been social, long before the advent of social media. Yet, we rarely pay attention to the antecedents of today's media phenomena. Most observers only stress the novelty of today's social media trends, describing our story-sharing practices as revolutionary and unprecedented. To balance out this bias, I include dozens of story collections from the past. Most of my examples come from three historical periods: The Enlightenment, the 1930s, and the twenty-first century. I focus on these three periods because they share some important common characteristics: namely, they were all marked by new means of mass communication (the book, broadcast media, and the internet), a rising concern about datafication and aggregation, and social unrest. The fact that all three of these historical periods saw a large number of story projects is not a coincidence. People in those eras were particularly concerned about how best to share their experiences with each other and how their stories could lead to collective insights and action.

As the following chapters show, collections of "lives" have been popular since antiquity, but it was not until the eighteenth century that people began to assemble autobiographical stories with a collective purpose in mind. In Western modernity, Enlightenment philosophers were the first to openly praise the communal value of autobiographical stories. Inspired by new methods of data collection and systematization, they were also the first to call on their fellow citizens to share their stories. Some proposed to use these "insider" stories to build libraries of human experiences; others compiled them to document social conditions and as a means of political mobilization. In the 1930s, the convergence of mass movements and the birth of mass media contributed to a second boom in story activism, so the book offers several case studies from this era as well. Finally, the rise of the internet and the current era of data collection and social media mobilization offer further exciting examples of assembled stories. My broad range of case studies makes it impossible to offer an in-depth analysis of the specificities of each historical era. My selection of case studies is also heavily limited by digital inequalities, and it is biased towards the global North. Nevertheless, these historical collections are worth closer attention because as forerunners of today's projects, they help nuance our contemporary debates.[29]

The biggest advantage of a historical perspective is that we can better see what is truly unique about our contemporary practices. Most importantly, by contrasting earlier print projects to today's digital story-sharing platforms, we can highlight the advantages of reciprocity, meaning that we are now able to instantaneously access the stories of many of our fellow citizens en masse. Sharing personal stories has always been a central ritual of social life, but the invention of the printing press meant that people no longer had to sit around the same fire to share their stories but could circulate them in book format. Paradoxically, the wider circulation of books led to greater separation, in that people now sat alone in their homes, reading each other's personal stories in isolation. Enlightenment philosophers were the first to lament this situation. As a response, they sought to recreate the sense of intimacy that storytellers around a fire would experience, by compiling personal stories into collections. Their hope was that reading each other's assembled stories would make people more aware of the similarities and differences between their parallel experiences, which in turn would expand their knowledge and solidify their sense of belonging.

Unfortunately, the limited circulation of print media meant that only a few people had access to these collections. The feedback loop therefore remained open, since people who shared their stories could not necessarily access each other's stories. All of that changed in the early twenty-first century when digital crowdsourcing technologies closed the feedback loop. Today, stories can get back to the people who shared them, often instantaneously and on a large scale. For instance, memoirs of sexual abuse published in print (and even on Web 1.0 blogs and websites at the turn of the millennium) had a limited impact due to their small and unidirectional circulation. When Tarana Burke first launched her Me Too site in 2006 on MySpace, sexual assault victims could share their stories in a safe space, but they only had a limited network of supporters. Later, however, as social media expanded and story sharing became fully integrated into daily life, people began to connect and socialize through stories on a broader scale.[30] By the time the #metoo hashtag took off in the fall of 2017, people could share their stories instantaneously and with a much wider audience. They could also react live to each other's stories, strategize, and form communities of support. This feedback mechanism presents us with an unprecedented opportunity. The question is: how are we going to use it?

A Critical Perspective

The third missing piece in current discussions about story activism is a critical perspective on community and what it means to create community through empathy. Many scholars take an uncritical stance and celebrate the role of stories in building community. Sharing is encouraged in many contexts today: in the sharing economy, in collaborative models of learning and healing, in big data analyses, in crowdsourcing, and in social and political activism. As story-sharing practices become increasingly crowdsourced, collaborative, and participatory, critics are beginning to turn their attention to the collective aspects of story sharing. Yet, most do not engage critically with the concept of community, choosing instead simply to embrace the "participatory condition" and the role of storytelling in community action.[31] What is missing, therefore, is a critical engagement with the idea of community, as well as more reflection on what it means to use stories to build community.

Since the major debate in the 1990s between communitarians and individualists, there have been numerous important critiques of "community." Joseph Miranda, in *Against the Romance of Community*, showed how community is described as an alternative to capitalism, when in fact the two mutually supplement and enable each other. The "Romantic narrative of community" locates "community as prior in time to 'society,' locating community in a long-lost past for which we yearn nostalgically from our current fallen state of alienation, bureaucratization, rationality."[32] This romanticized understanding of community distinguishes it from capital, both spatially (community is local and face-to-face, whereas capital is global and faceless) and structurally (community is based on ethical values, whereas capital is based on economic value).[33] In Miranda's alternative reading, "community functions in complicity with 'society,' enabling capitalism and the liberal state."[34]

Jean-Luc Nancy took a different but equally important approach when he tried to strip community of its immanentist interpretations. According to Nancy, the problem with all prior definitions of community (including the "organicist view" that presupposes community as a common depth and a shared origin from which subjects come into their social being, and the "contractual theory," which understands community as an association whose members come together freely to form a community) is that they think of community as an essence.[35] They all start out with the concept of the human as an immanent being that is only later marked by difference (born individuals who join communities), when in fact togetherness precedes individual existence. Therefore, Nancy tried to redefine community as a mode of resistance. "Community is, in a sense, resistance itself: namely, resistance to immanence."[36]

How to talk about community in non-essentialist terms, while also questioning its status as an alternative to capitalist values, is my challenge for this book as well. Both Miranda's and Nancy's critique are needed to nuance the celebratory ethos that currently surrounds story sharing. First, I want to highlight the illusions and deceptive practices that this new story-sharing trend generates. I will show how companies imbue their corporate missions with idealist visions about community participation and cooperative behavior so that under the guise of community-building they can produce more sellable data. Second, following Nancy's lead, I also want to dig deeper and examine the essentialist terms in which story-sharing platforms describe community. To this end, I will adopt a thematic approach and will study several concepts of "wholeness" that buttress the contemporary discourse about community. Chapters 4 and 5 are dedicated to time and space, respectively. We often think of communities as sharing "one time" (like the community of contemporaries) and "one space" (like the population of a city). Our personal stories, especially when arranged into collections, have a profound effect on how we imagine our being together in time and space. I argue that crowdsourcing thousands of diaries from a single day, or mapping the stories of a single city, do indeed promise a potentially revolutionary way to see our communities, but only if we can resist falling back on convenient, supposedly neutral categories of time and space. I also dedicate two sections to our methods of aggregation (chapter 6) and ideas about knowledge production (chapter 3). I argue that as we build increasingly large digital archives of human experiences, it is urgent to clarify what exactly it entails to aggregate large quantities of personal stories, and what kind of knowledge we hope to gain by doing so. The danger here is that we create the illusion of more open and information-based communities while algorithmically reinforcing old divisions and community boundaries. We need more rigorous debate about how to design archives and platforms which do not rely on essentialist, homogenizing categories of time, space, scale, knowledge, and so forth.

The answer, promoted by this book, lies in the open-ended and transgressive nature of stories. Assembled stories do indeed have a potential to positively transform our communities, but only if we preserve their unique, transgressive qualities. In my mind, the power of today's "collective lives" movement lies not in bringing people together in solidarity, as many claim. That would only mean reinforcing prior conceptions about who belongs to a group and who does not, which is exactly the danger of automated, algorithmic aggregations that silo us into prefabricated communities. Rather, the greatest promise of story sharing lies in the capacity of stories to constantly renegotiate borders of inclusion and exclusion. Narratives, which are tied to the specificity of individual speakers, have a unique role to play in resisting the standardization inherent in our traditional concepts of community. Personal stories are a promising tool of social transformation precisely because they can unsettle simplistic notions of community, cutting across the binary logic of belonging and exclusion by creating spaces where our alliances can shift continuously. How to preserve this unique quality while building new algorithms and databases to aggregate stories is our challenge for the future.

1 TOWARD COLLECTIVE INTIMACY

I share therefore I am.
—SHERRY TURKLE

Vaughn Allex was a gate agent at the American Airlines ticket counter on the morning of 9/11, checking in passengers on Flight 77: families, student groups, couples ... and two terrorists. The next day, people would not talk to him. They would not even look him in the eye: "I had this wild thing in my mind that everything that happened on 9/11 was my fault."[1] Because 9/11 support groups were for victims, there was no way for Allex to attend one, so he struggled with his guilt alone. It took him fifteen years to be able to talk about it, and when he finally did, he chose StoryCorps. StoryCorps is the largest story-sharing platform "recording the lives and stories of everyday Americans."[2] StoryCorps was established in 2003, when a soundproof recording booth called "storybooth" was installed between tracks 13 and 14 of New York City's Grand Central Terminal. StoryCorps invites people to take a moment out of their busy lives to sit down with friends, family, or strangers and share stories from their everyday lives. "This is not a project about statesmen or famous people," notes founder David Isay. "It's just the opposite. It's a project about the struggles, small victories and heroism of everyday people."[3] Isay's idea quickly took hold, and StoryCorps today has mobile booths in many cities. According to its website, the StoryCorps archive forms "the largest single collection of voices ever gathered in history."[4] The company also encourages people to listen to each other's stories, not just in the booth, but also via the web and the radio. StoryCorps stories are available in a wide range of formats, including podcasts, books, and animated shorts. In addition, the archive also has thematic collections, such as the Justice Project, which is about incarceration; Military Voices, which is about veterans; or the September 11th Initiative.

The success of StoryCorps is a symptom of a cultural shift from storytelling to story sharing. What matters today is not simply that we *tell* our story, but that we *share* it with someone. "Telling" a story puts the teller in the center, even if we assume that there is a listener as well. By contrast, "sharing" evokes a more egalitarian setting, where the person sharing the story and the person listening to the story are in a more even relationship. While storytelling is unidirectional, story sharing is reciprocal, even communal. Our prepositions also mark this difference: I tell my story *to* someone, while I share my story *with* someone. Today, thousands of websites and organizations, not to mention the invitations of social media, beckon people to share their story. Some platforms invite us in with a simple question: "What's your story?" Others assure us of their interest: "We want to hear your story." And in case we doubt whether anyone really cares to listen, we will be promptly reassured: "Your story matters." Marketers and community organizers praise the persuasive power of story sharing, while psychologists promote it as an essential component of individual and collective mental health. In our culture of care, the phrase "your story matters" appears everywhere from T-shirts to mugs to inspirational stickers. What matters is not so much the quality of the story, but the fact that someone has lived it and is willing to share it. But how did we get here, and is there something unique about how and why we share our stories today?

StoryCorps's mission is "to preserve and share humanity's stories in order to build connections between people and create a more just and compassionate world."[5] This mission has perhaps never felt as urgent as in the social isolation caused by the 2020 pandemic. StoryCorps responded to the crisis by diversifying its outreach so that the conversations can now also be recorded remotely. This singular moment in history raised the value of both the documentary aspect of story sharing (to "preserve humanity's stories") and its community-building promise (to "build connections between people").[6] As I will argue in this chapter, this double objective—one epistemic, the other social—is at the heart of the mission of all contemporary story-sharing sites. To clarify its significance, I will first trace recent trends in collective story sharing and then develop the idea of collective intimacy. I end the chapter by exploring the productive tension between the ethos of amateur community voices and the commercial media logics that govern these story-sharing sites.

From My Story to Our Story

Autobiographies are supposed to be about oneself, or at least that is what the word's Greek root suggests (*autos* = self). Yet, this relatively young word (the practice of life writing originated in antiquity, but the word "autobiography" did not enter circulation until the nineteenth century) says more about the worldview of those who coined it than about the actual practices of autobiographers. Romantic poets who first used the term "autobiography" may have been a bit too infatuated with the idea of individuality and selfhood to notice that autobiographers throughout the ages had been just as concerned about the lives of others as they were about their own. One of the first modern Western memoirists, Michel de Montaigne, published his *Essays* not because he considered himself unique but because he was convinced that "every man bears the whole form of the human condition."[7] In the eighteenth century, French autobiographer Rétif de la Bretonne justified his intense self-scrutiny by noting: "I'm not writing my life; this is the history of a man."[8] And in the twentieth century, writer André Gide made it a point to contrast the false ideal of autobiographical uniqueness to his own perceived representativeness: "Rousseau said he wrote his confessions because he believed himself to be unique. I am writing mine for the exact opposite reason, and because I know that a great number of people will recognize themselves in my autobiography."[9]

In the twentieth century, the rise of mass society, collectivist ideologies, and identity politics favored a more collectivist interpretation of autobiography. While the myth of the self-made author who overcomes hardship through perseverance remained popular, there was an increasing emphasis on the collective aspects of life writing. As more and more people got to tell their stories, authors and readers emphasized the shared nature of their experiences. Instead of merely seeing autobiographies as individually empowering (liberating authors from the burden of secrets or helping them discern patterns and overcome challenges through self-study), life writing came to be seen as a collectively empowering practice. Previously marginalized communities used autobiographical stories to call attention to their plight. In one of the more well-known cases, the Guatemalan Nobel Peace Prize winner Rigoberta Menchú began her memoir with a powerful statement of representativeness: "it's not only my life, it's also the testimony of my people."[10] Similarly, Maya Angelou, describing in an interview the process of writing her autobiography *I Know Why the Caged Bird Sings*, explained how she saw herself as a symbolic character for every Black girl growing up in America: "I wasn't thinking so much about my own life or identity. I was thinking about a particular time in which I lived and the influences of that time on a number of people . . . I used the central figure—myself—as a focus to show how one person can make it through those times."[11] Publishers also pushed such representative readings. As a rather extreme example, when the anonymous diaries of a German woman from World War II first came out, editors dismissed the importance of her particularity by stating: "Anyway, her identity is insignificant, for hers is not a unique case, but the dark mass-fate of countless women."[12]

As claims of autobiographical representativeness proliferated, the collectivist rhetoric came under attack. "Representative" readings were criticized for overemphasizing the struggle of collective subjectivity to the detriment of singularity and for concealing the fact that communal identities (just like personal ones) were discursively constructed. The feminist critic Nancy Miller was among the first to protest the collectivization of autobiographical expression. In *Getting Personal*, Miller complained about a "certain overloading in cultural criticism of the rhetorics of representativity (including feminism's)—the incantatory recital of the 'speaking as a's and the imperialisms of 'speaking for's.'"[13] Miller identified the idea of representativeness with scholarly abstraction and promoted instead a certain "situated writing."[14] Soon, the ideas of positionality and situatedness were widely embraced as an alternative to abstract and universalist claims of representativeness. Felicity Nussbaum underscored that by "displac[ing] the universality of human nature and substitut[ing] a historically located subject," autobiography "resist[s] a self made whole by humanist ideology."[15] This emphasis on situatedness served to authenticate many hitherto unacknowledged life stories, but it also led to intense debates concerning the notion of authenticity and autobiographical witnessing.

Aside from the risk of "limited personalism,"[16] one issue with the concept of situated autobiographical writing was that it did not reflect the intersubjective and relational aspects of selfhood. Again, feminist critics were instrumental, in recognizing that selfhood was not only constructed, contingent, and fluid but also relational. The idea of relationality is different from the notion of representativeness in that it acknowledges the intersubjective dimension of self-reflection while also respecting the limitations of situated positions. Susanna Egan's *Mirror Talk* (1999) was a pioneering study that foregrounded the dialogic nature of life writing, while Paul John Eakin's *How Our Lives Become Stories* (1999) offered a useful definition of relational selfhood. According to Eakin, it would be misleading to suggest that women's identities are formulated relationally, in terms of their relationships to others, while men write in individualistic, monologic ways. Instead, Eakin argued that "all identity is relational, and that the definition of autobiography, and its history as well, must be stretched to reflect the kinds of self-writing in which relational identity is characteristically displayed."[17]

The idea of relationality has since become a dominant paradigm. Sometimes the "other" in the story is a single other to whom the autobiographer is related intimately (a parent, a child, a sibling, a significant other); other times the story involves many others. Relationality can apply to family memoirs and friendship or companionship memoirs, as well as to stories involving larger social environments such as religious communities, environmental groups, artist cooperatives, or regional and ethnic communities. StoryCorps's model based on oral history, where autobiographical stories are born out of a conversation between two people, is a good illustration of relationality. Relationality does not necessarily involve collaboration, but critics in disability studies and ethnic studies often study collaborative forms of life writing and the ethical issues raised by such practices. For instance, they highlight the ambiguity of collaboration in Native American autobiography: "'Collaboration' can apply to life-narratives produced jointly by two or more people (in 'as told to' or 'ghostwritten' productions), as well as those articulated within political circumstances that compelled the narrators to cooperate or collude with governments, people, ideas, images, stereotypes, materials, funding institutions, and/or representational modes alien to them and to their manner of expression. It includes relations of complicity and of symbiosis."[18] In short, autobiographical relationality implies something more complex than the mere idea that we exist in relation with proximate others whose lives and stories shape ours. Rather, it suggests that I cannot say who I am without also saying who we are.

From Our Story to Our Stories

The demise of the self-made, autonomous autobiographer was also hastened by the rise of digital culture and the accompanying multiplication of autobiographical modes of expression. In *Reading Autobiography*, Sidonie Smith and Julia Watson attempted to catalogue the recent explosion of autobiographical genres. While the 2010 edition lists sixty different autobiographical genres, the point is not so much the nomenclature as the amazing diversity itself. No longer limited to writing (as the *graphein* in the word "autobiography" would suggest), autobiographers in the last decades have adopted multiple modalities and technologies to mediate their lives. Autobiographical self-expression remains an incredibly vibrant cultural practice, as demonstrated by the sheer variety of ego media, including life-logging, podcasts, books, Instagram stories, graphic memoirs, audio and video diaries, blogs, vlogs, body-maps, selfies, and so on.

To briefly trace recent trends in story sharing, the first version of the internet led to a wider dissemination of personal stories via websites and blogs. Later, companies developed specialized apps and platforms to encourage personal storytelling. Early storytelling startups such as Storylane, Storify, or Steller Stories encouraged people to share compelling stories online and to diversify their media: "Everyone has a story. Tell yours with photos, videos and text."[19] The rapid growth in personal storytelling was facilitated by greater access to digital tools but also by the recognition of the commercial and socio-political potential of personal stories. Seeking to harness the much celebrated "power of stories," marketers and activists turned "strategic storytelling" into a veritable weapon. In the business world, companies were encouraged to use autobiographical stories to articulate their business philosophy and to strengthen organizational structure. Strategic story sharing also flourished in the nonprofit sector, as personal stories were used to optimize services in health care, social services, and education. Activists also recognized the enormous potential of story sharing as a form of advocacy strategy. Story activists argued that in order to change our understanding of social issues, we need to listen to the stories of those whose voices have not been heard. Since policy-makers are often far removed from the problems they seek to address, providing them with the first-person perspective of those involved is said to lead to more informed decisions. The term used for this new type of activism is "storytelling for social justice" or "transformative storytelling," and it is a growing trend globally.

Another factor contributing to the explosion of personal story sharing was the gradual integration of storytelling into daily life through social media. Thanks to the rapid growth of mobile technologies, by the early 2010s people no longer needed to use special websites or apps to share their stories. Originally, specialized storytelling apps such as Storylane defined themselves in contrast to social media: "Storylane combats social media glibness with a sharing platform for in-depth stories and opinions." announced *TechCrunch*.[20] According to its founder, Jonathan Gheller, Storylane sought "to create a deeper impression of the individual, which is often lacking on other social media sites, and to position the user as a storyteller."[21] Soon, however, the companies promoting more meaningful modes of story sharing were bought up by or integrated into social media companies. Storylane, for instance, was acquired by Facebook in 2013, and Gheller suddenly saw a profound similarity between his own mission and that of the social media giant. "Facebook's mission of connecting the world has always been at the center of our work, and like our friends at Facebook, meaningful connections are what our team is most passionate about," he noted.[22] The most recent step in this process of expansion and integration happened around 2016–17, when social media platforms developed their own "story products," which made prior platforms and apps obsolete.[23] This last step completed the full integration of story sharing into daily life. Today, people produce a mind-boggling number of personal stories every single day. Nearly 1.7 billion accounts use the Instagram Stories format daily, and many users set themselves the goal of contributing at least one story daily.[24]

The increased production raised the urgent question of how to handle such large quantities of stories. Personal stories have become a part of what we call "big data," and just as the explosion of big data called for new methods of data aggregation, the boom of personal story sharing prompted the development of new techniques and principles for arranging stories. First, network concepts and tools (including social media) broadened the idea of relational selfhood, positing it as constituted by networks of social, cultural, political, and biological relations. The new emphasis on networks made it clear that autobiographical storytellers are not just plural but also interconnected. For instance, when mommy bloggers or vloggers curate their lives for online consumption, they engage in a "purposive and deliberate social engagement, a creative as well as interpersonal practice" that creates community by producing an interlinked, collective "autobiography in real time."[25] To maximize these networks' potential, story activists use social network analysis (SNA) to measure the "effectiveness" of each story and of various strategies of aggregation. Some use traditional data-mining techniques to plot the use of keywords and topics in stories, employing data visualization tools to render these as snapshots or evolving networks. They can thereby analyze the formation of story-sharing networks, including the position of the storyteller within social networks, the paths that stories follow as they are reposted or embedded into other stories, and the formation of central nodes in story networks. As one blogger explains, "The effectiveness of non-profit storytelling is best measured when taking this big picture view. When we look at the big picture, or the story arc over the long term, patterns can emerge through the stories we tell. It's these patterns that will make our organization's stories more effective in building relationships with our audience."[26] What is more, stories can now also be "reverse engineered," meaning they can be strategically developed to improve their "networking potential" from the start, from the moment that they are written or told. As noted by an analyst, "given the emotional appeal of individual stories over general descriptions, analysts may want to direct some of their efforts towards finding those individual stories within the larger collection of data that can best serve as representatives of the whole."[27]

Second, since social media favors visual and ephemeral modes of storytelling over narrative, long-form expressions, the explosion of social media also called for new algorithms to sort, curate, and archive these billions of "small stories."[28] The new algorithms offered automated ways to structure posts and curate stories, which further broadened the notion of relationality by expanding the notion of autobiographical agency. Alison Booth is a leading scholar in the field of digital humanities who studies collective biographies.[29] Booth argues that life writing is always multiple and relational in that its subject is always already embedded into networks of individuals and collectives: "Life narratives in any form both reveal networks of persons and distribute authorship and agency. Collective or multiple forms of life writing, which make these networks of association explicit, are surprisingly pervasive in print."[30] While such networks existed already in print, the internet and big data have made it more urgent to shape particularities into patterns, which is why "collective lives" have gained such prominence in recent years. Booth expands the idea of collective lives to social media and argues that social media itself is a "massive, crowd-sourced life-writing project."[31] She cites, for example, Facebook's Timeline as an example of "extreme collective narration":[32] "Facebook or Twitter resemble piecemeal ghosted memoirs in their collaborative production of what appears to be first-person testimonials."[33] Booth goes on to show how these companies engineer life stories with the help of algorithms and how they use the data from these stories to then classify people into categories. I fully agree with Booth that we need to pay "more critical attention to the many texts and genres that make an explicit theme of this *multiplicity* by taking the form of a collection of short narratives."[34] Yet, while Booth is mostly concerned with collections of *biographical* stories, my focus remains on *autobiographical* collections. Booth does not always distinguish between biographical and autobiographical narration, and she is right in doing so, in that digitization, social editing, and open formats have complicated the question of authorship and agency to such a degree that even when we are convinced that we are the primary authors of our own stories, the level of automation built into the media that generate these stories makes this a questionable assumption. Nevertheless, I will continue to distinguish between biographical and autobiographical narratives because of the strong illusion of agency that accompanies the latter. It seems to me that the question of ownership and agency, of who owns and who aggregates whose personal story for what purposes, continues to matter a great deal in the digital age. Therefore, we should not automatically collapse biographical and autobiographical narratives into a single category, not even (or certainly not) when we talk about large quantities of personal stories.[35]

Collective Intimacy

I have traced above the shifting emphases from "my story" through "our story" to "our stories" in order to highlight a trend towards relationality, diversification, increased production, and new means of aggregation. In describing this diversity, however, we need to be careful not to treat media as mere carriers of content. As Smith and Watson also underscore, media are not "'tools' for rendering a pre-existent self"; rather, "the materiality of the medium is constitutive of the subjectivity rendered. Thus, media technologies do not simplify or undermine the interiority of the subject but, on the contrary, expand the field of self-representation beyond the literary to cultural and media practices. New media of the self revise notions of identity and the rhetoric and modalities of self-presentation, and they prompt new imaginings of virtual sociality enabled by concepts of community that do not depend on personal encounter."[36] Likewise, in *Stories of the Self*, Anna Poletti cautions against treating autobiographical media as transparent channels. Inspired by Karen Barad's and Lisa Gitelman's arguments regarding the social and relational nature of media and materiality, Poletti concludes that we do not use media as tools to express a preformed vision but rather as storytellers we "co-emerge" with media.[37] Autobiography is not "a process through which lived experience is narrated and therefore represented"; rather, "our use of media—and our engagement with its material potential and limitations—is a fundamental process in life itself."[38] As we co-emerge with new media and our notions of personal identity get revised, our understanding of collectives and communities also change. In Smith and Watson's wording, new media "prompt new imaginings of virtual sociality," and the same observations made above apply to these new imaginings as well: we do not use media to express who we are as a community; rather, our collectives co-emerge along with our use of new media. But how exactly and in what ways is our understanding of sociality changing?

Media theorists and sociologists have spent the last two decades discussing emerging forms of "network sociality,"[39] including the influence of networked communications on social interactions and virtual communities, the erosion of boundaries between private and public, and the formation of new "intimate publics."[40] Lauren Berlant was among the first to foreground "intimacy" as both a cultural imaginary and a key political and market force. In Berlant's reading, "what makes a public sphere intimate is an expectation that the consumers of its particular stuff already share a worldview and emotional knowledge that they have derived from a broadly common historical experience."[41] For instance, when "women's culture" is advertised and sold to women, this makes women feel as though what they are buying or viewing expresses what is common in them, as though "there existed a world of strangers who would be emotionally literate in each other's experience of power, intimacy, desire, and discontent."[42] Berlant pays particular attention to modes of narration but carefully avoids limiting intimacy to personal or autobiographical literature only. Sure, autobiographical confessions play an important role in organizing the intimate public sphere, but we read all sorts of narratives "as autobiographies of collective experience,"[43] so in Berlant's view, we should not limit public intimacy to autobiographical storytelling alone.[44] While I agree with Berlant that the intimate and the public are deeply connected and that public intimacy entails more than autobiographical storytelling, I do think it worthwhile to examine our culture of personal story sharing with a special attention to how it engenders "collective intimacy." Berlant focuses mostly on individual lives and stories, and most critics of autobiographical practices continue to study single texts or acts of self-expression.[45] To expand this conversation, I study *collections* of personal stories, where many stories get assembled, arranged, and aggregated into a single collection, either through live story-sharing events, editorial practices, or through algorithmic processing. I am particularly interested in the new imaginings of sociality co-emerging with our new, aggregating technologies of self-expression and the role that story sharing plays in this process.

To try to pinpoint what is unique about our contemporary practices, I will borrow a term from marketing. Today, the most sophisticated versions of algorithmic personalization rely on what marketing professionals call "collective intimacy." To put it simply, collective intimacy relies on insights from big data analytics to deepen companies' relationships with each individual customer. In contrast to previous models of personalization, collective intimacy is no longer based only on the company's intimate relationship with a single customer; rather, to offer an even higher level of personalization, the model also draws inferences from the company's intimate relationships with many other customers. In other words, "if customer intimacy entails *multiple independent* pairwise relationships between a firm and each of its customers; *collective* intimacy deepens *each* relationship via insights developed across *all* relationships."[46] This is how *Forbes* magazine explains the difference between collective intimacy and earlier forms of personalization: "Collective intimacy represents more than a century of evolution: from handcrafting, to mass production, to mass customization, and then on to personalization, mass intimacy, contextualization, and now collective intimacy. It's more than simple personalization, which at its heart is not much more than selecting a photograph for your lock screen or monogramming your shirt. It's more than mass intimacy, which is personalization at scale."[47] Marketing professionals acknowledge that the level of intimacy achieved through collective intimacy can feel creepy and intrusive. But when it is done right, the result can be a powerful feeling of belonging, like "a company understands and *is one of us*."[48] As the term itself suggests, "collective intimacy" promises a powerful combination of two things: (1) valuable collective insights and (2) a sense of intimacy and belonging. This highest level of personalization feels particularly intimate because it is informed by both individual and collective insights. Its elusiveness is exactly what makes it attractive, for it is necessarily made to feel genuine even though it is the result of carefully crafted, intentional, and highly automated processes.

The notion of collective intimacy is also useful when describing the current story-sharing scene. Collections of personal stories promise a unique way to achieve the double objective of collective intimacy, in that we can now mine large databases of personal experiences for collective insights while also creating a sense of belonging and intimacy. This double promise was well articulated by the founder of Storylane when he explained his objective as trying "to build a *library* of human experiences by crafting a *community* where people can share things that really matter."[49] The mission statements of many story-sharing platforms emphasize this same double objective of archiving personal stories as a form of collective knowledge while also building connections between people. For instance, the site Cowbird, which catalogued close to a hundred thousand stories from nearly two hundred countries in five years, describes its mission as follows: "Cowbird is a public library of human experience. It consists of a community of storytellers, sharing heartfelt personal stories, focused on a slower kind of self-expression than the frantic world of tweets and social networks."[50] Similarly, StoryCorps shares stories "to remind one another of our shared humanity, to strengthen and build the connections between people, to teach the value of listening, and to weave into the fabric of our culture the understanding that everyone's story matters. At the same time, we are creating an invaluable archive for future generations."[51] Note that what gets personalized here is not the intimate relationship between customer and company, but storytellers' relationship to the community of humans. Story sharing promises to offer better knowledge about our communities (data-driven insights gained through aggregation, based on people's lived experience and experiential authority) as well as more bonding (more open, less segregated communities with more flexible boundaries and more mutual support based on shared experiences). The assumption is that collective intimacy could benefit communities just as it does businesses, leading to more informed and more personalized definitions of "our community" and "our democracy."

Relational Knowledge and a Sense of Belonging

The first advantage of collective intimacy is epistemic. Assembled personal stories are said to offer new, personal data–based knowledge about our communities. Documenting life's conditions has of course always been an important aspect of autobiographical storytelling, but in recent years, easy access to recording and crowdsourcing technologies has made this documentary function even more prominent. For instance, when post-election violence erupted in Kenya in 2007, there was no way for media to know the extent of the killings in remote regions. As a response, activists created an online crowd-map, Ushahidi, which allowed people to directly upload their personal stories about the violence and the destruction they experienced (*ushahidi* means "witness" or "testimony" in Swahili).[52] People used their mobile phones to upload their stories to a database, which aggregated all the individual reports. Since then, the platform has been used in over 160 countries to share more than ten million stories. According to their mission, Ushahidi aims to bring "global attention to their problems through the aggregation of their voices."[53] In recent years, this emerging form of social and political engagement has completely transformed the fields of journalism and politics, and the role of personal storytelling in participatory democracy is now a subject of substantial scholarly interest.

Ushahidi is relatively traditional, in that its story collection is centrally managed and the collected and aggregated data is mostly used as evidence in a campaign or monitoring project. However, an epistemic advantage of many contemporary story collections is the *circularity* of knowledge production. In collective intimacy, knowledge is not just crowdsourced, but can also be widely distributed back to the same individuals who shared their stories. The information gained from the stories gets reflected back, creating a relational knowledge that promises both individual and collective insights. This circularity is often described as "participatory research" or "participatory narrative inquiry" (PNI), "in which groups of people participate in gathering and working with raw stories of personal experience in order to make sense of complex situations for better decision making."[54] A pioneer in this field, the StoryCenter in Berkeley, California, has always emphasized the participatory nature of knowledge production and the importance of keeping the knowledge in the community by which it was produced.[55] A basic principle of community-based storytelling is that community members hold expert, experience-based knowledge of their life conditions, which can be expressed through situated, personal stories, and that the very process of story sharing can be valuable in itself in that it can help aggregate member input, articulate community goals, and help the community represent itself to others and to decision-making agencies. The participatory ethos is particularly dominant in story projects in health care, social policy programs, and education, but the participatory design of Web 2.0 encourages all users to form virtual knowledge communities through user-generated content.

The second advantage of collective intimacy is said to be precisely that: a sense of belonging and intimacy. In recent years, scientists confirmed what we have always known, that our brains connect through stories. This means both that we understand things better when they are presented to us in the framework of a story, and that stories allow us to establish more profound connections to each other.[56] Paul J. Zak, a researcher who studies the neurobiology of storytelling, used brain imaging to prove that stories literally change the brain's chemistry as they help "connect us with strangers."[57] Zak says he watches the "amazing neural ballet in which a story line changes the activity of people's brains."[58] According to Zak, the power of storytelling is due to the release of the neurochemical oxytocin, which makes people engage in cooperative behavior:[59]

> Emotional simulation is the foundation for empathy and is particularly powerful for social creatures like humans because it allows us to rapidly forecast if people around us are angry or kind, dangerous or safe, friend or foe. Such a neural mechanism keeps us safe but also allows us to rapidly form relationships with a wider set of members of our species than any other animal does. . . . By knowing someone's story—where they came from, what they do, and who you might know in common—relationships with strangers are formed.[60]

Note that while Zak does not distinguish between different kinds of stories, his wording suggests that *personal* stories about "where [we] come from, what [we] do, and who [we] might know in common" have a stronger potential to connect people to each other than, say, fiction or fantasy.

To begin with, the intimacy generated by collections of personal stories is said to be grounded in shared experiences. As pointed out earlier, the formula "not just my story" has been a common trope in autobiographical literature throughout the ages, and it remains equally popular today. For instance, when the child migrant Abdi Farah recently protested against the detention of migrant children, he introduced his story with these words: "My story is not just my own story. It's about thousands of other lives";[61] when a teenager named Rose Love posted her story of abuse on the internet, she entitled it "not just my story, my life";[62] and when Lucia Jang from North Korea recently testified in front of the UN, she used the exact same formula: "My story is not just my own . . . it is the story of so many North Korean women & children."[63] Collective story sharing ritualizes this formula by demonstrating the commonality of human experiences, since seeing or hearing many stories together (at the same time or in the same collection) will automatically reveal their similarities as well as their differences. In traditional print publications, single authors may have made those connections with single readers, establishing one-to-one similarities, but readers had to conjecture to accept the claim that someone's story reflected thousands of lives. By contrast, when large numbers of stories are aggregated into a single collection, audiences can readily see emerging patterns based on similar experiences. To foreground similarities, story-sharing platforms often praise the commonality of human experience. The Moth, for example, is a cross-media platform that offers storytelling events on a regular basis in all major cities around the US, and the only condition of participation is to be able to tell a true and well-rounded story about oneself. The Moth's mission is "to promote the art and craft of storytelling and to honor and celebrate the diversity and *commonality* of human experience."[64] To celebrate the company's twentieth anniversary in 2018, the website announced: "We honor and celebrate the diversity and commonality of human experience, with 25,000 stories to date, shared live and without notes."[65] And indeed, Moth fans often express a sense of intimacy and connectedness: "I love The Moth because its very origin is deeply rooted in our desire to connect with each other through *shared experiences* in stories."[66]

Moreover, as presented by these sites, intimacy is not just a source to draw from but also a goal to work towards. Collective intimacy is presented here as a means of community development. The Moth, for example, has recently introduced The Moth Community Program, which aims to "*deepen connections* within and between communities."[67] The program's objective is to "honor the individual experience" in order to "challenge dominant narratives, inspire greater confidence in storytellers, deepen connection in community and spark empathy among listeners around the world."[68] Note that community becomes here something to work towards, a shared vision of unity. StoryCorps, like The Moth, stresses this instrumental role of story sharing. The mission of StoryCorps is "to preserve and share humanity's stories *in order to build connections* between people and create a more just and compassionate world."[69] Recently, the company also introduced a new feature called "StoryCorps communities," which is described as "a new place to share your stories, to *connect with others* who record, and to contribute [to] a growing archive of our time in America."[70] The platform also offers custom programs designed to "strengthen relationships within your community."[71]

Ultimately, the sense of intimacy generated by collective autobiographical storytelling is said to form a basis for actionable solidarity. Story activists view the "listening, collecting and sharing [of] life stories as a critical process in *democratizing* culture."[72] As Amy Hill, the founder of the digital storytelling project Silence Speaks put it: "I am not interested in 'collecting stories' just for the sake of creating an archive of stories; I am interested in critically examining the ways in which the process of sharing and listening to stories can lead to specific changes across multiple levels of human experience and influence."[73] Sharing stories is indeed a deeply social act in that our social relations do not entirely precede the act of storytelling but are partly constituted by it. This implies that story sharing can cause transformation on two levels: in storytellers themselves, who will be inspired and empowered by their renewed understanding of collective issues, and in the collective, which can become more conscious of its members' values and priorities. This back and forth is a key principle of transformative story sharing. As the company Transformative Stories explains, sharing my personal story is a way to shape *my community* and *my democracy* by allowing for the rediscovery of connections between *my story* and *our story:*

> Stories don't offer answers. They invite the audience to make their own meaning, and this is part of their power. Democracy and social justice are nothing if not collective endeavors, so *how are connections made between personal stories and the shared narratives*

of social action? A sense of recognition and empowerment is part of what makes someone a citizen who is able to act on his or her own behalf. Personal storytelling can help to build these capacities. But the transition to shared narratives requires something else: a way of connecting personal stories to collective issues which are political, in the sense that they address relations of power. When people connect to these political issues through personal stories, they see them in a different way. They don't just see democracy in the abstract, they see "my democracy"—"what it means for me, in my life, and in the lives of others who I know."[74]

The hope is that by reconnecting people's personal stories to the larger narratives of collectives and social action, we can grow as citizens and develop our personal sense of "my community" and "my democracy."

Through this notion of collective intimacy, "the age of sharing" is fomenting a new, personalized understanding of community.[75] Political philosophers throughout the ages have relied on a binary model to oppose individualism to communitarianism: individualists are said to overemphasize the single individual's rights and independence at the expense of shared interests, while communitarians are said to sacrifice the single individual on the altar of the common good. These political philosophies pit the individual against the community, as if the two were necessarily in conflict. By contrast, the emerging notion of personalized communities sees the personal as a way towards the communal. Instead of being in conflict with the collective, the personal is seen today as a means of deepening our connection to others. The notion of personalized communities suggests that we can personalize our communities the same way we personalize our media content, services, or entertainment, and personal story sharing plays a key role in this process.

Social Media's Collective Intimacy

In the last decade, social media companies have eagerly embraced this notion of collective intimacy. Facebook, for example, built its product on the principle of sharing. CEO Mark Zuckerberg declared "the power to share" to be "the cornerstone of Facebook."[76] To enhance the "sharing experience," Facebook built an entire "sharing ecosystem" by providing both groups of its users—people who share and advertisers who mine the information that people share—with "sharing tools" such as "Share a link" or "Share a like."[77] Later, the company fully automated the process so that people could share without even thinking about it (frictionless sharing). In 2016, however, data showed an alarming tendency. There was a double-digit decline in "original" sharing, meaning that people were less willing to share details about their personal lives. The decline in intimate sharing made the company so worried that Zuckerberg set up a special team to try to reverse the trend. At around the same time, the 2016 US elections made people more aware of the potentially harmful effects of algorithmic sharing. Critics complained that while Facebook did indeed connect people to each other, the company "didn't push for any specific positive outcome from connection. Technically, [posting and sharing] could encompass digital voyeurism via the News Feed, trading in-person friendship for online acquaintanceship or the filter bubbles and echospheres that have further polarized the United States," as one analyst noted.[78] In short, the connections that Facebook created lacked a positive collective purpose.

Under pressure, Zuckerberg announced a monumental shift. On February 16, 2017, he surprised the world with an open letter entitled "Building Global Community." The letter described a transformational moment, calling for a qualitative change in our sharing culture. Zuckerberg encouraged people to replace shallow modes of sharing with deeper, more meaningful modes of communal engagement. Addressed "to our community," the five-page letter contained eighty-one instances of the word "community":

To our *community*,

On our journey to connect the world, we often discuss products we're building and updates on our business. Today I want to focus on the most important question of all: are we building the world we all want?

History is the story of how we've learned to come together in ever greater numbers—from tribes to cities to nations. At each step, we built social infrastructure like *communities*, media and governments to empower us to achieve things we couldn't on our own.

Today we are close to taking our next step. . . . Progress now requires humanity coming together not just as cities or nations, but also as a global *community*. . . . For the past decade, Facebook has focused on connecting friends and families. With that foundation, our next focus will be developing the social infrastructure for *community*—for supporting us, for keeping us safe, for informing us, for civic engagement, and for inclusion of all.[79]

Zuckerberg stressed social responsibility: "We have a responsibility to do more, not just to connect the world but to bring the world closer together"; "I used to think that if we just give people a voice and help some people connect that that would make the world a whole lot better by itself."[80] The aim, he argued, was to bridge social divisions: "Facebook stands for bringing us closer together and building a global community."[81]

At around the same time, Facebook launched a new product. Within a month of Zuckerberg's open letter about "building global community," the company released Facebook Stories. These "story products" encourage users to curate and share stories about their daily lives. The first company to popularize the story format was Snapchat. In 2013 the company introduced a feature whereby Snaps could be brought together into a single chronological Story. The new format was an immense success, and in 2016 Instagram and in 2017 Facebook copied the idea. Since then, the story format has exploded. *Tech Crunch* commented that "stories creation and consumption is up 842 percent since early 2016" and that the story format is growing fifteen times faster than feeds.[82] According to analysts, the potential repercussions of the storification of social media are vast. Zuckerberg noted that he expected stories "to overtake posts and feeds as the most common way that people share across all social apps."[83]

While the original story products were aimed at individual users, companies have since introduced collective story products as well, such as "Our Story" and "Community Voices."[84] This new type of story product allows people to combine their stories into larger wholes. For example, Snapchat created a feature called "Our Story" in 2014 that "gets away from the individual experience and embraces the collective." According to the company's description, "Our Story is a place where Snapchatters can build big community narratives together. Snaps you submit to Our Story can show up on Snap Map or in Search, grouped together with other Snaps from the same location, event, or about the same topic!"[85] In other words, while "My Story" allows users to share their individual experiences, "Our Story" is about individuals joining a community *via* their stories. According to Snapchat, "We built Our Story so that Snapchatters who are at the same event location can contribute Snaps to the same Story. If you can't make it to an event, watching Our Story makes you feel like you're right there!"[86] In a similar vein, in 2017 Facebook renamed its Facebook Stories site "Community Voices": "Facebook Stories is now Community Voices. Welcome to our new Page! Facebook's mission is to give people the power to build community and bring the world closer together. Community

Voices from Facebook celebrates how people like you are doing just that through our new video series."[87]

It is hardly a coincidence that Facebook published its open letter about the value of community at the exact same time as it developed its first story product. As I argue in this book, the contemporary storification of our culture and the somewhat nebulous goal of community-building go hand-in-hand. Strategic storytelling, as its name suggests, uses stories as strategic tools to reach specific goals. Whether in marketing, social services, or political activism, the objective is "to get the message out there." The purpose of sharing one's personal story might be collective—for instance, gathering information about events or showing support for a cause—but the strategy remains distributive. It's all about sharing *out*. By contrast, the kind of story sharing more recently promoted by social media companies and other story-sharing platforms prioritizes sharing *in*. It embraces the ideal of collective intimacy, both as a shared ground and as a shared goal to work towards. As Facebook's redefinition of its mission also illustrates, building connections is no longer seen as a satisfying outcome; instead, people are calling for more meaningful definitions of what it means to be in community.[88] In short, in the new millennium collective story sharing has become a key mode of collective engagement, promising the double advantage of collective intimacy.

A Critique of Collective Intimacy

Meanwhile, a strong current of criticism has also surfaced around story sharing. Some critics target the naïve tone of celebrations of community and the fuzzy feelings evoked by the notion of commonality. For instance, in *Facebook Society: Losing Ourselves in Sharing Ourselves,* Roberto Simanowksi traces the effects of social media on our practices of self-reflection, lamenting the fact that "on social networks self-representation is mostly delegated to the mechanism of the camera and rooted in a profound lack of self-initiative. The result of this development is a network autobiography that emerges automatically and posthumanly, simultaneously bypassing its object/subject, the act of reflection, and meaningful experience altogether."[89] Many complain that these emerging communities are meaningless because they are transitory and superficial. As Zygmunt Bauman proposed, such initiatives "can spawn 'communities' only as fragile and short-lived, scattered and wandering emotions, shifting erratically from one target to another and drifting in the forever inconclusive search for a secure haven; communities of shared worries, shared anxieties or shared hatreds—but in each case a 'peg' community, a momentary gathering around a nail on which many solitary individuals hang their solitary individual fears."[90]

Others argue that a vague celebration of "community building" is not only naïve but downright harmful in that it preempts social critique. Alexander Freund, among others, contends that story-sharing platforms do the opposite of community-building. He singles out StoryCorps to show how "storytelling conflates history and individual memory and thus depoliticizes public discourse." In Freund's words, "StoryCorps wants to make the point that every American is the same. It does so under the cover of democratization, inclusion, and humanism.... They are Americans, and whether they are white or black, poor or rich, StoryCorps's underlying message is that the story would be the same. Such a move, however, together with populist claims that all debate is divisive, is a political strategy to preempt social critique."[91]

There is criticism of both elements of collective intimacy: (1) the idea of story sharing as knowledge production and (2) the idea of story sharing as a means to create intimacy. Regarding the idea that story sharing will offer better knowledge about our communities because we can mine large databases of personal experiences for collective insights, critics are quick to point to the drawbacks of participatory methods. For instance, Sujatha Fernandes in *Curated Stories: Uses and Misuses of Storytelling* studies specific interactions between storytellers, activists, and media organizations to show how political agendas and financial priorities distort individual stories to make them more palatable or actionable. Fernandes argues that personal stories are often being mobilized for social justice issues without accounting for the deeper context of issues and lives.[92] Furthermore, the ideal of stories told by us and for us becomes even more questionable when viewed in the context of surveillance capitalism. Surveillance capitalism thrives on personal data, which it commodifies with the purpose of profit-making.[93] Seen from this perspective, storytellers who eagerly post their personal stories are complicit members of the surveillance market and surveillance state. Note that "participatory media," in this context, does not subvert but rather drives the system, as the urge to make our voices heard becomes a way to commodify our personal and relational knowledge. The aggregated knowledge we gain will indeed produce new insights, but those insights serve other purposes than intended.[94]

The idea that collective story sharing will lead to a greater sense of intimacy and belonging is also up for debate. José Van Dijck, among others, has questioned the motivation behind social media companies' approach to community-building. In *The Culture of Connectivity*, Van Dijck demonstrates how companies such as Facebook purposely conflate connectivity with community participation and cooperation so as to generate more sellable data. She argues that people "erroneously attribute" the participatory potential of social media to the Web's technological design,[95] which in turn helps corporations adopt the ethos of communitarianism for commercial purposes.[96] Indeed, most people fail to distinguish between the words "connectedness" and "connectivity" (the former refers to the connectedness of human networks while the latter means the ability of electronic devices to connect to each other). In Van Dijck's view, this minor detail is symptomatic of a larger conflation: "Companies tend to stress the first meaning (human connectedness) and minimize the second meaning (automated connectivity) . . . connectedness is often invoked as the pretense for generating connectivity, even now that data generation has become a primary objective rather than a by-product of online sociality."[97] Van Dijck's point is that companies intentionally conflate the two meanings so as to imbue their corporate missions with idealist visions about community participation.[98] In the end, "under the guise of connectedness, [companies] produce a precious resource: connectivity."[99]

Jodi Dean, with her notion of "communicative capitalism," mounts a particularly fierce attack against the idea that personal story sharing can improve communities.[100] Dean's prime target is "the seemingly unquestionable connection between publicity and democracy."[101] Like Van Dijck, she evokes the "New Communalists" of the 1960s Bay Area counterculture, who were seen as transforming the computer from a tool of military, industrial, and state control into a means of grassroots organization and personal empowerment (as exemplified by the Whole Earth Catalog, personal computers, internet, etc.). In Dean's view, New Communalists actually "failed to acknowledge how their ostensibly countercultural practices themselves served as conduits for spreading the communication and control mechanisms"[102] that "produced the networks through which communicative capitalism ensnares speech and action."[103] Communicative capitalism is characterized by an endless reflexivity driven by the circuitry of feedback loops established by our constant urge to post and to share, which turns the very practices that connect us to each other into new forms of control. I would argue that the practice of autobiographical story sharing is key to the operation of communicative capitalism, because it responds to the injunction to participate. We are responsible for making our voices heard so that each and every member can be accounted for in our shared co-creation of communities, but this pressure to individuate ourselves for the sake of the common good actually captures "users in intensive and extensive networks of enjoyment, production, and surveillance."[104] This system is particularly intense in its affective dimension, since every retweet or comment is rewarded with enjoyment, "a smidgen of attention," a "tiny affective nugget."[105] These affective links function as "a binding technique," and they do produce "feelings of community, or what we might call 'community without community.'"[106] As a result, even our potential acts of resistance become inscribed within the circuits of communicative networks, so that in the end, "Our participation does not subvert communicative capitalism. It drives it."[107] Following Dean's logic, one could argue that story sharing sites are harmful in that they create online filter bubbles that lead to an increased polarization of social and political views. These self-isolating communities, based on shared stories of personal experiences en masse, are founded on essentialist ideals and may become so authoritative that they end up silencing or actively discrediting dissenting voices.

Complementary Practices

These critics raise valid points, and I agree that there is an urgent need to ask critical questions, not just about the feel-good messages of the story-sharing industry, but also about the complex role of aggregated stories in imagining new communities. I share their skepticism about the contemporary techno-euphoria, and I am concerned about the erosion of the line between "collective (non-market, public) and commercial (market, private) modes of production."[108] It is evident that in contemporary practices of story sharing, nonprofit peer production, with its invisible labor, is being exploited for profit-oriented production and surveillance, which leads to the commodification of audiences and communities. I also agree with Dean that given the extent of our entrapment in the very mechanisms that control us, critical media theorists "should forswear affective offerings of hope and reassurance."[109]

Nevertheless, I will argue that neither the freedom implied by self-expression nor its consequences for our democratic publics are as illusionary as Dean and others insist. First, to grasp the full potential of story sharing, we should avoid positing the two sides as a binary—top-down exploitation versus bottom-up liberation—and focus instead on the morally messy ways in which the two intersect in communicative capitalism. As the creation and circulation of personal stories can serve a wide range of interests, the traditional boundaries between users and producers, creativity and disruption, "complicit passivity and subversive participation,"[110] become less and less tenable. As producers and users of these platforms merge, "to some extent, all self-curators [become] self-produsers, cobbling together presentations of selfhood within networks of consumption and exchange that still bear the traces of a market economy. Even if they aren't seeking 'instafame' and commercial gain, online auto/biographers remain subject to an imperative to produce appealing products in an environment shaped by more or less friendly competition."[111] Also, looking at the phenomenon from a historical perspective, it is questionable whether the notion of agency and privacy attached to the subject position has ever been a reality, especially in those populations that have long been aggregated, observed, and managed along racialized and gender-based lines. I agree with Jenkins, Ford, and Green, who argue that "in order to accept this more morally complex account of collaboration, it's crucial to move beyond seeing the relations between producers and their audiences as a zero-sum game."[112] Collective story sharing is a messy and unpredictable process of negotiation, with some complementary interests and no single optimal strategy.

Second, just as the non-zero-sum game of collective story sharing creates an open field of possibilities, so does the unique, open-ended nature of stories. We need to remember that personal stories constitute a unique kind of data in that they are never "raw"; they are already the product of interpretation while also being up for interpretation. What makes narratives particularly powerful is their "subjunctive quality," "*to make it so by saying it so*—and the inevitable relationship, as a consequence, between narrative and judgment." Narratives rely on "the slippage between the real and the imagined," and "the impossibility of unraveling aesthetic from moral judgment."[113] "The configuration of events into a temporal frame with a beginning, middle, and end involves numerous acts of judgment, including the translation of 'difference into similarity' and the leaving out of some things and inclusion of others."[114] On the one hand, this subjunctive quality of narratives and their ability to cover their tracks means that narratives can normalize exclusions by folding them into a familiar narrative form—that is, they can create storylines that resonate with familiar values and assumptions about who belongs and who does not. On the other hand, the same qualities also mean that stories are uniquely positioned to challenge existing answers and categories, and unlike other types of data, they even offer the luxury of not knowing to which question they seek the answer. In analyzing contemporary practices of story sharing, therefore, we need to emphasize how personal stories can disclose new possibilities for being, not only on a personal but also on a collective level.

Third, in talking about collections or databases of personal stories, it is tempting to again set up a binary and emphasize the competing motives between databases and stories. As the contemporary surge of datafication seems to exacerbate the rivalry between stories and numbers, many observers argue that narratives are threatened by the dominance of database technologies. Among others, Lev Manovich argues that the "database and narratives are natural enemies": "As a cultural form, database represents the world as a list of items and it refuses to order this list. In contrast, a narrative creates a cause-and-effect trajectory of seemingly unordered items (events). Therefore, database and narrative are natural enemies. Competing for the same territory of human culture, each claims an exclusive right to make meaning out of the world."[115] I see the relationship between database and narrative as competitive but also complementary. I side with commentators such as Katherine Hayles, who argues that narrative and database are more like "natural symbionts" whose "complex ecology" can expand the capabilities of both databases and narratives. Databases of personal stories are perfect examples of this symbiosis, because they illustrate how, on the one hand, database technologies and the algorithmic processing of digital data have come to dominate the process of interpreting personal stories and, on the other hand, how databases themselves are fluid like narratives in the sense that they allow for ever-new queries and readings depending on who uses them for what purposes.[116]

Therefore, in analyzing various story-sharing practices, we need to first acknowledge the complementary nature of top-down and bottom-up practices, of databases and stories, and of the inclusive and exclusive tendencies of narratives. I will even argue that it is because of these complementarities, and not in spite of them, that collective story sharing has such power and potential. Collections of personal stories can create new ways to imagine our connections to others and our communities, but only if we are attentive to the deep complicity between these various forces. The following chapters all raise critical questions about what it means to come together as a community via personal stories. How does the materiality of the medium shape these story collections, and what inherited paradigms about community, time, space, statistics, and knowledge guide us when we try to imagine our "shared humanity"? I argue that assembled stories ritualize shared time, shared space, and shared knowledge as a way to build bridges, often in the name of justice and democratic dialogue. While acknowledging the importance of shared dreams, I will urge caution about the new sense of intimacy promised by story-sharing platforms, as well as about the new insights that aggregated personal stories are said to generate. Our newest crowdsourced, aggregated story collections do indeed offer more democratic ways to source insider knowledge about our collectives and more intimate ways to experience our communities. Nevertheless, the ideas of a neutral story library of human experiences and of a worldwide community of storytellers remain just as problematic today as they were in the eighteenth century, when they were first proposed.

2 EARLY STORY COLLECTIONS
Setting the Stage

> *Indeed, the strange property of political statements is that their task—an eminently temporary, risky, fragile task—is to produce those who formulate them!*
> —BRUNO LATOUR

The previous chapter showed how, in the age of social media and algorithmic processing, personal stories are being used to create collective intimacy. I borrowed the term "collective intimacy" from marketing to explain how each citizen's relationship to their community deepens via insights developed across all relationships. The present chapter traces this notion of collective intimacy back to eighteenth-century Germany, because late Enlightenment philosophers were the first to simultaneously lament the breakdown of traditional communities and to celebrate the potential of personal stories to bring people back together. The Enlightenment is a unique point in the history of story activism because it was the first time that autobiographical stories had been assembled into print collections. The Age of Reason, with such canonical texts as Jean-Jacques Rousseau's *Confessions* and Benjamin Franklin's *Autobiography*, has often been described as the first golden age of Western life writing. According to scholars, the Enlightenment values of self-education and autonomy found a suitable literary expression in the genre of autobiography, and vice versa, the rising memoir culture bolstered the Enlightenment ideals of self-fashioning and autonomy. Some even argued that "the very idea of autobiography has grown out of the political necessities and discoveries of the American and French revolutions."[1] The problem with this account is that it overemphasizes the myth of autonomy and the role of individual authors in developing democracy. To challenge this account, I present an alternative story in which many people gather their personal stories into print collections, thereby creating the spectacle of a democratic, public forum.

Collective intimacy, we said, promises a powerful combination of two things: collective insights and a sense of intimacy and belonging. These two priorities, the epistemic and the social, converged in the Enlightenment when a few visionaries began to ponder the connection between autobiographical self-reflection and collective insights and intimacy. In terms of collective insights, the eighteenth century saw the first modern efforts to systematically collect, classify, and publish all human knowledge. Scholars in the Age of Reason were enamored with the possibility of establishing a universal set of rules for nature, as well as for social, political, and moral order. It made sense to seek empirical knowledge based on people's own self-observations and to want to systematize that knowledge in archives of autobiographical stories. The Enlightenment was also the first time that social philosophers lamented the rise of modern society (*Gesellschaft*) as opposed to the cozy, humanizing communities (*Gemeinschaft*) of earlier eras.[2] As philosophers sought ways to reconstitute those bonds that tie community into an organic totality, some realized that sharing personal stories had a "campfire effect," that by reading each other's stories people could develop empathy and be able to create a sense of unity in the community.

Karl Philipp Moritz (1756–1793) and Johann Gottfried Herder (1744–1803) were contemporaries who both championed autobiographical story sharing. They both believed in the value of publishing not just individual memoirs but collections of them, although they had different priorities. Moritz was more interested in the knowledge that people could gain by assembling their stories. He described these "crowdsourced" story libraries as an innovative way to increase society's knowledge about the amazing variety of human experiences. Herder, meanwhile, was more interested in the idea of social bonding and the political consequences of assembling personal stories. He wondered what would happen if people had access to each other's diaries and stories and could hear about the similar fates and thoughts they shared and about all the injustices they suffered. I have chosen Moritz and Herder as case studies to stress the epistemic focus of the former and the political concerns of the latter. Of course, knowledge production and politics are inseparable, since knowledge is always socially produced and also because whose stories we collect depends on "the role of history in the community."[3] I only separate them here for heuristic reasons, to show this double priority of collective intimacy.

In their commitment to diverse autobiographical voices, Moritz and Herder both went against mainstream Enlightenment science in that they rejected its universalizing objectives. Enlightenment scholars aspired to universal truths unattached to particular places, times, and individuals. By contrast, Moritz and Herder believed in each and every human being's capacity to self-reflect, and they championed the value of limited perspectives and diverse voices. At the same time, neither of them was immune to the scientific and progressivist urges of their age. Moritz and Herder marveled at the diversity of individual voices, but they also wanted to rein them into collections. What makes their projects fascinating is precisely the productive tension between their simultaneous desire to, on the one hand, individualize and democratize and, on the other, collectivize and centralize. As such, Moritz's and Herder's public forums of individual voices are perfect illustrations of the crucial role that assembled stories can play in political imagination.

Moritz: A Common Mirror in Which Humankind Could Inspect Itself

Karl Philipp Moritz was a German novelist, editor, and essayist who tried his pen in many genres. Having received only a haphazard education, Moritz's intellectual authority was often questioned by his contemporaries, and his eccentricity rubbed many the wrong way. Yet, his outsider status also had its advantages, as demonstrated by the originality of his undertakings. Moritz's most lasting contributions include *Anton Reiser*, a fictionalized autobiography, and the journal *Gnothi Sauton; oder, Magazin zur Erfahrungsseelenkunde*.[4] *Gnothi Sauton* ("know thyself" in classical Greek) was the first periodical ever devoted to experimental psychology. Moritz was drawn to stories about pathological behaviors and wondered what the description of such cases could contribute to knowledge about humanity. He believed that "the collected reports of several careful observers of man's heart could form an experimental psychology, which could by far surpass in terms of practical usefulness all that our forebears have done in this respect."[5] If people could all share their personal stories and assemble them into collections, those archives "could one day serve as a common mirror in which humankind could inspect itself,"[6] he enthused.

Moritz's idea clearly had appeal, since the journal lived for an entire decade (1783–93), during which it published roughly thirty volumes and close to one hundred authors. The contributions include a wide range of materials: diaries, dream reports, descriptions of unusual behaviors, and letters, as well as court cases and school reports. Some of the narratives are autobiographical, such as diaries and confessions, others biographical, such as case studies describing pathological and pedagogical cases.[7] The collection includes stories of murders, suicides, self-mutilation, mental illness, melancholy, somnambulism, hypochondria, kleptomania, and more. Moritz encouraged his readers to share their stories of "obvious and hidden faults,"[8] as well as stories about how they struggled with and overcame their vices.[9] Overall, the journal presents a highly eclectic, fascinating series of unusual case histories, representing a wide range of social classes ("those who fell from the highest echelons of society to the lowest and the other way around, those who rose to wealth and power").[10] In Moritz's words, these "true reports about life or observations about oneself"[11] are "worth more in terms of practical knowledge than a thousand observations taken from a book."[12] Indeed, the individual cases were described in such detail that two centuries later a team of psychologists could evaluate them based on their own diagnostic criteria.[13] The journal's material greatly influenced the development of modern psychology and psychiatry, and it also contributed to the nineteenth-century literary fascination with the grotesque and the criminal.

To some extent, Moritz's project was a product of its age. Self-observation was an imperative of the Age of Enlightenment, and systematic self-observation was prescribed in the vocabulary of the natural sciences. Rousseau famously declared: "I shall perform upon myself the sort of operation that physicists conduct upon the air in order to discover its daily fluctuations. I shall take the barometer readings of my soul, and by doing this accurately and repeatedly I could perhaps obtain results as reliable as theirs."[14] Moreover, the dictate to self-observe was also extended to the observation of others. Historians, statisticians, and scientists from the emerging fields of pedagogy, psychology, and psychiatry exhorted people to report not only their own behaviors, thoughts, and emotions but also those of others. In Germany, for instance, teachers encouraged their pupils to "write down their thoughts about everything that they have read, heard and seen" and to share these diaries with their teachers and classmates as a means of mutual accountability.[15] Echoing this mantra, Moritz's journal sought to document "observations from real life" and "real facts," and he described the journal's contributors as "people observers" (*Menschenbeobachter*).[16]

Moritz also adopted the Enlightenment ethos of progress. On an individual level, he believed in the therapeutic function of autobiographical storytelling, as well as in its corrective function. Autobiographical narratives have long been framed in terms of self-optimization, and self-improvement has always been a part of the ideal of a well-lived life, from the Confucian virtue of *ren* and the Socratic ideal of an "examined life," to the confessional practices of later centuries. During the Enlightenment, however, the idea of self-optimization became inseparable from to the idea of societal optimization. Ralph Köhnen, who has traced the history of self-optimization through diary-writing, argues that starting in the sixteenth century, the ancient practice of self-reflection became more and more focused on perfectability, as diary writers internalized external pressures from various other discourses, such as the pietistic emphasis on the value of confession, the celebration of new empirical methods, new state interests in demographic and social research, and advances in medical and economic knowledge. Together, these discourses created a context in which autobiographical writing became not simply a technique to improve one's own personal life, but also a way to put self-reflection into the service of society.[17]

Benjamin Franklin's *Autobiography* is often cited as an example of this connection between personal and collective improvement. Franklin's story has been praised as a testament to the self-made man, but Franklin himself considered autobiographical self-reflection a form of communal engagement. His motto (*communiter bona profundere deum est*, "to support the common good is divine") was deeply community-oriented, and he viewed the act of self-reflection as a form of public service. His famous list of thirteen virtues that he tracked throughout life,[18] as well as his daily question in his diary about "What good have I done today?" served as tools in his quest for personal "moral perfection." The ultimate purpose of his personal perfection, however, was always the common good, and it was in the process of self-reflection that Franklin could identify the strengths and weaknesses in his character that made him a better citizen.

Moritz's journal bears the imprint of these same empirical and pietistic principles in that it treats personal stories as part of the common good. Moritz framed the value of personal stories mostly in epistemic terms, stressing the unique kind of knowledge that individuals and society can gain from them. He subtitled his journal a "reader" (*Lesebuch*) and addressed it to the "educated and the uneducated," which suggests that he wanted to popularize psychology as well as create new knowledge. Observing others via their own self-observation could be therapeutic on a personal level, he argued, since reading about "how someone managed to overcome faults such as anger, pride or vanity" could help readers correct their own weaknesses.[19] Moreover, dissecting life could also have a preventive and corrective function on the level of society. "We executed thousands of criminals" without ever asking what had led them to those paths, complains Moritz.[20] Using the metaphor of the social body, he suggests that his collection could help detect "little unnoticed splinters" and early signs of inflammation in society before they require more drastic intervention.[21]

Given Moritz's enthusiasm for self-observation and observation, it would be tempting to read his journal as an instrument of early modern state-centered biopolitics, as described in Foucault's *Discipline and Punish*. Foucault argues that over the course of the eighteenth century, biographical and autobiographical reports, along with other types of documentation, began to form archives of knowledge that supported institutions of power and control such as prisons, schools, psychiatric wards, and various government offices. As Foucault explains, this "whole mass of documents" created a "network of writings," a "field of surveillance" that "capture[d] and fix[ed]" people. It turned people into "describable, analysable objects" as part of a "comparative system that made possible the measurement of overall phenomena, the description of groups, the characterization of collective facts, the calculation of the facts between individuals, their distribution in a given 'population.'"[22] As a result, individuals became correctable and classifiable "case studies" based on their own self-observations or the observations of others, and self-discipline became inseparable from the disciplinary measures of state power. One could certainly read the magazine's material in terms of Foucault's panoptic vision, especially those passages where Moritz praises the correctional and regulatory promise of his journal, noting that these personal stories bring attention to minor details that previously may have passed under the radar of scientists and authorities. Clearly, the epistemic desire to want to know everything is a slippery slope, politically.

Yet, reducing the journal to a mere tool of surveillance would not do it justice. First, Moritz was determined not to fall into the trap of premature generalizations and resisted the urge for inductive reasoning. He insisted that the journal should contain mostly "facts and no moralistic verbiage."[23] He also averred, especially in the beginning, that there should be as few added reflections and interpretations as possible: "All these observations should first be collected under various rubrics in a special magazine dedicated to this material, presented without reflections, until enough facts have been accumulated, and then, at the end, take all this material and arrange it in useful ways into a whole, what an important work this could be for humanity."[24] With his commitment to unsystematic exploration, Moritz went against mainstream eighteenth-century science. The fields of psychology and psychiatry were on the cusp of professionalization, which made them particularly eager to embrace the Enlightenment values of classification and universal knowledge. Moritz, however, was adamant about wanting to create a "censor- and moral-free space for experiential reports from the inner world of empirical individuals."[25] Later in his life, as he struggled with his own autobiographical recollections, Moritz began to doubt the value of narrated facts. Nevertheless, he stuck to his original method, arguing that the self-deception of autobiographers could be counterbalanced by the insights gained from aggregating a sufficiently large number of stories.

If Moritz sought to avoid premature analysis, it is because he recognized the limitations of empiricism in matters of psychology. He made every person an authority on their own life and elevated the epistemic authority of experience. Convinced that "experience contains its own redemptive coherence,"[26] he maintained that every single life, even those traumatized by oppression and deprivation, were worthy of scientific interest and social investment. Lack of education should not be a barrier, he stressed, for no one else could possibly invent the unique perspective from which each individual sees and experiences the world: "The one at the very bottom of humankind would still remain a masterwork on earth, if he were the only one of his kind."[27] Moritz was particularly adamant about the epistemic authority of autobiographical narratives. He studied the role of memory and language in developing one's life story, and he wanted to share the full story of people instead of merely using their stories to present the history of their disease or crime. He also resisted the advice of friends who recommended that Moritz accompany each issue with a contextualizing essay to "brighten the view" and to "dissolve dissonances in harmony."[28]

The magazine was also revolutionary in the way it decentralized observational power. Although Moritz called for a shared, "crowdsourced" effort to gather knowledge, this did not imply the existence of impartial observers. Instead, he promoted the idea of what Donna Haraway calls "situated knowledges," acknowledging that all knowledge comes from the positional perspectives of socially situated observers. He wrote: "Should people from various social classes divide this labor among them, each making observations about those few people with whom office or class brings him in close contact?"[29] This reference to "office" (*Amt*) and "class" (*Stand*) highlights the subject position occupied by each observer within society and the special epistemic value of their situatedness. As Andreas Gailus suggests, Moritz actually "out-Foucault's Foucault," in that "for Foucault, the case is an administrative invention generated 'under the gaze of a permanent corpus of knowledge.' By contrast, *Erfahrungsseelenkunde* is an exploratory investigation criss-crossing a number of professional discourses, and the *Magazin*, . . . is a messy archive emphatically located outside institutions of power and knowledge (university, state, professions). Whereas Foucault, for all his anti-law rhetoric operates with an essentially sovereign model of panoptic surveillance, Moritz out-Foucault's Foucault by stressing that truly detailed knowledge of society can be generated only from within society, that is: through the multiplicity of partial and situated observers spread across the entire social body."[30]

Finally, Moritz's enterprise was also groundbreaking in its creation of a reading public. With close to eight hundred readers, the journal was a successful venture and its readers represented a wide range of professions, including teachers, doctors, lawyers, and priests. From the very beginning, Moritz insisted that creating a public library of human experiences would have to be a collective effort. He therefore called on "all observers of the human heart, no matter their social rank and position, who wish to actively promote truth and happiness among men."[31] Moritz's crowd-sourcing efforts were highly successful in that many of his readers turned into active contributors themselves. People began to recognize the value of their own "insider knowledge" and sent in enthusiastic submissions from all over Germany. As a result, the *Magazin* was not only the first journal devoted to experimental psychology, but also the last one in that subject area to have a lay readership and lay contributors. Editors of the 1981 reedition argue that the magazine "deserves to be viewed as a collective statement" in that it created "a communication medium for citizens who were beginning to remember, in full public view, and who were becoming more certain of their experiences."[32] Indeed, by keeping his journal purposely fluid, open, and democratic, Moritz created an important public forum for private citizens, laying the foundations for a civil society in the Habermasian sense. And although Moritz himself did not dwell on the political implications of such a public forum, seen from our twenty-first-century perspective they are hard to miss.

Herder: A Sense of Belonging and Community for German Citizens

Johann Gottfried Herder was a German philosopher, poet, and literary critic who, like his contemporary Moritz, enthusiastically promoted autobiographical story sharing. Herder dedicated several philosophical treatises to the subject, and he was also actively involved in assembling collections of personal stories.[33] Herder saw many advantages, both private and public, to the practice of life writing. He argued that as a form of personal reflection, autobiography could help to heal and clarify; as a family document, it would allow parents to transmit their experiences to their children; as a scientific document, it could contribute to both self-knowledge and to the knowledge of humankind; and as a document of collective existence, autobiography could enhance communal spirit.[34] Herder was so enthusiastic about the benefits of life writing that he urged his contemporaries to get into the habit of writing down and sharing their reflections. At least two collections appeared as a direct result of his prompting: *Autobiographies of Famous Men,* edited by David Christoph Seybold, and *Memoirs of Remarkable Men,* edited by Johann Georg Müller.[35]

At first, the titles of these collections referring to "famous" and "remarkable" men seem to suggest an elitist enterprise. Herder's introduction to Müller's edition, in which he encourages his contemporaries to collect "the life histories that notable people have left for others," further reinforces this elitist impression: "First of all, I wish for autobiographies of select, remarkable men."[36] At the same time, Herder also valued personal stories for their democratic potential. He insisted that collections of autobiographies should make room for people from all walks of life: "Everyone who experiences or performs anything memorable has the right to tell about it; and if he can write a clear and entertaining narrative, then even better."[37] He went as far as to argue that all who are alive have the authority and even obligation to share their experiences. As he put it, a valet's reminiscences may actually be more interesting than those of his master.[38] It would be wrong, in Herder's view, for a collection of personal stories to only include a "select" group of texts. In theory at least, the entire population should be able to contribute to it.

Herder seemed particularly interested in the political promise of such democratic archives of personal experiences. For instance, he argued that such collections could help keep the justice system fair. He mentions a concrete example, the case of Friedrich Daniel Schubart, whom the *Fürst* locked up without sufficient evidence. Schubart protested against this injustice by writing down and circulating his personal story.[39] Herder comments that true stories such as Daniel Schubart's should be transmitted "by word of mouth, from diary to diary."[40] As Herder notes, "When a hundred accusing voices rise, and they name specific names and describe faithfully all the circumstances, then no ears will remain deaf, not even the most hardened and insensible ones."[41] As the rousing tone of this passage demonstrates, Herder believed that personal stories en masse could not only reflect but also transform social reality.[42] Besides matters of justice, one important way in which assembled personal stories could transform societies is by making people conscious of their political power as a community. Understandably, Herder was particularly concerned with the fate of his own political community, the German nation. In the late eighteenth century, Germany (more precisely, the Holy Roman Empire of the German Nation) was highly fragmented, comprised of many small independent territories. Herder viewed this fragmentation as the major cause of Germany's social, cultural, and economic underdevelopment. While efforts were underway to administratively and militarily unify the country, Herder sought alternative ways to accomplish unity. Somewhat surprisingly, he singled out autobiographies as one of the means to unify the German nation.

Herder used autobiographies as a paradigm for how collectives, such as nations, can evolve through self-reflection. He was one of the first cultural relativists, meaning that in opposition to the "universal reason" celebrated by French philosophers he promoted a pluralist stance.[43] Herder was ambivalent about the universalizing principles of the French Enlightenment. His early studies explore the possibility of portraying the individual as an object of universally applicable "human sciences," while also treating it as a subject, "as an individual phenomenon, as an identity." "Based on the knowledge of single individuals, I get to know classes and nations," he noted in his travel diary.[44] Yet, while he believed in the inductive nature of scientific generalization, he was skeptical about deducing the individual from the general. He insisted that every phenomenon, person, and culture needed different sets of value criteria: "Each people, each age had its own form of happiness, its own form of excellence, its very own aspirations. Each of these could only be understood in its own terms, its specific conditions through time—that is, its history."[45] According to Herder, just as the idea of a unified humanity guarantees the sovereignty of every unique and irreplaceable nation, the idea of a unified nation is necessary to secure the value of the diversity represented by the individual members of the national community. This pluralist stance led to an unusually generous idea of what constitutes history. According to Frank E. Manuel, "Herder broke the bounds of what could be included in history with an impetuosity that makes previous enlargements of the historical vision puny."[46] He made "all moments of time in all cultures worthy of respect," which democratized the historic process to "a degree that had never been achieved before."[47]

Herder coined the term "collective individuality" to refer to cultures, nations, peoples, and civilizations, and he described their functioning in highly dynamic and fluid ways, like the life cycle of an individual. To emphasize the unique history, value, and potential of each collective individuality, he compared their history to the life story of an individual.[48] He imagined the German nation as a unique person in the family of humankind, one that could only be understood in its own terms, through its own history. Over the course of his career, Herder's attention shifted from the role of Germany as a unique member in the family of humankind (a collective *individuality*), towards the question of the inner constitution of the nation's unity (a *collective* individuality). Autobiographies played a key role in Herder's thinking, because in his view, autobiographies could help articulate the connectedness within collective individualities, just as they help individuals see the connections within their own lives. As Hallberg explains, "Herder view[ed] language as a kind of tool to gain consciousness of one's self and one's relations to others, thus making community life possible."[49] In sum, he used the genre of autobiography to illustrate the dynamic processes whereby collective individualities can shape themselves through self-reflection.[50]

According to Herder, autobiographies could shape a nation's sense of unity and solidarity both externally and internally. On an external level, collections of personal stories by ordinary Germans could help disseminate and popularize German culture abroad. Lamenting the lack of such literature, he compared Germany to other nations and concluded that Germany was far behind: "How far behind we are, Germans, behind other nations such as the French, the British, and the Italians!";[51] "Our old biographies have not been collected; the French, the British have been";[52] "we Germans painfully lack personal reminiscences written in the first person."[53] To underscore this backwardness, Herder contrasted German autobiographies to the prestigious French life-writing tradition.[54] Not only did French autobiographies contribute to the formation of good taste within their own country, he noted, but they also helped popularize French language and culture abroad. Germans should do the same, he urged: "Write memoirs, you quiet, hard-working, too modest, too timid Germans!"[55]

Furthermore, he proposed that a nation also needed to recognize its own cohesion *internally* and that sharing personal stories among citizens was a perfect way to do it. A nation could only fulfill its world-historical potential, he noted, if its powers were first joined into a shared, unified vision. Herder lamented that, historically, Germany had lacked such a unifying vision and urged Germans to develop such a shared voice: "Indeed, it is our fatherland's fault that we never had a shared voice, a place to gather where we could raise our voices in unison. Everything is so divided here."[56] He again contrasted Germans to other nationalities and noted how the French or the British could be confident in the importance of their own personal voices because they felt that they all belonged to the same community: "the feeling that they belong to a fatherland, that they belong to themselves, and that they are responsible for their lives to themselves and to the world, gave them courage to judge."[57] In Herder's view, the solidarity that French and British citizens felt for each other was grounded in their shared autobiographical readings: "nothing in our life can lift us up, strengthen and revive us, as much as the compassion of an other."[58] That is why he sought to persuade Germans to also share their stories, to make them conscious of their unique power as a community. The nation was not something fully formed, but it was always in the process of becoming, and the dynamism of personal stories could guarantee that the process remained open-ended.[59]

It would be difficult to overestimate the significance of Herder's emphasis on the social and political function of aggregated personal stories. Collections of biographies have long been used to instill a sense of pride in collectives, but Herder was among the first to apply the same logic to autobiographical narratives. He criticized state power and "envisaged a political community in which all citizens, individually or in groups, co-operated within some sort of pluralist scheme where power and control were not centralized but widely diffused."[60] To Herder, collections of shared personal stories were both symbolic and practical representations of such a diffused democratic power. The number one priority in the project of nation-building should be the creation of a unified "public sphere" (*Öffentlichkeit*), he wrote, "I don't wish for a court or a capital; instead I wish for an altar of honest faithfulness where [citizens] can gather in spirit and heart."[61] Forget about building a capital or a parliament; it is not the buildings that we need to start with, he urged. Focus instead on people's diverse voices and concerns, because once people start reading about each other's joys and tribulations, they will realize that they share similar concerns and experiences, which in turn will instill in them a sense of solidarity.[62]

It would not be an overstatement to call such a public forum of individual voices revolutionary. As a matter of fact, we have a concrete example from the eighteenth century that demonstrates the political potential of such story collections. In the same decade that Moritz and Herder were active, the French Revolution shattered the *ancien régime*. Realizing that he had lost touch with his people, in March 1789 King Louis XVI ordered every Estate to draw up a list of their grievances in so-called *cahiers de doléances* (notebooks of complaints).[63] This was a rather democratic idea, since it allowed even members of the Third Estate, such as peasants from poor villages and urban workers, to speak out against the injustices they suffered. The king, of course, did not intend this collection of personal experiences to challenge his regime, he merely wanted some ideas and suggestions about how to reform the country. However, once people began to air their complaints and hear each other's stories, this made them aware of the magnitude of the problems, which in turn fueled widespread political discontent. As Zaretsky points out, "given the world-altering events that followed later that year, the seismic rumble of the cahiers de doléances is often overlooked. Yet it was an unprecedented exercise, not just in 18th century France but throughout Europe, in uncensored and unbound popular expression."[64] As such, these *cahiers* could be considered the earliest examples of the type of story collections discussed in this book, and they underscore the enormous potential that Herder also attributed to them.[65]

The Spectacle of a Public Forum

To conclude, I want to emphasize the role of Moritz's, Herder's, and other similar story collections in social and political imagination. The explicitly political nature of the *cahiers de doléances* helps highlight a key paradox at the heart of all story collections. Whether framed in epistemic or political terms, crowdsourced story collections offer a common mirror in which communities can examine themselves. Moritz hoped that his magazine "could one day serve as a common mirror in which humankind could inspect itself,"[66] while Herder described them as "mirrors of the age" that could reflect social and political conditions.[67] The metaphor of a "common mirror" is of course tricky, for it assumes that the community exists already prior to looking into the mirror, when in fact both Moritz and Herder viewed story collections as transformative in the sense of being *performative* of personal and collective identities. Assembling personal voices was a means of creating a sense of commonality, a way to make connections between private stories and shared narratives.

Herein lies the paradox of all political expression, for in order for individual voices to become transformative social force, people need already to have formed an audience or public—that is, they need to already think of themselves as a collective in order to authorize one of their members to speak, to share their story. To put it succinctly, political speech assumes what it sets out to create, in the sense that it has to "produce those who formulate [it]."[68] This is how Bruno Latour explained the paradox in the example of the *cahiers*: "The historians of the Revolution have clearly shown the effect of the birth of the citizen and even to some extent of the French people themselves, as they reacted to King Louis XVI's summons to write ledgers of complaints, yet in 1788 no one would have bet a farthing on the ability of these same 'people' to express themselves."[69] The "citizen-capable-of-expression,"[70] in other words, was created by their own act of self-expression. This paradox is at the heart of all the story collections in this book. The projects I present all assume some shared knowledge or shared human condition and community as the basis on which they call for people to make their stories public; at the same time, they describe the act of sharing stories as the very process whereby people join each other as members of a community.[71]

This paradox of the "we," both preexisting and coming into being as a result of "collective speech acts,"[72] is in fact what drives political imagination, since it opens a space that invites constant negotiation. Western democracies prize this space of dialogue and even fetishize it as a key spectacle of democracy. People in democratic societies do not just discuss and debate, they also create spectacles of their discussions and debates so as to self-authorize their regime as being founded on the exchange of ideas. Jürgen Habermas traced the emergence of this modern type of "public sphere" to eighteenth-century Europe. He showed how literary salons, coffee houses, popular journals, and other forums of discussion created new, inclusive, and discursive spaces where "private people [could] come together as a public" and form a public opinion.[73] What mattered was not only that people formed a public, but that they created a spectacle of togetherness and that they viewed themselves as a diverse but unified public: "The fantasy of a unified public links together powerful utopian energies of inclusivity, equality, transparency, and rationality. It holds out the promise of democratic institutions in which free and equal citizens collectively deliberate over the principles that should govern their lives"[74]

Autobiographical collections such as Moritz's and Herder's, I argue, were one of the forms that this emergent public sphere took in the eighteenth century. One could even argue that collections of autobiographical narratives are paradigmatic of this ideal of a public forum. Stories are important tools in creating spectacles of togetherness, and not just those grand narratives that societies tell themselves, but also the small stories that people share around the proverbial fire or in story collections. Habermas tied the emergence of the public sphere to the bourgeoisie and to their adoption of the print culture as a forum of exchange. Whereas in aristocratic societies the "public" meant a public representative of power, by the eighteenth century "public" came to mean the democratic, institutional procedures that legitimized state power and held it accountable.

Print as a medium of intellectual exchange embodied the utopian vision of this "communicative rationality," in that "it seemed to promise both interpersonal transparency and universal accessibility. Paradoxically, the very 'dispersal of persons' seemed to yield a 'universality of judgments.' The moral autonomy of the reader as solitary consumer, insulated from the social or political effect of the author's presence, grounded the moral authority of the public as a whole."[75] Moritz and Herder shared this emancipatory view of print culture, and they were committed to the ideal of a public exchange of personal reflections. The vision of a modern public, understood as open communication among citizens, is clearly what inspired their projects.

However, contrary to Habermas, Moritz, and Herder did not subscribe to the idea of a homogenizing and universalizing public. Whereas Habermas was inspired by Kant's universalist values and aspirations (including his "principle of publicity"), Moritz and Herder viewed such universalist objectives with suspicion. The advantage of their nonhegemonic view was that it acknowledged the ambiguity of these collective speech acts. In their eyes, the unclassifiable peculiarities of life, including linguistic and national specificities, were not obstacles in the way of a universal consensus, but unique perspectives that provided richer insights and more profound points of connection. Moritz and Herder envisioned their projects within the boundaries of a nation-state rather than in a Kantian cosmopolitan dimension, and they both foregrounded the embodied—spatially, historically, linguistically, and socially situated—position of their storytellers. What saved them from the temptation of dogmatism was their respect for the open-ended nature of personal narratives. It is not that they were unattached to the hope that publicly shared private stories would ultimately generate consensus, either in the form of scientific knowledge (Moritz) or political will (Herder). But their process did not presume a unified public grounded in abstract universality.[76]

In sum, Moritz's and Herder's groundbreaking projects offer an alternative perspective on the intersecting histories of personal expression and political imagination. In today's age of political polarization and fragmentation, they should be of interest not only to life writing scholars but also to political scientists who study political imagination. Political imagination often gets sidelined in political science, even though it has a profound effect on our political actions. Imagination, of course, is not an abstract exercise but it is shaped by social and material circumstances, as seen in these story collections. Assembling large numbers of personal stories is a way to imagine and to stage community. In bringing their stories together, people create a theater of democracy, a spectacle where they co-appear in front of each other as a diverse but unified community. Moritz and Herder may have been among the first to articulate the importance of such autobiographical forums, but they were certainly not the last ones. Women, for instance, have long used collaborative forms of life writing to develop friendships, to network, and to sustain communities. As Amy Culley, Felicity Nussbaum, Linda S. Coleman, and others have shown, in the eighteenth century women preachers, courtesans, and other women formed networks and used collaboratively produced life writing to articulate relationships and communal affiliations. As Culley argues, "women often wrote their auto/biographical works collaboratively and attempted to preserve the voices of others, record a threatened history, and perpetuate a shared tradition across the generations. Their life writing was shaped by their relationships and communal affiliations and articulated identifications with individuals and communities (both actual and imagined)."[77]

The following chapters all build on this expanded notion of collective intimacy. The projects I present all embrace the fantasy of a unified and transparent public forum even as they set out to create it. The next four chapters examine various shapes that these fantasies of unity and community can take. The ideas of universal knowledge (chapter 3), shared time (chapter 4), shared space (chapter 5), or the totality of statistical categories (chapter 6) are all universalizing concepts that help create the stage design of the spectacle, so to speak. For instance, the idea of a universal time and space helps create a background to the spectacle, projecting a world in which humans all coexist simultaneously and in the same space. Story collections often visualize these abstract concepts by arranging stories on a single globe, map, or timeline. Similarly, the abstract idea of universal knowledge, often visualized as an all-inclusive library of human experiences, helps create a common scene on which to stage our togetherness. We need to remember, however, that these abstract concepts, often presented unequivocally as common goods, are never a static, neutral background "in front of which" people act out the stories of their lives; rather, they are dynamic components of the performance itself, serving particular interests. For instance, although the technological platforms of platform capitalism (Srnicek) provide the stage, the foundation on which people play out the stories of their lives, these platforms are not neutral play areas but active forces that shape the performance.

The tensions that characterized Moritz's and Herder's project are also present in contemporary collections. As we aggregate more and more diverse personal stories with the help of increasingly efficient and automated algorithms, activists express the same two priorities: to produce better knowledge about our collectives and to enhance people's sense of community. A key advantage of twenty-first-century "assembled lives" is that those who contribute their stories today can also access, often simultaneously, the stories of others. This feedback mechanism is exactly what Moritz and Herder envisioned, but they lacked the affordances. Herder's collections were severely limited by their small circulation, and even Moritz's relatively wide journal audience had limited interactivity. By contrast, today's interactive, participatory technologies enable a circular, back-and-forth process between individual and collective self-reflection. As I argue in the following chapters, such projects can indeed democratize our knowledge production and political participation, but only if we are careful to uphold the critical spirit and productive tension that energized Moritz's and Herder's projects.

3   LIBRARIES OF HUMAN EXPERIENCE

> *Our knowledge and wisdom could live on in the commons, as a resource for others to look for guidance.*
> —JONATHAN HARRIS

Imagine a public library containing all of humankind's experiences. Not just yours and mine, but everyone's. What would such a library look like? What kind of collective knowledge could we gain from it and what would we use it for? Who would curate this knowledge for us? And most importantly, what kind of experiences should we include and in what format? Some have argued that the best way to compile such a collection would be to record people's own personal stories, since everyone is an expert on their own life. Karl Philipp Moritz and Johann Gottfried Herder were among the first to propose such a collection in the eighteenth century (see chapter 2). Moritz hoped that a library containing stories of personal experiences would be a valuable source of scientific knowledge and that it could also serve "as a common mirror" for humanity to inspect itself in. Today, with the advent of digital crowdsourcing and archiving technologies, Moritz's dream is becoming more of a reality.

The number of story libraries aiming to "preserve humanity's stories"[1] is growing rapidly. StoryCorps, for instance, seeks to establish "an invaluable archive for future generations." As one commentator noted, StoryCorps "stories become a library for learning. What you have at your disposal are resource persons who really live through the stories. This carries an unquestionable authority because these are their stories and they are living witnesses to what transpired."[2] Like any public library or archive, StoryCorps prides itself on the size and accessibility of its collections ("StoryCorps' archive comprises one of the first and the largest born-digital collections of human voices, featuring tens of thousands of conversations recorded across the United States and around the world").[3] Cowbird is another story library committed to preserving humanity's history, one story at a time. Cowbird grew out of the online diary of its founder, Jonathan Harris. Harris imagined a platform that would function as "a community of storytellers [who] build an online library of human experience."[4] In order to "gather and preserve" all the "exceptional stories of human life," Harris invited people to upload photos and stories from their lives. Between 2012 and 2017, the library collected close to one hundred thousand stories from nearly two hundred countries. Cowbird had all the characteristics of a traditional library while also offering the advantages of interconnectivity. As the website explains, "Stories are guidebooks for living and lifeboats for memory: they help us not to forget, and then later, not to be forgotten."[5] Harris hoped that "our knowledge and wisdom could live on in the commons, as a resource for others to look for guidance." Today, the site no longer accepts new submissions, but as a library it seems to have fulfilled its mission. The site functions as a searchable catalog of human knowledge, as "a single interconnected place where the stories get interwoven, allowing people to find and share stories they might otherwise not discover."[6]

Today, thousands of similar story libraries exist, each with a slightly different emphasis. Memory of Mankind, for instance, presents itself as "one of the most ambitious time capsules of humankind."[7] Concerned about the disappearance of the digital traces of our age, the organizers of Memory of Mankind propose to convert our collective knowledge into ceramic-based data tablets and preserve them two thousand meters deep in an Austrian saltmine. Although the program's primary focus is on bestsellers, the site also encourages people to include their own personal stories: "Everyone can participate within drawing this portrait of our era: You can contribute a personal story, your favorite poem, or newspaper articles which describe our problems, visions or our daily life." "The main point of what we are doing is to store information in a way that it is readable in the future. It is a backup of our knowledge, our history and our stories," says founder Martin Kunze.[8] Other story libraries are less ambitious about material preservation and more invested in documenting the stories of particular communities, events, or places. For example, The September 11 Digital Archive contains fifteen thousand personal stories from 9/11, the Ellis Island Oral History Collection consists of approximately 1900 stories by those who passed through that immigration station, while the Memory Project documents the stories of Hungarians displaced by the 1956 Revolution.[9] Also, some companies archive the stories of their employees in order to preserve institutional knowledge. Besides public and corporate collections, there exist also private story libraries. The genealogical industry has an army of "personal historians" who stress that individual memories are worth preserving because they are part of "the history of a community." As the website Personal Story announces, "Our stories are our heritage. They offer insights into who we are, remind us where we've been. Beyond the history of one family, our stories are the history of a community, a people, a world. And so we must preserve them."[10]

What sets these story libraries apart is their emphasis on the role of personal stories in generating and transferring knowledge. Indeed, as semantics scholars maintain, stories are crucial in capturing and conveying both explicit and implicit knowledge, which is why they are essential for successful knowledge exchange:

> Stories are an intrinsically attractive form of communication that outperform logical arguments.... There is some evidence to show that stories may enhance our ability to remember (Hayne 2009; Oaks 1996), and storytelling possesses great potential as a teaching–learning tool (LeBlanc and Hogg 2006).... Narrative methods focus on experiences and implicit knowledge, which are not only difficult to access, but can hardly be disclosed and conveyed by listing facts alone (Erlach 2003). By transmitting context-laden knowledge, stories can be seen as a bridge between implicit and explicit knowledge that helps to unmask some implicit components (Meyer et al. 2005).... By helping to exchange implicit meanings, narratives aid in establishing shared meaning structures, which are needed to interpret all other forms of knowledge (Meyer et al). Thus, narratives may be seen as a means to cohere meaning structures amongst people. Those shared frames of reference then build the prerequisites for effective knowledge exchange (Meyer et al. 2005).[11]

Story libraries promise to document the human condition through the exchange of individual stories and to thereby establish "shared meaning structures."

The present chapter focuses on this epistemic promise as well as its attendant challenges. I start with examples of a special kind of story collection from the first half of the twentieth century, in which participants were invited to freely describe their experiences of certain historical periods. These "memoir contests" from the 1930s were important precedents of today's digital story libraries in that they sought to grant greater autonomy to storytellers, while also hoping to establish scientific truths based on storytellers' individual experiences. In the second half of the chapter, I move to contemporary story libraries to trace a shift in emphasis from documentation toward social transformation. In contrast to early collections, today's story libraries pride themselves on their ability to overcome traditional categorizations by valorizing the "lived experience" of each and every storyteller and by generating more reliable data. They also seek to put these new insights into the service of social justice by cultivating empathy in "library visitors." I will argue, however, that for these story libraries to accomplish their mission, they will first have to reevaluate their positivist belief in their story data, as well as their uncritical acceptance of the authority of "raw," lived experiences and the emotions they elicit.

Historical Background: Oral History and Memoir Contests

Nineteenth-century social scientists faced a dilemma. In order to lay solid epistemological foundations for their fields, they embraced positivist principles and statistical methods, but many found themselves conflicted between their commitment to the ineffability of individual human experience and the pressure to make objective and generalizable statements about the human condition. As Wilhelm Dilthey famously asked, "How are we to overcome the difficulty that everywhere weighs upon the human sciences of deriving universally valid propositions from inner experiences that are so personally limited, so indeterminate, so compacted and resistant to analysis?"[12] This question led to an unfortunate division between two research paradigms. The individualizing and the generalizing approaches were given distinct names: the "ideographic" approach (from the Greek word *idio*, meaning "one's own") focuses on what is contingent, unique, and subjective about knowledge, while the "nomothetic" approach (from the Greek word *nomos*, meaning "law") relies on types and categories to establish generalizable laws. The ideographic approach often corresponds to qualitative methods, while nomothetic studies rely on quantitative measurements. The individualizing and the generalizing approaches can of course be seen as complementary, but a hundred years later the verdict is still out whether the resulting "hybrid" or "mixed method" studies are epistemologically congruous.[13]

To document people's perception of their own conditions, in the twentieth century, most scholars interested in ideographic research adopted oral history's qualitative method: "Oral history is a field of study and a method of gathering, preserving and interpreting the voices and memories of people, communities, and participants in past events."[14]

Oral history uses a particular method based on the interview, whereby trained interviewers (some paid, some volunteers) prepare a set of questions and the recording involves a conversation between the interviewer and interviewee. In the US, the first story libraries were compiled by oral historians who wanted to study individual stories of particular individuals while also documenting the larger context in which those individuals were situated.[15] The 1930s saw a host of large-scale oral history projects, such as the collection *Born in Slavery: Slave Narratives from the Federal Writers' Project, 1936–1938*, which collected more than 2,300 first-person accounts of slavery.[16]

Some researchers, however, found oral history's methods too restrictive. They wanted to grant greater freedom to storytellers and further democratize knowledge production, which led them to the notion of "memoir contests." The idea can be traced back to a Polish-born sociologist named Florian Znaniecki. In the early 1900s, Znaniecki and his colleague William I. Thomas set out to document the lives of the first Polish immigrants to the US. They decided to use immigrants' own personal stories, arguing that these were "the perfect type of material": "We are safe in saying, that personal life-records, as complete as possible, constitute the *perfect* type of sociological material, and that if social science has to use other materials at all it is only because of the practical difficulty of obtaining at the moment a sufficient number of such records to cover the totality of sociological problems, and of the enormous amount of work demanded for an adequate analysis of all personal material necessary to characterize the life of a social group."[17] The two researchers set out to collect personal documents by immigrants, based on which they coauthored one of the classics of empirical sociology, the five-volume *The Polish Peasant in Europe and America*. Yet, the practical difficulty of obtaining personal records in large quantities continued to plague researchers.

In response, Znaniecki came up with an original idea. Upon his return to his native Poland, he and his colleagues began to organize so-called "memoir contests," inviting people from all walks of life to come forward and share their stories. Widely publicized by the press, in schools and through political organizations, these memoir contests became highly popular public events in Poland. Certain groups of society, such as workers, peasants, youth, immigrants, and the unemployed were emphatically encouraged to write. As Katherine Lebow explains, "By the late 1930s, some 20 competitions, the largest receiving over 1,500 entries, had resulted in around 25 published volumes that were widely discussed in the press at the time."[18] Lebow also provides the following information:

The 1922 competition announcement "for the best life story of a worker written by himself," for example, began by specifying the prizes being offered (usually money, books, or travel) and laying out the competition's minimal eligibility requirements: "Anyone may take part in the competition who supports himself through physical labor.... If you do not know how to write, you may dictate to someone else. Grammatical errors, bad style, and poor handwriting will not in any way prevent you from getting a prize. One should not imagine that writing the history of one's own life is a very difficult thing.... All that matters is honestly, truthfully, and precisely to describe one's whole life from childhood to the present moment. It is easiest to describe everything in order, year by year, event by event. In the end, write however you like."[19]

At first, the concept of a "memoir contest" may seem rather unorthodox. After all, memoir-writing does not seem like a highly competitive sport. Nevertheless, the idea was well received and Znaniecki's method inspired scholars in other countries as well. Memoir contests were particularly popular in the Scandinavian countries. For example, starting in 1926, the Finnish Literature Society regularly organized contests, many of them specifically designed for life stories. The public was eager to participate and Finnish scholars found a convenient way to collect data about the population. By the end of the twentieth century, the Finnish Literature Society had archived "oral and written material about Finnish traditions and culture comprising 515 shelf meters of manuscript notes, 14,500 hours of sound recordings, 950 hours of video recordings, and 110,000 photographs."[20] Swedes have also been collecting personal stories for decades,[21] and Norwegians organized at least two major contests in the twentieth century. The 1988 contest in Norway was titled "Write Your Life" and it was announced with the following questions: "Have you ever thought about how your life has become what it is today? Which events have influenced you the most? Did you ever consider writing your life story? You now have the opportunity to participate in a contest with this as an aim."[22] No fewer than 630 Norwegians answered the call.

Collecting Firsthand Knowledge about Nazi Germany

While the history of oral history has been richly documented, memoir contests have been largely forgotten. I present here four examples to trace the changing perception of the role of these collections. The "Polish method" never gained quite as much prestige among academics in the US as it did in Europe, but a few American scholars did organize memoir contests in the 1930s and 1940s. Theodore Abel, a sociology professor at Columbia University, was among the first to launch such a contest.[23] Abel studied the effects of Nazism on the psyche of ordinary people, and seeing the party's sudden rise in popularity, he wondered why people joined the Hitler movement. From what background did they come, and what experiences had shaped their worldviews? Like Znaniecki, Abel believed that "there are questions to which autobiographical data alone hold the proper answer,"[24] so he decided to ask the Nazis themselves. After having interviewed about a hundred of them, he realized that his interviewees had a lot more to say than could fit into the restrictive framework of an oral history interview. He therefore decided to self-finance a memoir contest and published the following call for contributions:

400 MARKS IN PRIZES
For the Best Personal Life History of an Adherent
of the Hitler Movement

Any person, regardless of sex or age, who was a member of the National Socialist party before January 1, 1933, or who was in sympathy with the movement, may participate in this contest.

Contestants are to give accurate and detailed descriptions of their personal lives, particularly after the World War. Special attention should be given to accounts of family life, education, economic conditions, membership in associations, participation in the Hitler movement, and important experiences, thoughts, and feelings about events and ideas of the post-war period.

The prizes will be awarded to authors who have submitted the most detailed and trustworthy accounts. Style, spelling, or dramatic story value will not be considered. Completeness and frankness are the sole criteria, so that even the simplest and most undramatic story will receive full consideration.

The prizes will be awarded as follows:

First prize . . . . . . 125 marks
Second prize . . . . 50 marks
Third prize . . . . . . 25 marks
Five prizes . . . . . 20 marks each
Ten prizes . . . . . . 10 marks each

The prize money is deposited in the German Bank. The contest is organized under the tutelage of the sociology department of Columbia University, whose members will be the final judges. The purpose of the contest is the collection of material on the history of National Socialism, so that the American public may be informed about it on the basis of factual, personal documents. The contestants whose contributions are published in part or in full will receive an additional honorarium of two marks per printed page. Manuscripts will not be returned, and must be submitted on or before September 1934.[25]

Abel received an unexpectedly high number of contributions (683) with which he was highly satisfied.[26] He called these autobiographical sketches "biograms," and he praised them for being more "open-ended, free-association" in character than traditional oral history interviews and questionnaires[27] He wrote: "I recommend the use of biograms whenever an investigator's problem involves change or development over a period of time and when it can be assumed that there is a common factor or pattern that accounts for similar or concerted behavior by the members of a particular social category."[28] Abel used the personal stories to write his book *Why Hitler Came into Power: An Answer Based on the Original Life Stories of Six Hundred of His Followers* (1938), which became a major success.[29] Abel was so satisfied with his results that in 1939 he decided to call for "another prize-contest in Germany for the best life-story of a Nazi Party worker to gather material for a second study on how Hitler stayed in power."[30] The sudden outbreak of the war, however, forced him to flee Germany, and he never completed his second project.[31]

A few years later, a team of researchers from Harvard University organized a similar contest. Psychologist Gordon Allport, historian Sidney Bradshaw Fay, and sociologist Edward Y. Hartshorne launched a $1000 memoir contest to investigate the effects of Nazi politics on the everyday life of Germans. The contest called on "all who have known Germany well before and since Hitler":

$1,000 Prize Contest

*

ATTENTION

To all who have known Germany well before and since Hitler!

*

For the purely scientific purpose of data collection, which will be used to study the social and psychological effects of National

Socialism on German society and on the German people, we are offering one thousand dollars as a prize for the best unpublished personal life-histories on the theme

"MY LIFE IN GERMANY BEFORE AND
AFTER JANUARY 30, 1933"

The contest is being personally sponsored by the following faculty members of Harvard University, who will also serve as judges. They will assume sole responsibility for reading the manuscripts and for awarding the prizes

GORDON WILLARD ALLPORT — Psychologist
SIDNEY BRADSHAW FAY — Historian
EDWARD YARNALL HARTSHORNE — Sociologist

The following prizes are offered:

FIRST PRIZE $500   SECOND PRIZE $250   THIRD PRIZE $100
    FOURTH PRIZE $50   5 FIFTH PRIZES, $20 EACH

Manuscripts may be submitted under a pseudonym or anonymously, but they must be truthful.

You may write in English or in German, your choice of language does not influence your chances.

There is no limit as to length, but 20,000 words should be regarded as the minimum.

The contest closes April 1, 1940. (Manuscripts must be mailed by then.) Prizes will be announced as early as possible.

The manuscripts will be treated as strictly confidential.

SPECIAL INSTRUCTIONS

No manuscript will be accepted if it does not state clearly on the first page the following information: AGE (approximate) and GENDER of writer; the REGION of Germany where writer lived, and SIZE OF COMMUNITY; RELIGION professed by writer;— and other relevant information about the writer's SOCIAL POSITION in Germany (e.g. married or single, children, approximate income, education, etc.) (Your societal position as such has no bearing on your chances of winning.)

Your life story should be written as simply, directly, fully, and concretely as possible. You should aim to describe, in so far as you can remember them, THINGS WHICH ACTUALLY HAPPENED,

THINGS PEOPLE DID AND SAID. The Judges are not interested in philosophical reflections about the past but in a record of personal experience. Quotations whenever possible from letters, diaries, notebooks and other personal documents will help to give your account the authenticity and completeness desired. This is not a literary contest. Even if you have never written before, if you have a good memory, sharp observations and a good insight into human nature, you should try. Even if you do not win a prize, your manuscript will be of value as a source of information about Germany and National Socialism.

Address all communications to: S. B. FAY

776 WIDENER LIBRARY, CAMBRIDGE, MASSACHUSETTS, U.S.A.

Additional copies of this announcement will be gladly furnished upon request.[32]

Allport and his colleagues advertised the contest on flyers and in the newspapers of the German expatriate community.[33] Approximately 250 stories were submitted, some of them book-length. Participants represented a broad range of socioeconomic strata, but most were educated, exiled German Jews with strong anti-Nazi sentiments. According to Allport and his colleagues, the submissions "averaged one hundred pages in length. All were read and analyzed by a corps of psychologists and sociologists working in close collaboration. Of these documents, ninety were submitted to particularly detailed psychological analysis."[34] The three researchers developed a standardized nineteen-page questionnaire to judge the manuscripts, and winners were announced in 1940. Allport and his colleagues published their findings in the *Journal of Personality* in 1941 under the title "Personality under Social Catastrophe: Ninety Life-Histories of the Nazi Revolution." The collection then went largely forgotten before it was rediscovered and catalogued in the 1990s.[35]

The true interest of these memoir contests lies in the wealth of stories they occasioned. Nevertheless, for my purposes here, I will focus on their research design in order to discern their epistemic presuppositions. The two contests clearly had a lot in common.[36] Although their target groups were different, Abel and Allport et al. both wanted to study the individual effects of a collective experience and they both relied on personal stories as their main source of information. They both assembled the submissions into collections and drew scientific conclusions based on their aggregate data. In terms of method, they both employed what is now call "mixed methods" research, meaning they integrated qualitative and quantitative data within a single investigation. In fact, Allport was the first to introduce the terminology "nomothetic" and "ideographic" to American social scientists.

On the one hand, Abel and Allport et al. were both committed to the value of qualitative analysis. To briefly summarize, "a qualitative approach to research aims to understand how individuals make meaning of their social world.... This approach is committed to multiple views of social reality whereby a researcher's respondent becomes 'the expert'—it is his or her view of reality that the researcher seeks to interpret. Social reality is assumed to be subjective and varied; there is not just one story but multiple stories of lived experience."[37] Abel and Allport et al. both believed in the value of personal experience and individual insight, which is why they opted for free-form personal stories instead of the customary oral history interview or questionnaire. Admittedly, the submissions do not fully meet the description of "unsolicited" material since they were occasioned by an invitation. Also, they would hardly conform to the requirements of an "unconstrained" expression, given the numerous criteria listed in the calls. Still, it is clear that organizers wanted to grant substantial freedom to contestants, emphasizing the value of each individual contributor's subjective perspective. They wanted "descriptions of [contestants'] personal lives,"[38] a "record of personal experience."[39]

On the other hand, they were also committed to quantitative analyses. They designed their projects as contests because they wanted a statistically viable sample size. They also both requested specific data so that they could analyze their respondents' profiles.[40] Beyond the kind of information usually requested in surveys (name, date, place of birth), they asked for other types of data (size of community, number of children, approximate income, social position, etc.). In Allport et al.'s case especially, asking for such data is ethically questionable, given that the study focused on a regime that manipulated statistics to harm its citizens. But setting this ethical question aside, we can presume that the researchers requested this data because they were in search of statistically representative respondents. In fact, there was a selection bias in both surveys, favoring man-in-the-street experience over the experience of highly educated respondents.[41] According to Abel, the fact that most of his storytellers were uneducated was actually an advantage, in that their lack of education "would predispose them to present a straight-forward story rather than fiction and deception."[42] In the end, they both reported their quantitative results in tables. Abel even aggregated his results to establish the "fictitious, average type of follower of the Hitler movement."[43]

Eighty years after these memoir contests, scientists are still debating whether such hybrid methods can produce scientifically valid results. The more important question, however, is not whether hybrid methods are acceptable but what justifies their employment. If the epistemology of these memoir contests seems incongruous, it is not because they employed mixed methods but because they maintained a positivist methodological orientation. Exploring this underlying positivist ethos is important, because as I will show, the same tension continues to shape our story libraries today. First, regarding the epistemic authority of first-person testimony, Abel and Allport et al. both maintained the positivist view that social reality is objective and scientifically verifiable. As a result, they discredited the subjective evidence found in the stories, insisting that personal documents were neutral and factual. Abel argued that his contestants were under no pressure or obligation to write, which made their stories more objective and authentic. He also insisted that most of his material was neutral, because it concerned people's childhoods and everyday lives, and that even the more openly political passages could be considered unbiased since their authors' views were not yet distorted by outsiders' later judgments about Nazis. Anticipating potential charges of subjectivism, Allport et al. were similarly keen to stress the factual nature and objective value of his material. Allport et al.'s call asked for "complete," "full," and objective "descriptions" of "real events." His wording ("describe . . . things that actually happened") echoes Leopold von Ranke's famous criteria for documenting history "as it really happened."

Their narrow, positivist interpretation of documentation is even more evident in their definition of what they consider evidence. For instance, Allport et al. requested that participants substantiate their personal stories with objective evidence (he asked for "quotations whenever possible from letters, diaries, notebooks and other personal documents," to "help give [the] account the authenticity and completeness desired"). How exactly a quote from one's own diary could authenticate a personal story is not quite clear, but Allport et al.'s request is symptomatic of his positivist interpretation of documentary evidence.[44] His statement, according to which "the manuscripts can be submitted under a pseudonym or without a name; but they must be authentic," is similarly paradoxical. The epistemological incongruence is rendered particularly sharp by Abel's request for "factual, personal documents." It is important to stress here that researchers using mixed methods need not sacrifice the subjective type of evidence found in personal stories for the factual type, since the point of the hybrid approach would be precisely to grant equal authority to both kinds of evidence. Abel and Allport et al., however, felt compelled to justify subjective stories as factual documentation, which distorted their project design.

Finally, these memoir contests were also limited by their narrow definition of audience. Allport et al. insisted that their contest was strictly scholarly in that it had "purely scientific purposes" (as stated in the call for participants: "For the purely scientific purpose of data collection, which will be used to study the social and psychological effects of National Socialism on German society and on the German people"). Abel, too, underscored the scholarly nature of his project: "The purpose of the contest is the collection of material on the history of National Socialism, so that the American public may be informed about it on the basis of factual, personal documents." Abel's bestselling book did reach a wider audience than Allport et al.'s journal article; however, what matters here is not only the size of the audience but also its identity. Recall the eighteenth-century dream about story libraries serving as mirrors in which humankind could inspect itself. The point is that the stories people contribute about their own lives should be made accessible to the very same people who produced them. That is how these archives could fulfill their socially transformative role. Instead, what we have here is a group of scholars studying a group of people, but the people who contribute their stories never get to see each other's stories or the collection as a whole. Abel and Allport et al. both asked Germans to observe themselves, but the results were aimed at scholars and the American public and not at Germans. This meant that the fascinating insights offered by the stories never reached the community from which they came.[45]

Bringing the Knowledge Back to the Community: YIVO and MOA

My next two examples were also conceived as scholarly projects, but their organizers further recognized their socially transformative potential. Instead of merely assembling stories to gain new knowledge about a particular historical period or group, these scholars also sought to bring the knowledge back to the community from which it was sourced. In 1942, the Yiddish Scientific Institute in New York (YIVO) organized a memoir contest for Jewish immigrants on the theme "Why I left Europe and what I have accomplished in America." The call for contributions was publicized in the Yiddish press, and it asked participants to write about their daily lives before as well as after immigration.[43] The contest was open to "every adult Jew, man or woman, not born in the United States or Canada, without regard to level of education, background, occupation or party affiliation."[46] Like Abel and Allport et al., organizers stressed the scientific value of individual life stories. They assured contestants of strict confidentiality, asking participants to use pseudonyms. They asked participants to be "detailed" and "sincere"[47] and, if possible, to support their stories with other personal documents. More than two hundred people responded, contributing approximately twenty-five thousand pages of material, forming a rich resource on Eastern European Jewish communities and their migration.[48]

Organizers of the YIVO contest were clearly influenced by Znaniecki's "Polish method."[49] In contrast to Abel and Allport et al., however, YIVO scholars also stressed the "social therapeutic" function of collective story sharing.[50] As Daniel Soyer explains, researchers at YIVO believed that "social research could not only uncover the sources of social and cultural dislocation, . . . but also come up with an antidote."[51] They believed that immigrants needed to be "compensated" for their psychological losses and that a positive sense of cultural affiliation and appreciation could help their adjustment. Therefore, to make young immigrant Jewish Americans more conscious of their need to belong to a strong ethnic community, YIVO scholars designed the contest in such a way as to allow immigrants to familiarize themselves with their own community's past. The idea was that if immigrants considered their own personal past and then read about other people's similar experiences in both the old country and the new one, then they would recognize the many commonalities that bind them together into a single community. Organizers therefore used the contest to try to define the "elements that make up the essence of this community."[52] In other words, YIVO's objective was not merely to document Jewish migration, but also to strengthen immigrant Jews' sense of belonging to their ethnic community: "The significance of the autobiography contests, therefore, lay not only in the documentation they produced but also in the way they brought young people into Yivo's orbit and connected them to a new form of Jewish spiritual and intellectual life."[53] This is a key difference compared to Abel's and Allport et al.'s projects, and it raises crucial questions about the purposes of knowledge transfer. While the role of curators was similar in all three contests, YIVO scholars had a more inclusive idea about who the knowledge in the stories was supposed to serve. And although there is little evidence that the Jewish community used the stories for the purposes envisioned by the contest's organizers, their intentions gestured in an important direction.

My last example is not a memoir contest in the strict sense of the word, since participants were not always financially compensated, but it was assembled along similar principles. It is not coincidental that this project was also initiated in the 1930s, since that decade saw the emergence of mass movements and the idea of "mass science." England was on the brink of a constitutional crisis in 1936 when Edward VIII decided to abdicate, and citizens felt that the press did not accurately reflect their opinions. As a response, three former students from Cambridge, Tom Harrisson, Humphrey Jennings, and Charles Madge, proposed to develop a "mass science" based on people's personal observations. "Only mass observations can create mass science,"[54] noted Madge. "The real observers in this case were the millions of people who were, for once, irretrievably involved in the public events."[55] They therefore called for "voluntary observers" to report their experiences back to the Mass Observation office.[56] The number of volunteer observers grew rapidly, from 25 to 592 in the first year alone.[57] Over the next decade and a half, the archive grew rapidly. Between 1939 and 1945, more than 500 individuals sent in diary entries, and around 2500 individuals responded to the archive's open-ended questions ("directives").[58] After the war, the project lost steam as public interest began to wane. By the late 1970s, however, social historians expressed renewed interest for the archive's rich material. The revival of the Mass Observation Archive (MOA) marked again a royal event. In July 1981, on the day of Princess Diana and Prince Charles's wedding, the newly reopened archive asked people to send in their diary entries, responding to the simple question: "Celebration or bore?" The project was a resounding success. Today, the MOA remains a well-known public institution with close to five hundred volunteer participants. According to its website, the archive is "dedicated to the collection of views and experiences of 'everyday' people across the UK."[59] People's contributions take many different forms, including diaries, letters, and "day surveys."[60] Recently, the archive also added a searchable online catalog, and they now accept email submissions as well.

Just like Abel and Allport et al., organizers of the MOA believed in hybrid approaches and sought to balance statistical analyses with the liveliness of individual voices. As founder Harrison put it, "It is clear that in most sociological research we require an adequate admixture of words and numbers, of penetration and tabulation, representation and interpretation, understood situations and unimpeachable correlations, the raw material of life with the authentic statistic of validity."⁶¹ This balancing act is of course easier said than done, and the hybrid methods have caused heated debates throughout the archive's history. One key difference between the memoir contests about Nazi Germany and the MOA is that the latter was also concerned with the effects of the project on storytellers themselves. Whereas Abel and Allport et al. collected stories by Germans so that Americans could better understand them, the MOA asked Brits to observe themselves *as* British citizens. Unlike Abel and Allport et al., Mass Observation archivists were committed to the spirit of collaboration and treated their observers as research partners. The relationship between observers and archivists was so close, in fact, that in the early days every single submission was acknowledged with a letter from the archivists. This personal touch served to counterbalance the anonymity and mass scale of the project. At the same time, it also deepened the paradox about the exact function of these storytellers. The archive never quite managed to clarify the role of the observers: Were they objects of study whose reactions and opinions were to be studied by other researchers like any other document? Or were they subjects who actively participated in research? The questions matter, because if observers are to be regarded as objects, then it is important to make sure that they are representative of British society or a certain segment of it; whereas, if they are to be regarded as active researchers, then their lack of scholarly training would become problematic.⁶²

The words "observer" and "observation" are also problematic in that they evoke the specter of Big Brother, which undermines the institution's democratic intentions. As a matter of fact, during World War II the archive did collaborate with the state, which raised the charge of "home front espionage."⁶³ Archivists, however, managed to turn the charge around by arguing that the collection was not only *by* the people and *about* the people, but also *for* the people.⁶⁴ To prove this, they democratized not only the sourcing of the knowledge, but also its distribution. In contrast to the other memoir contests, which only resulted in scholarly publications, the MOA regularly published collections from its materials for the people. In the early decades, they issued popular illustrated volumes such as *Mass Observation—Meet Yourself at the Doctor's* (1949), in which patients described their experiences in the waiting room and doctor's office, or *Mass Observation—Meet Yourself on Sunday* (1949), which offered a composite portrait of a typical British Sunday. And the tradition continues today with volumes such as *Our History of the 20th Century: As Told in Diaries, Journals and Letters* (2017), which draws on over one hundred diaries to offer "candid and intimate insights not only into the headline-grabbing events but also the domestic and personal moments of those who lived through it."[65]

The titles of these publications suggest that they function like mirrors in which Brits can inspect themselves ("meet yourself," "our history," etc.) The idea is that these aggregated stories reflect back an image of the collective called British society. This mirror metaphor is problematic for several reasons, we said: first, it downplays the performative role of stories, and second, it deemphasizes their transformative capacity (see chapter 2). The point of self-reflection is never just to confirm a status quo but to imagine alternatives—that is, the knowledge that British citizens gain by sharing what they observe about themselves and others is supposed to be reflected back to the people, so that based on what they learn citizens can initiate certain transformations. In this fashion, collective self-observation can create a productive, circular process of observation, interpretation, and transformation. To cite the founders again, the MOA "does not set out in quest of truth or facts for their own sake, or for the sake of an intellectual minority, but aims at exposing them in simple terms to all observers, so that their environment may be understood, and thus constantly transformed. Whatever the political methods called upon to effect the transformation, the knowledge of what has to be transformed is indispensable."[66] Note the emphasis on the transformative potential of the knowledge gained through citizens' self-observation.

The MOA demonstrates the continuity of the practice, since the project now spans more than eight decades. Over the course of the twentieth century, what started out as oral history collections and memoir contests mostly only available to scholars, became increasingly open and accessible public story libraries. They also expanded beyond the question of documentation and began to consider the potential impact of their collections on storytellers and their communities. This transformation was driven in part by the rise of social history and its emphasis on microhistory and the experiences of "ordinary people," and in part by technological advances including new digital archiving tools and new audio recording technologies that eliminated the need for interviewers. While some insist that we need to maintain the distinction between libraries (meant to collect and provide access to previously published materials) and archives (designed to collect unpublished materials to preserve institutional and cultural memory), the increasing fuzziness about what counts as "published" has recently led to a convergence of the two. As both story libraries and story archives become more interactive, foregrounding not just the role of scholars and storytellers, but also that of curators and users in shaping the collections, these libraries raise further urgent questions.

Contemporary Story Libraries Based on Experiential Encounters

In the twenty-first century, the enthusiasm for story libraries has not waned one bit. Even memoir contests remain popular. For instance, in 2018, *Memoir* magazine published a call for its "#MeToo Trigger Warning Nonfiction Essay Contest," with a $500 monetary and publication award:

> The theme for the *#MeToo Trigger Warning Nonfiction Essay Contest* is Sexual Violence and Domestic Abuse. As in, have you or someone you know survived sexual harassment, assault, rape or abuse? Perhaps you are married or related to a survivor and you've witnessed the emotional journey that is so rarely spoken of. If so how did it change you? How does it affect your daily life? You were strong enough to get through that, and your story matters. Why? Because Memoir is a movement. Our jam. Our way of cultivating global consciousness. And few issues today require more enlightenment than the way the pain of abuse can affect us as a person, a family, a society. Sexual violence is a public health, human rights and social justice issue. So, here's your chance to use your voice to Change the Culture. You are not alone. *Memoir Magazine* stands with you! Together we can shatter the silence and end sexual violence. Your essay may be humorous, sad, upsetting. It can be one paragraph long, or several pages. It's all up to you, but most of all it should be your untold truth expressed in your unique voice.
>
> Pseudonyms are allowed.
>
> The winning story receives $500 + publication in *Memoir Magazine,* and a note from our judge on why the story was chosen. Short and Long listed applicants will receive publication.[67]

Just like the memoir contests from the twentieth century, this one also seeks "untold truth expressed in your unique voice" while reassuring contestants that they can remain anonymous by using pseudonyms.[68] The crucial difference is that the 2018 call also appeals to contributors' sense of solidarity and communal awareness. Sharing personal stories becomes here a means to "shatter the silence." People are called upon to "use [their] voice to Change the Culture." Organizers stress the power of stories to connect people to each other: "You are not alone." They refer to their act of assembling stories as a "movement," "our jam", "our way of cultivating global consciousness." They reassure future storytellers that they stand "together," that abuse is a shared concern, a "public health, human rights and social justice issue." In short, contemporary story libraries reject the scholarly ethos of neutrality in favor of mobilizing society around pressing issues, which they hope to achieve by building empathy through experiential encounters between storytellers and audiences.[69]

Collective intimacy, we said, promises a powerful combination of two things: (1) valuable collective insights and (2) a sense of intimacy and belonging. Contemporary story libraries, presented as means of knowledge production and knowledge transfer, offer both. For instance, the story library Cowbird was not originally designed to be a social platform, but users ended up building a community by sharing and liking each other's stories. The media celebrated the project as a "new cultural force on the Internet," praising it for "deepening" the Web by allowing people to experience each other's stories in a more reflective environment. Users described the site as an "almost sacred space,"[70] praising it for revealing what is universal in our experiences: "You've not just gotten together a collection of experiences, but are on your way to creating an experiential taxonomy of everyday life, one that crosses generations and classes and brings us to regard what's universal even in each unique entry."[71]

Note that Cowbird and most contemporary story libraries operate with the term "experience." One of the first story-sharing platforms to foreground experience was the Experience Project. An early social networking website, the Experience Project (2007–16) had millions of users who submitted stories of personal experiences and then joined groups based on shared experiences.[72] The site did not refer to the stories people uploaded as "stories" but as "experiences."[73] The Experience Project functioned as a free, communal library of experiences, seeking to "harness social media to bring empathy and understanding to all."[74] As of May 2016, the site contained over sixty-seven million of these "experiences," by hundreds of millions of people.

More recently, "lived experience," a variation on the word "experience," is becoming particularly popular in the context of story archives. The slight difference originates in the German: *Erfahrung* and *Erlebnis* both mean "experience," but the former refers to a more active form of experience (as in "being experienced" or "having experience"), whereas the latter has a more passive connotation, as in "having lived through" something. The validation of "lived experience" (*Erlebnis*) as a legitimate source of knowledge has been a slow and contested process. As Einstein famously said, "The only source of knowledge is experience," but it was his contemporary Edmund Husserl who first made "lived experience" an object of scientific study. Originally a philosophical concept, the phenomenological notion of "lived experience" is meant to highlight the essence of phenomena from the perspective of the individual who has "lived through" those experiences. As a concrete qualitative research method, however, phenomenology is not easy to implement, which is why it took such a long time for researchers outside philosophy to embrace it.

Recently, however, "lived experience" has become a popular epistemological category, and story libraries often use the term to stress the uniquely situated knowledge of storytellers. For instance, The Moth is said to bestow empowerment on "immigrant women to use their unique voice to embrace and share stories of lived experience";[75] StoryCorps interviews often carry the title "lived experience interviews"; mental health story-platforms use the expression "lived experience storytelling";[76] and story archives documenting the 2020 Covid-19 outbreak ask contributors to focus on "the local, lived experience of a global pandemic."[77] What gets foregrounded here is the lived experience of the storyteller. The phenomenological focus on lived experience prioritizes the local, embodied, and uniquely intersectional nature of each individual storyteller's knowledge of the world. It is also used to highlight marginalized lives, since lived experience is often associated with "being thrown" (*geworfen*) into a situation involuntarily. Moreover, sharing one's "lived experience" also opens a path towards others' lived experiences. In these story libraries, it is not just storytellers who process their lived experiences, but those who access the stories are also said to be transformed by their encounter with the storyteller's experience. As filmmaker Claudia Stack put it: "We can learn so much about people's lives and trends in history by concentrating on the actual personal experiences as they were lived. To me, each person is the authority on his or her own experience."[78] While Stack uses the traditional term "learning," in contemporary story libraries the process of learning is mostly understood as social emotional learning. Knowing is helpful, but what we need to sustain our collectives is emotional knowledge, empathy, and compassion. Storytelling, in particular storytelling about personal hardships, is said to generate empathy and foster pro-social action, and story libraries often evoke their socially therapeutic function.

For instance, the traveling exhibit *A Mile in My Shoes* invites people "to walk a mile in someone else's shoes—literally. Housed in a giant shoebox, this roaming exhibit holds a diverse collection of shoes and audio stories that explore our shared humanity. From a Syrian refugee to a sex worker, a war veteran to a neurosurgeon, visitors are invited to walk a mile in the shoes of a stranger while listening to their story. The stories cover different aspects of life, from loss and grief to hope and love and take the visitor on an empathetic as well as a physical journey."[79] Interactive story libraries that aim at generating empathy are increasingly popular. For example, the Humanity House in The Hague offers a virtual meeting with eight refugees: "eight remarkable people, all with remarkable stories of their escape from war or conflict." This "empathy museum" promises a rich, embodied experience:[80] "Embark on a journey through the museum and see, hear and experience personally what it must feel like to have to survive in an area affected by conflict or disaster. It's an impressive journey on which you imagine the unimaginable. It's as if you find yourself in the place of a refugee."[81]

Indeed, futurists predict that the library of the future will no longer be a dusty place with shelves, but an interactive, multidimensional space where we can participate in experiences. Instead of merely accessing or viewing the description of an experience, thanks to emerging technologies, library visitors will be able to embody all kinds of experiences, including other people's lived experiences.[82] According to organizers, the ultimate purpose of partaking in each other's lived experiences is to collectively process the injustices of having been thrown into certain involuntary and harmful experiences. While listening to each other's wildly different stories may at first spotlight the differences between our lived experiences, story sharing creates an opportunity to process and to recombine our disparate lived experiences into a more just and voluntary experience (*Erfahrung*). Hence, contemporary story libraries are no longer satisfied with just documenting and informing, but they seek to mobilize storytellers and audiences around specific, shared lived experiences.

Human Libraries: A Critique

However, for these story libraries to accomplish their mission, they will first have to reevaluate their positivist belief in their story data, as well as their uncritical acceptance of the authority of "raw," lived experiences and the emotions they elicit. I will support this argument with the example of the popular story library called Human Library.[83] Founded in 2000, the international organization aims to challenge prejudices by encouraging people to "read" other people. The library has "depots" of "human books," which are available for "checkout" and can be "read" together at various public events: "The Human Library is a place where real people are on loan to readers," announces the website. "We publish people as open books."[84] The key mission of the Human Library is to create empathy, hence their motto: "Unjudge someone." The way it works is: organizers set up special "dialogue rooms" at various public events, where the "human books" share stories about their lives as well as stigmas and prejudices that they have experienced, and the audience can engage with them, ask questions, and so forth. Currently, the Human Library is operational on six continents in more than eighty countries, and as a "hands-on learning platform" it is embedded in high school and university curricula as well as in medical and civic training.[85] The project underscores the social nature of knowledge by reimagining the traditional story library as an interactive exchange between people. The Human Library describes itself as an interactive community space where one should not remain silent: "No silence please! This is a human library."

The Human Library, like most similar contemporary projects, appeals to the authority of "lived experience." It prioritizes the experiences storytellers have lived through, especially the unique ways in which each individual life defies stereotypes. Organizers prompt "human books" to use their uniquely situated knowledge. The website encourages participants to consider the unique value of their individual experiences: "Are you like an open book and do you have valuable experiences that readers could benefit from learning about?"[86] Audience members' experiences are similarly prized, and users are encouraged to allow themselves to be transformed by others' knowledge. There is a special emphasis on the social emotional learning experience of those listening to the stories. As one of the human books, a deafblind person explains, "I am not angry about my situation. I don't even get angry with cab drivers that refuse to pick me up because of my guide dog. But I think it important to give people a chance to understand what life looks like through my eyes."[87] These last words, especially poignant coming from someone without sight, express equal concern for the value of the storyteller's own experience (for what the world "looks like through my eyes") and for the experience of the audience (for their "chance to understand"). A visit to a story library is an opportunity to place oneself in another's embodied position, quite literally, and to see the world through their eyes.

As attractive as this opportunity may sound, there are important risks in wanting to build such "libraries of human experience." The first is that we forget the crucial role that narratives play in mediating experience. By using the word "book" as a metonymy for "person," the Human Library short-circuits the connection, assuming that others' experiences can reach us directly, when in fact those experiences are narrativized before they are shared, and then they are interpreted by others. Narrativization, our capacity to tell stories about our experiences, is both an obstacle and an advantage: an advantage in that language is what creates a shared space for critical reflection on experience, and an obstacle in that the opacity of language makes shared interpretation both necessary and historically conditioned. By arguing that "human books" are directly accessible to audiences, organizers suppress the role of narrative mediation in order to focus on how realities are felt in our bodies. By foreclosing the field of narrative interpretations, organizers allow, contrary to their intentions, some experiences to masquerade as human universals, instead of acknowledging that there are no such things as "pure" experiences (since all experiences are filtered through and shaped by historical and cultural acts of interpretation). They thereby run the risk of phenomenological dogmatism.

Given the motto of the Human Library, "don't judge a book by its cover," it is particularly ironic that, to catalog their collection, organizers resorted to pigeonholing human books into highly restrictive, one-dimensional categories such as "young single mother," "homeless," "polyamorous," "Muslim," "molested," and so on. The website explains that they purposely choose representative "books": "Every human book from our bookshelf represents a group in our society that is often subjected to prejudice, stigmatization or discrimination because of their lifestyle, diagnosis, belief, disability, social status, ethnic origin etc."[88] Of course all libraries operate with classifications to organize their knowledge, but the extension of this notational logic to "human books" reduced to a single defining feature of their lives seems to undermine the very purpose of the project. The ultimate aim of the Human Library, and of many contemporary story libraries, is to "challenge stereotypes." For that, however, we first need to gain critical, interpretive distance on the structures, forces, norms, and meanings that shape our experiences, as well as our own epistemic relevance as authors of ourselves. In short, there is no direct way to experience others' experiences.

The second issue has to do with the idea of empathy. As critics of naively formulated notions of empathy have cautioned, empathy can actually turn "toxic" when we start to "feel good about feeling bad."[89] Lisa Nakamura studied documentaries that use VR (virtual reality) technologies to put audiences in the shoes of marginalized and threatened bodies. She showed that whereas early VR technologies promised to produce "new kinds of knowledge," the new genre of "VR for social good, or virtuous VR" aims to generate new kinds of feelings by immersing users in others' disadvantageous experiences.[90] Nakamura argues that this mission is "founded on the concept of toxic re-embodiment: occupying the body of another who might not even own their own body."[91] The practice allows users to temporarily feel good and it "provide[s] absolution framed as information."[92] Similarly, in contemporary story libraries, feelings are prioritized over arguments, and feelings of empathy are sold as a way to compensate for our feelings of disaffection and exhaustion caused by alienating technologies. There are several risks here. For one, when doing good feels impossible, affective experience replaces tangible action and lulls us into social and political passivity. Just visiting the Human Library may seem like a virtuous act. Moreover, being so attuned to audiences' sentiments means that the emotional needs of users might trump the needs and intent of storytellers. This seems to be the case in those story collections that are searchable based on how "you want to feel" after listening to the story. For instance, The *Seattle Times* has a story library called Her Story: Our Story, which invites users to "experience the world through the lives and lenses of women."[93] Users first click on "I want to feel" and then choose, from a pull-down menu, between "proud, resilient, powerful, defiant, heartbroken, inspired, or joyful." Predetermining affective reaction in such deliberate ways suggests a false sense of control and deprives users of potentially transformative experiences. Finally, while it may seem that curated encounters such as those arranged by the Human Library are based on trust, one could also argue the opposite, since overemphasizing emotional identification suggests that "you cannot trust marginalized people when they speak their own truth or describe their own suffering, but you have to experience it for yourself."[94]

The third issue that the Human Library helps spotlight is the positivism of contemporary story libraries. In the case of the Human Library, this positivism is rooted in the certainty of feeling. As Nakamura warns, being so attuned to mood and affect may lead to an erroneous sense of epistemic certainty grounded in feeling, so that the story "not only needs to be felt to be believed, but cannot be doubted once it is felt."[95] Positivism in story libraries can also take other forms, such as data positivism and the fantasy of comprehensiveness. Even though many story libraries operate with small data, they are clearly marked by the fantasy of comprehensiveness promised by big data. Users are constantly urged to produce more knowledge by producing more stories, because more inclusive and more comprehensive collections are said to lead to more accurate and more complete knowledge about the human condition. Organizers stress our shared responsibility in crowdsourcing this knowledge, as well as the shared custody of these collectively produced archives ("our knowledge and wisdom could live on in the commons").[96] To play up their dream of completeness, story libraries often reference a "global community of storytellers,"[97] and they pride themselves on their number of contributors.

The fantasy of comprehensiveness is particularly tempting in the gigantic story archives created by social media. Here, the illusion of comprehensiveness is grounded in a certain "digital positivism,"[98] which treats stories as a "datum": given, observable, empirical evidence capable of producing objective and accurate knowledge. Data positivism in this case suggests a representational view of data, meaning that stories are treated as "reliable representations of reality" and an "objective foundation for the acquisition of knowledge," especially when their accumulation allows for inductive analysis.[99] More stories are taken to automatically mean better, more precise knowledge. Vincent Mosco was among the first to caution against "big data's imperious and dangerous digital positivism,"[100] which not only fails to acknowledge the limits and context of knowledge production, but also threatens to undermine other ways of knowing. Mosco complained that computational social science often fails to connect big data analytics to a broader analysis of human interpretations, values, and experiences, and the same may be said of the way story data is presented without broader questions.[101] Curators' excessive confidence in the definitive knowledge produced by story libraries turns downright dangerous when it becomes the basis of predictive analyses. Once story sharing is treated as a data-centric form of inquiry, researchers can formulate predictions and create justifications for any possible interpretation of the story data. Abel's and Allport et al.'s positivist perspective gets magnified here. The portrait of the "fictitious, average type of follower of the Hitler movement" created by Abel through the quantitative analyses of Nazis' stories had limited impact due to its low circulation. However, today's predictive analytics are much more powerful in that they can make sensitive inferences and circulate them widely.

To conclude, it seems that digital technologies have not resolved the nineteenth-century challenge to derive scientifically "valid propositions from inner experiences that are so personally limited, so indeterminate"—if anything, our technologies have only exacerbated it. On the one hand, the expansion and democratization of story libraries meant that they became a means of mobilization rather than just documentation; on the other hand, the phenomenological dogmatism celebrating lived experience and the digital positivism promoting the value of large-scale story data risk short-circuiting the process of interpretation that is key to unlocking the true potential of narratives. Therefore, as we build increasingly inclusive and dynamic story libraries, especially through the automated archiving functions of social media, we should keep in mind that there is no such thing as a neutral repository of knowledge, not even when that knowledge comes from ourselves, is about ourselves, and is circulated to ourselves.

4   TO-GATHER IN TIME

> *This was a most ordinary day. On Earth, as always, snow fell, flowers bloomed, people were born and died, they loved and hated, they tilled the earth, achieved the unknown, tempered steel and wrote poetry.*
> —DEN MIRA

One Day in the Life of Us

Diaries may seem like intensely private affairs, but people have been sharing and even co-creating them for quite some time.[1] The present chapter focuses on a special kind of collective diary in which people crowdsource and compile their personal stories of a *single day*. Simultaneous, crowd-sourced diary-writing is a popular trend. According to the *New York Times*, "The crowd-sourced global diary, a new kind of documentary in which thousands of videos shot around the world at the same time are assembled into a concise chronicle of a day in the life of the planet, is an astonishing technological and organizational achievement. The visual feast it provides is inspiring and breathtaking, introducing audiences to cultures, customs and languages while underscoring humanity's inescapable connectedness."[2] The popularity of one-day diaries has greatly increased in recent years. The project One Day on Earth enlisted filmmakers and "other inspired citizens" in every single country on October 10, 2010, November 11, 2011, and December 12, 2012, to record the events of those particular days. According to the website, "The 10.10.10 collaboration was the first ever simultaneous filming event occurring in every country of the world."[3] The call encouraged everyone to contribute their voice: "Help document the world's story." A similar example, *Britain in a Day*, was a documentary of life in Britain on November 12, 2011, which was broadcast by the BBC before being released in movie theaters and as an online archive.[4] Yet another project, titled A Day, asked people around the globe to document their life on May 15, 2012. The images contributed by participants were later shown simultaneously worldwide across 85,733 major digital display screens in twenty-two countries. Organizers also planned to lock the whole collection "in a copper mine in Sweden, giving future historians a glimpse of just one day on our planet."[5]

A day in the life of a community is indeed a fascinating thing to imagine. Ever since spiritual traditions began to prescribe rituals of daily reflection, people have pondered the meaning of a single day. The temporal unit of a day plays a fundamental role in human life. The day, unlike the minute or the week, is based on the rhythm of our biological needs, which makes it a convenient unit for measuring lived time (the root of the word "day" lies in the Sanskrit *dah*, meaning "to burn," as in the burning of the sun, which creates a daily rhythm). The day also gives a rhythm to our personal practices of self-reflection, and the entire tradition of diary writing rests on the concept of a day (the Latin form of the word "diary," *diarium*, means "daily"). Importantly, our ability to imagine our contemporaries all "sharing the same day" can also increase our sense of social belonging. As I argue in the present chapter, narrative or visual snapshots of a single day, when arranged into public collections, can profoundly influence how we imagine our being-together in time as a collective. Artists and journalists have long used the theme of a single day to create composite portraits of communities. Early twentieth-century photographers experimented with montage (see Rodchenko's *A Day in the Life of the World*), and the technique remained influential throughout the century (see the acclaimed city-series *A Day in the Life of London, 24 Hours in the Life of Los Angeles,*[6] etc.). In recent years, new developments in time-lapse photography, as well as crowdsourcing and mashing technologies, have further increased the popularity of the one-day format.

In the following I present a half a dozen one-day diaries, mostly from the 1930s and the first decade of the twenty-first century. These projects vary greatly in terms of scope, objectives, and the methods they use to aggregate individual images and stories. Some promise snapshots of the whole world, while others focus on smaller communities; some involve a hundred thousand people, others only a handful. One thing that joins them is that they all promote the community-building effect of a shared sense of time. They celebrate the simultaneity of our parallel lives and the sense of community that this simultaneity engenders. Such snapshots of time, like a family photo, can indeed create a spectacle of togetherness. However, their mesh of temporalities, which connects "real" time to narrative time as well as to the time of the database, is a lot more complex than organizers generally acknowledge. Crowdsourced one-day diaries present us with perfect case studies of the interconnections between our concepts of time and community, because they show how time is constituted through social interaction and narrative organization, and how new possibilities of sharing time may mean new possibilities of being together.

Life in a Day, 2010 (and 2020)

In July 2010, YouTube announced a crowdsourced megaproject. To celebrate the company's fifth anniversary, they asked people from all around the world to film one day of their lives: July 24, 2010. The plan was to create the world's first crowdsourced documentary by taking the best submissions and molding them into a single, feature-length film. The idea spread virally, and to their great surprise, organizers received 4,500 hours of footage in 80,000 submissions from 192 countries. YouTube dedicated an entire channel to the project, and an army of film students and translators spent months sifting through the material. The gargantuan task was completed by director Kevin Macdonald and editor Joe Walker, who reduced and composed the material into a ninety-minute film. The premiere of *Life in a Day* was an instant success, and what started out as a cinematic experiment turned into widely accessible, popular entertainment. Ten years later, on July 25, 2020, Kevin Macdonald repeated the experiment, to great success.[7]

Organizers praised the democratizing effects of instant sharing and technology's capacity to establish a sense of wholeness: "Every day, 6.7 billion people view the world through their own unique lens. Imagine if there was a way to collect all of these perspectives, to aggregate and mold them into the cohesive story of a single day on earth,"[8] they appealed. Wholeness, or the wholeness of the community of humankind, was defined here in temporal and narrative terms as "the cohesive story of a single day," and the role of technology was to "aggregate" all these perspectives into a simultaneous present. The immediate reactions following the release of *Life in a Day* praised the film's community-building effect. As one viewer put it, "watching [the film] makes viewers feel like they must run out and meet all the new friends they're watching on screen."[9] Christopher Brian, one of the contributors, felt overwhelmed by this sense of connection: "I feel like so connected to the whole world. Now after seeing this movie just one time you realize how the things that you want in this life are the same things that other people want in Tanzania or wherever."[10] The project, according to many, celebrated our sameness despite difference: "we're actually far more similar than we are different,"[11] "there are things that divide us as humans, but far more things that unite us."[12] Many saw the film as a "powerful example of how people are beautiful in their diversity and yet we are still so obviously one.human.family."[13]

This sense of a universal siblinghood was based neither on shared parentage nor on common experiences. Participants and viewers of *Life in a Day* came from such diverse social, geographical, and economic strata that they had barely anything in common. The only thing that joined members of this eclectic group was the temporal quality of their existence. Editor Joe Walker stressed the importance of this shared temporality by presenting the history of that July 24th as symbolic of our lifetime, stretching from birth to death. "It's not just midnight to midnight," he explained, "but it's also from light to dark and from birth to death."[14] What matters is that we all exist in time: birth and death are markers of our temporality, reminders of the finite nature of our existence. *Life in a Day* thus defines the community of humankind in terms of our universally shared temporal condition. In addition, the project also refers to the community of all those who were alive on that particular day in July 2010. "The fact that we all experienced that day is part of what gives the documentary an unusual kind of relatability,"[15] opined one of the viewers. The project was considered groundbreaking in that all of it was "shot on the same day."[16] Many considered this sense of simultaneity awe-inspiring: "I really enjoyed watching the diversity on show here and I had to keep reminding myself that all these things happened on the same day."[17] The fact that all these diverse events happened simultaneously made viewers' sense of diversity more acute. Director Kevin Macdonald further reinforced this sentiment by praising the "sense of magic that is given to [the project] by knowing this was more or less all happening *at the same time*—all over the planet! That idea induces a bit of awe, for me anyway."[18]

A Day in the World, 1935

When asked in an interview about the possibility of making such a crowdsourced diary before the existence of the internet, director Kevin Macdonald responded: "It would have been an undertaking that maybe a Chinese emperor or Stalin might have undertaken."[19] As a matter of fact, Macdonald was not too far from the truth, for it was precisely the Soviets and the Chinese who first introduced the idea of crowdsourced, simultaneous diaries. Eager to engage the masses and to promote the spirit of proletarian brotherhood and collectivization, Soviet writers were among the first to invite their fellow citizens to describe their experiences of a single day and to contribute their stories to a single volume. At the First Congress of Soviet Writers, writer Maxim Gorky presented an original proposition: he called on writers from all around the world to describe a single, randomly chosen day of the year, September 27, 1935. The purpose was to convey the richness of the "powerful symphony of human life" created out of all the sounds of a single day. Contributors sent in material from more than fifty countries, which were then translated and arranged geographically. Each country was represented by a rich array of newspaper articles, letters, telegrams, small ads, realia, photos, caricatures, cinema, theater programs, and more. The resulting six-hundred-page volume with the title *Den Mira* (which could be translated as "A day in the world" or "Peace day") was published in 1937.

In conceiving his project, Gorky was at least partly motivated by Soviet propaganda. As the following letter to his co-editor Mikhail Koltsov indicates, he wanted the collection to serve as a "proof" of the "decay" of Western bourgeois societies: "We are writing that the bourgeoisie is decaying, rotting, etc. It sounds proofless, since it is not confirmed by facts—our newspapers are not suitable for the material on everyday life which would provide an obvious clear picture of how exactly the senile obsolete world of the bourgeoisie is decaying."[20] If they really wanted to present a convincing case about the decay of Western societies and the glory of the Soviet system, they should appeal to the experience of the man in the street and present people's own perception of their daily lives, urged Gorky. Such a bottom-up perspective would automatically reveal the superiority of the Soviet experience.

The "facts" of "everyday life" did find their way into the collection, mostly in the form of diary entries, telegrams, individual reflections, letters, and other autobiographical material. These personal snippets make *Den Mira* a complex and captivating document. For example, the following selection of telegrams from the night of September 27, 1935, shows the myriad concerns of individual participants. The condensed stories of these telegrams offer all the drama of a Tolstoy novel, and they also remind us that six-word memoirs and instant messaging are not twenty-first century inventions:

Exam passed excellent kiss mum, dad, granny Nadya

Been robbed stay Metropol stop send six hundred fifty kopek stop Blestyaschiy

Operation successful stop don't worry see you soon stop Vanya

Wonderful fall Moscow stop missing you dot Hugs and kisses Asenka stop Come soon waiting impatiently your Kolya

Malania Terekhova awarded Lenin order stop congratulate my behalf Merkushev

Tanchuk gossiped stop swear nothing happened stop cried all night Olya[21]

In the end, however, Gorky's intentions were undercut by the heavy-handed editorial board, who selected mostly material written by journalists. The politically motivated, strategic layout of the material also undermined the original intention. While *Den Mira* was meant to celebrate the voices of unknown individuals from around the globe, in the end, "every foreign country [was] depicted mainly in the words of its own ruling classes and groups." The collection was divided into two parts, the Soviet Union and the rest of the world, and the two were also separated by a smiling portrait of Stalin. There was special irony in the fact that, even in a proletarian regime committed to the well-being of the man in the street, the rich details of individual lives were overshadowed by grand narratives. Gorky himself seemed puzzled about the motley nature of his collection: "How should one read this book? . . . readers may feel confused and perplexed. . . . How should they relate to this book? Browse through it or read it from beginning to end, look through the sections that might be interesting to them personally, or read it according to its plan?"[22] By reading the book "according to its plan," Gorky meant "hear[ing] in the sounds of the present the voice of the worker" and the "powerful symphony of human life" created out of all the sounds of a single day.

One Day in China, 1936

Despite Gorky's slight disappointment, the idea of crowdsourcing the diary of a single day resonated with many, both inside and outside the Soviet Union. Less than a year after Gorky's announcement, newspapers and magazines all over China carried a similar advertisement, calling on all Chinese citizens to document a single, randomly chosen day: May 21, 1936. To their great surprise, organizers received over three thousand submissions, of which they published close to five hundred under the title *One Day in China* (*Zhongguo di yi ri*).[23] The number of contributors was even higher if we include all whose writing was submitted by others (people often enclosed others' letters or essays along with their own contributions). A selection of these stories was published in English in 1985, under the title *One Day in China: 21 May, 1936*.

The editor, Mao Dun, favored the contributions of "small" people, meaning he did not want *One Day in China* to only reflect the perspectives of educated and wealthy individuals. By advertising in newspapers, he hoped to reach all people, including the lower classes and those who had never published anything. He also made it a point to market the collection in a way that made it affordable to all. He summarized his editorial principles as follows: "we hope that all writers and unpublished writers who support this project of ours will ... write down their impressions (in a maximum of two thousand words).... Materials for writing may be drawn from episodes that take place within personal experiences at work on May twenty-first, may be drawn from personal impressions on any aspect of anything in sight on May twenty-first, and may also be drawn from private correspondence and personal reflections on May twenty-first."[24]

Mao Dun's democratic editorial policy paid off. Compared to the Soviet project, the Chinese one was much more successful in generating previously unpublished material. *One Day in China* offers pieces from an impressively wide geographical range and by authors from diverse social and educational backgrounds, as well as a great variety of genres, including pictures, diary entries, letters, short stories, and more. Just like Gorky's team, the Chinese editorial board struggled with how to arrange the rich material. They finally opted for a geographic approach, organizing the stories based on where their authors came from. They paid special attention to the "frontier provinces," even if that meant including the submission of a middle schooler over the piece of a Shanghai scholar. As they noted: "For example, among the essays from Yunnan, we included a piece by a middle school student. Both in content and in literary style, this piece is far inferior to essays from Shanghai, Jiangsu, and Zhejiang that were rejected. But we felt that *One Day in China* should not be *One Day in China* of the few provinces and areas which have a comparatively high degree of culture."[25]

Mao Dun echoed Gorky's reference to the "powerful symphony of human life" when he declared: "This is the spectacular orchestra heard on one day in today's China!"[26] He highlighted the contribution of each story to the harmony of the whole: "Truly, here there is everything: the dissipation and indulgence of the rich, the writhing masses on the edge of starvation, ... the rampant religious superstitions, the degeneracy of public servants, the overbearing swagger of the local bullies and evil gentry, the oppression of women, ... From the main streets and back alleys of cities, from the tall buildings and thatched huts, from the deserted little marketplaces of small towns . . . there have arisen anguished and strong calls to arms, grief-stricken utterance, bitter cursing, tearful smiles, restrained but boiling passions."[27] *One Day in China* inspired a whole series of similar crowdsourced reportages in China and beyond, such as *One Day in Shanghai* (1938), *One Day in Central Hebei* (1940), and *One Day in Anping* (1941), among others.[28]

These Soviet and Chinese examples may suggest a special connection between communist or collectivist ideologies and crowdsourced diaries. There is, indeed, a special affinity between the mass subject of communist ideologies and the mass public of these crowdsourced diaries. There is also an interesting tension between communists' rejection of the self-absorbed, "bourgeois" genre of diary and their use of it for ideological purposes. Nevertheless, one-day projects were popular in the West as well, as demonstrated by the May Twelfth tradition of England's Mass Observation Archive. Just a year after the Chinese project, three former students from Cambridge proposed to develop a "mass science" based on people's personal observations. They signed up fifty people from around Britain to "make observations on how they and other people spend their daily lives."[29] In February of that year, these people began to document a randomly chosen day, the twelfth of each month. May 12, 1937 happened to be the day of the coronation of King George VI, so organizers sent volunteer observers into the street, distributed questionnaires with the question "Where were you on May 12th?" and they also asked volunteers to share their diary entries from that one day. To make the results public, they published an anthology titled *May the Twelfth*.[30]

The tradition of one-day diaries continued in later decades as well.[31] The Mass Observation Archive still repeats its annual call for one-day diaries every May 12. The 2020 call resulted in five thousand contributions, and the most recent call, in 2021, announced: "We don't know how life will be on the 12th of May, but we would like your help to document it."[32] The Soviets also repeated Gorky's experiment, twenty-five years later on September 27, 1960. The 1961 edition of *Den Mira* is a giant almanac with a similar geographical arrangement, lots of photos, and journalistic material. Compared to the 1935 version, the 1961 edition buckles under the weight of propaganda. Editors included parallel maps and charts comparing the world in 1935 and 1960 so as to encourage readers to imagine diachronic historical development and to discover parallels between their own lives and the victory of socialism: "A quarter century has passed. People born at the same time as Gorky's book have left their youth and entered adulthood. Those who were young back then are now the creators of life, having been made wise by experience and knowledge. In the last quarter century all of humanity has made advances towards a great renewal. The world of socialism, born in October, already unites a third of the population of the planet."[33]

The idea of a quarter century of similar September 12ths or May 12ths only serves to highlight the potential and promise of every single day. The appeal of crowdsourcing the stories of a single day lies in its infinite repeatability with variation, in knowing that any random day will offer a similar wondrous mix of events and perspectives. That is why all these projects stress the fact of having selected the day randomly. "Any day will do," wrote Gorky. "September 25, October 7, or December 15, they're all the same."[34] The Chinese announcement also specified that "the day that has been selected was chosen at random."[35] One-day diaries rely on the longitudinal perspective to lend significance to any random day. What really builds community, however, is the cross-sectional perspective called "simultaneity," the idea that all of these different things happened on the same day, at the same time.

Simultaneity and Its Social Function

According to Gerard James Whitrow, the concept of simultaneity is as old as human consciousness, since humans have a "deep-rooted natural tendency to correlate the microcosm (oneself) with the macrocosm (universe)."[36] We imagine our lives in the context of other, simultaneously occurring events, and we are aware of the presence of contemporaries who live "in the same time" as us. The notion of simultaneity is born out of our tendency to spatialize time. As the etymology of the word also confirms, the idea of simultaneity implies "togetherness" (the Latin *simul*—deriving from the Sanskrit *sem* or *sema*—means "together"). In technical terms, simultaneity means the co-temporality of two or more spatially separated events—that is, two events will be called simultaneous if they happen "together."

The "togetherness" associated with simultaneity is not limited to temporal togetherness.[37] Being together in time also implies social togetherness. Consider, for example, the community of contemporaries who share the planet at a particular moment in time. In order to imagine this community, we need to establish the simultaneity of events happening far away. We can only do this, however, if we can communicate and compare our perceptions at distant corners of the world and agree that those events did indeed happen at the same time. This explains why the concept of simultaneity only gained practicality in the early 1500s, with the invention of the portable mechanical clock, because people needed two synchronized, locally placed clocks to establish the simultaneity of two faraway events. Hence, practically speaking, we can never observe the simultaneity of two distant events, only presuppose it by comparing our perception to those of others. That is why Whitrow states that simultaneity is "an intellectual hypothesis which far transcends our perception of phenomena."[38]

While simultaneity may indeed be nothing more than an "intellectual hypothesis," it can still have a powerful effect on our social life. To begin with, the very way we talk about time shapes our relationships to each other. When asked about the top five most commonly used English nouns, few people guess right. According to the *Concise Oxford English Dictionary*, the #1 noun is "time."[39] "Time" is followed in second place by the word "person." Although there need not be a correlation between the first two words, time *is* in fact very personal, or at least we experience it as such. It is hard to think about our lives without thinking about the passing of time, and the opposite is also true: thinking about time involves reflecting on our lives. It is no coincidence that one of the most prominent philosophers of time, Saint Augustine, was also one of our first memoirists. Of course, self-reflection need not take the form of written narratives, but most psychologists agree that we cannot say who we are without some reference to time, which, in turn, will take the form of some kind of narrative.[40]

Since humans are social, our ideas about time influence not only who we are as individuals, but also who we think we are in relation to others, as a community. Philosophers, sociologists, and anthropologists have long tried to clarify the relationship between time and social identity. As anthropologist Carol Greenhouse explains, in medieval times the agency attributed to God in "sharing out" time concealed the question about the relationship between time and society.[41] Later, however, people recognized that there was no such thing as an Absolute Time that "flowed uniformly,"[42] backstage so to speak. Time is not a passive, neutral background; rather it is us, people, who construct it through our social practices and imagination. By the end of the twentieth century the question was no longer *what* time was, but *how* societies use it as a tool to construct their relations to each other. As Johannes Fabian famously put it, "*geopolitics* has its ideological foundations in *chronopolitics*,"[43] because "time, much like language or money, is a carrier of significance, a form through which we define the content of relations between the Self and the Other."[44] Societies manage time in many different ways: through rituals, regulations, technologies, institutions, and last but not least, through collective acts of storytelling. As I will show, organizers of one-day diaries not only assume that our temporal condition binds us together, but they *ritualize* simultaneity in order to promote its community-building effect.

Simultaneity Based on Coincidence

Twentieth-century debates about simultaneity were mostly dominated by two competing interpretations. To simplify, I will associate the first one with Albert Einstein, and the second with Henri Bergson.[45] Einstein was mainly concerned with physical time, defining simultaneity as the temporal coincidence of two spatially distant events. Bergson opposed Einstein's views and focused instead on psychological time. In Bergson's view, time does not exist independently from our subjective experience of it. We experience time not as a series of distinct, measurable instants, but as an indivisible, continuous flow or "duration." In short, while Einstein understood simultaneity as the temporal coincidence of two artificially defined instances, Bergson thought of it as the parallel and continuous flow of our individual time perceptions. In Bergson's words, "We therefore call two external flows that occupy the same duration 'simultaneous' because they both depend upon the duration of a like third, our own."[46] Though these ideas may seem abstract, Einstein's and Bergson's competing theories left their mark on all these crowdsourced diaries.

In his classic study *Imagined Communities*, Benedict Anderson based his theory of nation-formation on the coincidence-based notion of simultaneity. According to Anderson, what facilitated the formation of modern communities was the emergence of a new mode of temporality, that of a simultaneity across time, which—unlike the earlier, prophetic understanding of simultaneity as a copresence of what was, is, and is to come—was "marked not by prefiguring and fulfillment but by temporal coincidence."[47] What allowed the synchronization of time, argues Anderson, was the idea of temporal coincidence created by the clock and the calendar. In the course of the last few centuries, this coincidence-based definition of simultaneity became instrumental to official time representations, and it also helped solidify the prestige of public time as linear, measurable, and unifiable. Anderson argues that the nation-state as a modern construct came into being when print capitalism first allowed people to imagine the simultaneous, anonymous, and parallel existence of other members of the nation. As he put it, "the idea of a sociological organism moving calendrically through homogenous, empty time is a precise analogue of the idea of the nation, which also is conceived as a solid community moving steadily down (or up) history. An American will never meet, or even know the names of more than a handful of his 240,000,000-odd fellow-Americans. He has no idea of what they are up to at any one time. But he has complete confidence in their steady, anonymous, simultaneous activity."[48]

To illustrate the functioning of this modern type of community based on simultaneity, Anderson cites the example of newspapers. We can easily grasp the homogenizing effect of this new print technology, he argues, if we imagine all the readers of the same daily sitting at breakfast reading about the same events of the same day and imagining themselves doing the same thing at the same time as all the other readers. I argue that what happened on the random days selected by these one-day diaries was not that different from the morning ritual described by Anderson. People around the world picked up their pens or cameras to record a segment of their lives, knowing that thousands around the world were doing the same thing at the same time, and this mass ceremony reinforced their sense of belonging to an anonymous community. The technological means that created this effect in 2010 or 2020 were of course substantially different from those referenced by Anderson or those in the 1930s. Also, while Anderson's newspaper readers were merely receiving the news, authors of these crowdsourced diaries were actively shaping them. Despite these differences, Anderson's description is relevant to crowdsourced diaries in that they all depend on modern processes of synchronization to create a unified vision of a single day in the world.

The "time capsules" created by these one-day diaries are all products of calendrical synchronization.[49] Organizers of YouTube's *Life in a Day* project openly embraced the value of synchronization: "Today, we're excited to announce the launch of *Life in a Day*, a historic cinematic experiment that will attempt to do just that: document one day, as seen through the eyes of people around the world. On July 24, you have 24 hours to capture a snapshot of your life on camera."[50] Choosing a single, specific date gave the project a historical dimension ("be a part of history" was one of the project's mottos), and more importantly, it allowed the synchronization of each participant's twenty-four-hour unit with those of others. Yet, the very idea of "a day in the world" is a fiction created by the modern concept of standard time: the "history of the world on the 24th of July 2010" as described in the call for contributions is a fiction, because even with standard time there is no single "24th of July" in the world. The "24th of July" refers to a different unit of twenty-four hours in each time zone, so it is entirely possible that what people filmed from their lives on the 24th of July 2010 happened on the 25th or 23rd of July in other parts of the world. Interestingly, despite the obvious conventionality of this concept, individual participants themselves sought to uphold the illusion of unity that it provides. For instance, some contributors redoubled the official acts of synchronization by incorporating into their video narratives image of clocks, mostly on cell phones, showing the exact time and date at the time of their recording. In one case, the narrator held up her own phone and that of somebody else next to her, thus tripling the process of synchronization.

The effects of calendrical synchronization are even more tangible in the diaries of the 1930s, given the journalistic nature of those projects and the time lag created by their medium. The temporal lag is particularly pronounced in the case of *Den Mira*, since the analyses of what happened on the 27th did not appear in newspapers until the 28th. Mao Dun also acknowledged the artificial idea of a single day: "Most of what appeared in the newspapers on the twenty-first took place before the twenty-first, but since these reached all readers through newspapers on the twenty-first, these deserve to occupy a place in this 'one day history' of the twenty-first."[51] Editors not only acknowledged but celebrated the synchronizing effects of standardized time. The 1935 edition of *Den Mira* opens with the following triumphal note: "At midnight, the Internationale played from the Kremlin tower, while two hours later, Big Ben played God Save the King."[52] The 1961 edition highlights the effects of synchronization even more explicitly, by offering a full chapter called "Midnight to midnight" which relates the events of the world hour by hour, tying them all to Moscow time ("Moscow 21:00" lists events that happened in the "same" hour in New York, Lagos, Prague, etc.).

The clock and the calendar are of course not the only means to establish a temporal coincidence among various moments. In the case of *Life in a Day*, for example, the edited version of the film itself became an important means of synchronization. To start with, since the cinematographic experience of film is based on the rhythmic sequence of indivisible and commensurable units of time editors had to convert the sixty different frame rates of the individual submissions into a unified rate.[53] This standardization sacrificed the incommensurable rhythm of individual moments for the sake of viewability, but it managed to create a unified temporal framework which made it possible to bring those individual moments into sync.[54] To create a cinematographic vision of a world in sync, editors also used two further techniques: parallel editing and montage.

Their choice of parallel editing (or cross-cutting) is hardly surprising, since the success of *Life in a Day* depended on viewers' ability to conceptualize the parallel relationships between simultaneously occurring events, and the objective of parallel editing is precisely this: to create a strong sense of simultaneity by alternating two or more simultaneously happening, but spatially distant scenes. For example, editors cut the video-narratives of certain characters into segments and inserted them into various sections of the film, so that the recurring appearances of these characters would reinforce viewers' sense of simultaneity; their reoccurrence reminds us that what cannot be seen momentarily is still there, happening simultaneously in the background. Somewhat paradoxically, they also used asynchronous music to reinforce viewers' sense of synchronicity. For instance, when we see a group of women singing while working, and then their work song accompanies us for the next couple of minutes as we watch scenes from various corners of the globe, the use of music establishes a temporal connection, reminding viewers that all those things were happening at the same time.[55]

The use of montage—a process of piecing together sections to form a whole—also helped to synchronize the final product. The advantage of montage is that it can reenact simultaneity as overlapping copresence, while minimizing sequencing. As the Soviet film theorist and director Sergei Eisenstein explained it: "montage is an idea that arises from the collision of independent thoughts" wherein "each sequential element is perceived not next to the other, but on top of the other."[56] The use of such spatial metaphors in discussing temporalities can be somewhat problematic. In this case, however, it seems justified because in the Western imagination simultaneity across time is about perceiving things "on top" rather than "next to" each other. The challenge in using montage is to avoid the impression of aimlessness (MacDonald emphasized that he "wanted to make a movie, not just best-of clips"), but without conferring too much meaning on this particular order of snapshots. This balancing act proved difficult. The danger of overinterpretation is most tangible in the scenes that employ intellectual montage, which is designed to allow new ideas to emerge from the conflict between shots. For example, the sequence of images showing first the brutal slaughtering of an animal and then a man eating his spaghetti Bolognese—two shots submitted by two different authors, brought together by the editors—may shock viewers into questioning their habit of eating meat, but it could be viewed as manipulative. Nevertheless, montage had several advantages:

besides creating the illusion of simultaneity, it also allowed editors to preserve, and even exaggerate the visual and spatial discontinuity of the collection.

In sum, one-day diaries are illustrative of the processes described by Anderson, in that they rely on the clock, the calendar, and various other techniques of synchronization to present a unified time.

Simultaneity Based on Parallel Time Flows

The problem with such a coincidence-based notion of simultaneity is that it betrays the decentralized heterogeneity of a crowdsourced product. If the whole point of creating these diaries is to acknowledge the multitudes of perspectives that make up the story of a single day, then totalizing them by way of consensus, standardization, and homogeneity is clearly not an optimal solution. This may explain why producers felt the need to also evoke a second, more decentralized notion of simultaneity. Bergson, we said, was the first to caution against limiting the idea of simultaneity to the coincidence of two instances. He argued that the coincidence-based simultaneity embraced by physicists was artificial, and that there existed a more natural kind of simultaneity constituted by the simultaneity of our parallel time flows. "The theoreticians of relativity never mention any simultaneity but that of two instants," complained Bergson. "Anterior to that one, however, is another, the idea of which is more natural: the simultaneity of two flows."[57]

Bergson's views are clearly reflected in all these one-day diaries. At the basis of Bergson's concept of simultaneity lies a phenomenological interpretation of time, which is more concerned with individuals' personal sense of time than with units of measurable, commensurable instances.[58] The genre of these diaries is significant here, in that autobiographical self-reflection is often seen as prioritizing the individual experience of time. Indeed, what people shared in these one-day diaries were intimate scenes from their private lives, stories of their innermost fears and joys. Participants felt personally invested in their stories, and organizers and viewers alike saw this as a powerful guarantee of authenticity. What authorized these first-person accounts as "authentic" was not simply the first-person perspective, but the temporal ideal of immediacy attributed to this perspective. According to this ideal of immediacy, the subject is present to itself in reflecting on its own life. One-day diaries promote this idealist understanding of autobiographical self-presence in several ways.

First, they celebrate participants' personal sense of "now" by favoring the iterative time of everyday rituals over the historical time of epochal events. Organizers purposely chose a historically insignificant day, because they did not want historical events or public commemorations to distort participants' personal sense of time.[59] Instead, they sought to record personal rituals of survival like people eating and sleeping, as well as the small luxuries and tragedies of life, such as daily gestures of care and neglect. All of these one-day diaries include stories describing "people's comings and goings,"[60] and in doing so they stress the priority of ordinary experiences and their idiosyncratic, personal rhythms. Second, they actively encourage a personal ownership of time. "Film part of *your* day tomorrow."[61] *Life in a Day* also complemented its twenty-four-hour definition of the day with a "more natural," even biological interpretation of the day. Celestial bodies have long served as references of time reckoning, and here they serve as symbols of a personal sense of time. For example, the film presents the visual history of that one day as a natural arc between the setting and rising moon. It begins with a dozen images of the moon, then shows the rising and setting of the sun before concluding with views of the dark sky. With these clips of the sun and the moon, participants establish their individual ownership of time: "my day" starts when "my sun" rises and not when standard time dictates it.

Note that, just as Bergson argued that the personal time flow–based simultaneity was more natural than its coincidence-based interpretation, organizers of these diaries celebrated this option as more natural than the artificial, homogenized time created by standardization. For instance, when asked about his decision to start the film *Life in a Day* "at midnight, with a full moon seen from a dozen different perspectives around the globe," the producer suggested that the image of the moon was "the most natural place to start." This shift in emphasis from "artificial" temporal *co-incidence* to "natural" temporal *co-existence* is significant. It is not that the latter replaces the former. The clear-cut, artificially defined temporal plane created by two simultaneous instances—such as a single date or a unit of montage—continues to serve as a convenient tool of organization in all these one-day diaries. Yet, just as the mechanical clock is often seen as the materialization of some universal sense of time, these diaries present the artificial simultaneities as mere "virtual stops" along a more natural, shared flow of personal and social time.[62] The film *Life in a Day* makes this particularly explicit in a scene that juxtaposes in quick succession two symbols, the alarm clock and the rooster, suggesting that the former is an artificial proxy for the latter.

The problem with presenting the simultaneity of our personal time flows as more "natural" than the artificial simultaneity of two instances is that it assumes that there is something natural about simultaneity. The thing to remember here is that it is us, humans, who give meaning to the very idea of a moment in which two or more things happen together.[63] In other words, simultaneity is not a natural phenomenon, but a form we give to our experiences. As Carol Greenhouse cautions, the idea of a universal or natural time is only a fiction which serves to "naturalize" the linear model of time, which in turn serves to legitimate, through its "intrinsic rationality," nation-states, empires, and other similar power formations. In other words, the paradox embraced by these crowdsourced projects about time being both culturally relative and universal is merely a cultural artifact.

Falling Back on a Totalizing Sense of Simultaneity

My point so far is that by acknowledging the artificiality of standardized time, organizers promote participants' personal sense of time as a more natural alternative, which in turn serves to conjure up the image of a unified time and a unified humanity. These one-day diaries seem to suggest that there *is* such a thing as what Eugen Fink describes as an "all-encompassing Present,"[64] in which everything around the globe or the country happens at the same time. This idea of a "universal simultaneity" is crucial to their success, since this is what allows people to imagine a unified community of contemporaries or national citizens. Positing the personal time flow–based simultaneity as more natural implies that not only are our individual stories synchronizable but they are always already synchronous. For example, in the scenes from *Life in a Day* where dozens of people are shown in quick succession getting out of bed, going to the bathroom, or brushing their teeth, the emphasis is not on these moments being calendrically anchored but on their relation to each other. Since these are repetitive actions, it is easy to allow them to "float" in the process of editing, so that one person's routine gets aligned with those of others without being tied to a specific point in time. To underscore the shared nature of these routines and the shared flow of time, editors also cut and mixed various submissions into temporal wholes. For instance, the scene in *Life in a Day* that shows a man getting out of bed in the morning is composed of five different submissions, so that by the time the man's feet touch the floor we have seen five different pairs of feet. Similarly, the scene about breakfast preparation shows several different pairs of hands cracking eggs, all composed into a single sequence.

The idea of a single, synchronous social time around the globe, however, is based on the controversial concept of a universal simultaneity. To put it simply, the concept of universal simultaneity extends the idea of a personal now to a universal, all-encompassing Now. The phenomenologist Eugen Fink explains the idea as follows: "The Here is the mode in which living beings 'experience' their place in the totality of space. And I experience the Now in the same way: to the extent that I experience it, it is 'mine'; but I never experience it as mine alone, but rather as something belonging to all beings; so now I am in the Now of all things. Now thus designates a worldwide Time in the sense of an all-encompassing Present, in which I am co-present with everything that is simultaneous." In short, "The fundamental meaning of the Now is that of a universal simultaneity.... it contains the whole world-wide extent of the simultaneous."[65]

One-day diaries eagerly embrace this idea of a universal Here and Now. They presuppose a unified Present, a "worldwide Time in the sense of an all-encompassing Present." This "Now of all things" is not the present that has been unified by standard time. Rather, it is the Present created by the supposed immediacy of many, simultaneous acts of living and storytelling. These diaries celebrate the universal Present by distinguishing themselves from other sources of information, like newspapers, which are by definition retrospective and secondhand sources. The creation of a one-day diary is supposed to be simultaneous with the events that it reflects on, as well as more authentic in that people reflect on their own lives in "real" time. At first, this may seem like a good way to "liberate" our experience of the present from the restricting progression of historical time. However, by liberating the present from the totality of historical time, these diaries end up reinscribing it into another form of totality: the totality of present immediacy. This notion ignores the fact that "to speak of the present already denote[s] the unification of several givens in a minimal unity of meaning."[66] The idea of a universal Here and Now conceals the fact that we are never fully "present" to each other, and that we are never fully "present" to ourselves either, since both relations involve the mediation of narrative reflection. In other words, "the worldwide Now" projected by Fink, "in which I am co-present with everything that is simultaneous" is no more than an illusion created by the very structure of the stories we tell.[67]

The idea of a worldwide, single time allows organizers to project a vision of a *unified* community of contemporaries. Evidently, this unity does not imply a lack of diversity. All one-day diaries present an impressive diversity of voices, and editors and contributors justly pride themselves on this diversity. The problem is, they portray this diversity as unified. For instance, when viewers of *Life in a Day* rave about how they feel "so connected to the whole world," or when the journalist at the *New York Times* concludes that these diaries "underscore humanity's inescapable connectedness," they adopt a vision of the world's population as diverse but unified. This vision of unity is interwoven with the idea of a totality of all whose stories and voices this diary is supposed to represent. Somewhat paradoxically, the idea of totality is created here by the very disclaimers that pronounce its impossibility: all the editors include disclaimers about the limitations of their project. For instance, the editors of *Life in a Day* acknowledged that the digital divide and other dominant patterns of representation had caused some distortions in their collection, but they maintained that the large number of contributors guaranteed a greater degree of authenticity (Walker: "I felt duty bound to represent as much as we could and really try to represent life on earth for one day";[68] Macdonald: "You have to show the reality of life; otherwise, it's not a true representation"[69]). These references to "true representation" and to the totality of stories give the impression that the moment these organizers could represent every single individual's story, these diaries could actually do justice to the original wholeness of some preexisting community. The issue, however, is never the limited number of contributors, nor the practical impossibility to represent the story of every single member of the population. The thing is, there is no such thing as a community of contemporaries that precedes the act of storytelling. Rather, it is the collective act of storytelling and the resulting vision of unity that creates the illusion of wholeness and unity among contemporaries. The unfortunate consequence of the promotion of such a universal, totalizing notion of simultaneity is that it reduces the utopian potential of these projects. The promise of one-day diaries lies in relativizing time and social homogeneity through individual narrative perspectives. Unfortunately, by falling back on the idea of a universal simultaneity, these one-day diaries end up undermining the very heterogeneity of time that they were meant to celebrate.

Time in the Making

Despite this shortcoming, I will conclude by venturing the optimistic statement that crowdsourced diaries could become an open-ended, socially transformative praxis. Herein lies the promise of these projects: the disjunctive, ephemeral temporality created by the many personal now's—constantly recreated through the decentered temporality of individual narratives as well as the ongoing possibility of renewed, creative use by viewers and readers—could transform the unidirectional linearity suggested by clock time and the calendar into a hybrid and socially transformative temporality. People's personal interpretations of the present through their personal stories do have the potential create a space alongside the homogenous time created by temporal coincidence for a heterogenous *time in the making*. The most promising aspect of these polyphonic and polyrhythmic mass reflections lies precisely here, in the incommensurability and constant tension of these competing temporalities. Yet, we need to remember that just as there is no personal now that unifies my experiences of past, present, and future into a single moment of unmediated access to myself, there is no all-encompassing Present that would unify the multitudes of now's experienced by various people into a single time and a single community.

To better grasp the utopian promise of simultaneity for how we think about our communities, I will briefly refer to comments made by Homi Bhabha and Ernst Bloch. Bhabha was famously critical of Anderson's interpretation of how a coincidence-based simultaneity allowed for the formation of modern nation-states. He argued instead in favor of the idea of a "double time." As Bhabha explains, the two modes of temporality—the homogenous time referred to by Anderson, which is constituted by people's "artificially" synchronized narratives, and the hybrid temporality constituted by people's ongoing performance of their stories, remain incommensurable, and they create a "double time": "In the production of the nation as narration there is a split between the continuist, accumulative temporality of the pedagogical, and the repetitious, recursive strategy of the performative. It is through this process of splitting that the conceptual ambivalence of modern society becomes the site of writing the nation."[70] In contrast to Anderson, Bhabha stresses that the "split" between these two temporalities is not a gap that can or should be closed but a source of creative and political potential. It is *because* of the incommensurability of these competing time perspectives, and not in spite of it, that communities can remain productive sites of continuous recreation.

Although Bhabha was not concerned with the particular case of one-day diaries, his concept of a "double time" highlights beautifully the potential of these diaries as well. A description of Bhabha's "double time" in terms of simultaneity would lead to the concept of "relative simultaneity," which, since Einstein, is widely accepted in physics. In the social sciences, however, the development of this concept is lagging, despite

Marxist thinkers' commitment to it. We get perhaps closest to the idea of a relative, frame-dependent simultaneity in Ernst Bloch's famous dictum, "not all people exist in the same Now."[71] Bloch maintained that people coexisted in a heterogenous non-simultaneity—that is, people living at the same time coexisted in various stages of social and personal development. Consequently, their different temporalities, voices, and spatialities could never be subsumed under a homogenous social time. Bloch's argument also implies that at any one moment in time there are a range of possibilities open, since the past never becomes completely past but coexists with the present. This also means that the unfulfilled hopes and projects of the past remain open and available to us in constructing the present.[72] The advantage of such a relative understanding of simultaneity is that it leaves room in the present for all of the past unfulfilled potentials and delayed expectations that were part of the original experience, as well as for all the diverging expectations of the present.[73] However, since documentation is never a purely archival relation to history as a sum of facts, but instead is an opportunity to creatively engage with latent futures in development, maintaining the heterogenous temporalities of the individual stories would have been essential to ensuring the openness of those latent futures. In other words, simultaneity is never a given or a finished project, but it is a "field[] of experimentation,"[74] always being actualized through everyday praxis.[75]

Thinking about simultaneity not as a given but as a "field of experimentation" would allow these story projects to acknowledge that "not all people exist in the same Now."[76] It would allow us to reread the 1930s Soviet and Chinese one-day diaries as testimonies of possibilities rather than facts, and to ask why *Life in a Day* had an overwhelming representation from the Global North. Such questions are particularly timely in our present moment as people become increasingly enthusiastic about new technologies' potential to create a perfect simultaneity and solidarity. Today's story-sharing technologies create a greater sense of simultaneity than ever before. To the age-old feeling of the simultaneity of our parallel lives, video technologies have added the quasi-simultaneity of living and recording the moment. Video promises a unique way to capture the moment as it unfolds, and this "live" character of video is also often interpreted as a guarantee of greater authenticity. Instant sharing has added yet another layer of simultaneity to this already doubled sense of simultaneity. Most recently, VR and AI are taking the illusion of simultaneity to a whole new level, especially in the domain of life-casting, where people stream live events in their lives through digital media using wearable recording technology.[77] This intensification of the illusion of simultaneity leads to the misleading impression that we are ever closer to the "perfect" simultaneity when events in our lives, and the stories we share about them, will overlap. Perfect simultaneity is often projected as a return to pre-technological, face-to-face experiences of community in which we will again be able to directly relate to each other as if we were sitting around the same fire. This is the dream that drives our contemporary experimentation with all kinds of digital, mobile, networked, and transnational simultaneities. However, as we continue to explore new forms of participation and imagination made possible by new forms of simultaneous storytelling, we should heed Carol Greenhouse's warning that while practices such as story sharing can indeed affect how we experience time, simultaneity itself will never function as a unifier or a universal equalizer.[78]

5   TO-GATHER IN SPACE

Maps are more about their makers than the places they describe. Map who you are. Map where you are. Fill the map with a story or paint your favorite cup of coffee. Map the invisible. Map the obvious. Map your memories.
   —BECKY COOPER

The Rise of Collective Story Mapping

The one-day diaries presented in the previous chapter ritualized the sharing of time, they celebrated the sense of community among contemporaries who live through the same twenty-four hours. Time is of course inseparable from space, and the two intersect in many ways in these story collections, so the present chapter shifts the emphasis from time to space. To illustrate the deep connections between space, stories, and communities, in this chapter I analyze story maps. Our creation and usage of maps yields important insights about our relationship to space and to each other. According to the cartographer Denis Wood, we live in the "Age of Maps" in that more than 99.99 percent of all the maps that humankind has ever created were made in the last one hundred years.[1] The same is true for personal stories: we live in the "Age of Memoirs" in that the vast majority of autobiographical stories have been published in the last decade, if not the last year.[2] Both mapping and storytelling are attempts to make sense of the world, and maps and stories have always been inextricably linked. Maps tell stories, and stories can be mapped: both internally, by tracing the events of a story on a map, and externally, by geotagging stories to create a map. It is hardly surprising, then, that the two activities have recently converged in the trend called "story mapping."

Narrative cartographers have a rather wide definition of what story mapping entails, including readers tracing the steps of their favorite book characters in the real world, writers providing their readers with factual or invented maps of the world they describe, or cartographers using oral histories to enhance maps.[3] While all story maps raise intriguing questions, this chapter focuses on the special practice whereby people map urban spaces by mapping their personal stories collectively. With the rise of Web 2.0, the number of projects that map cities by inviting people to share their personal stories has multiplied. The phenomenon is so recent that it does not yet even have a name. To use the existing term "story mapping," while also emphasizing the distinctly collective focus of this emerging trend, I will call it "collective story mapping." Collective story mapping owes its recent upsurge to two parallel developments: first, to the proliferation of online story-sharing sites where individuals can share their stories of personal experiences; and second, to the spectacular advance of technologies for mapping, geolocation, cameras, and mash-ups. Advances in these two fields have created an environment where individuals as well as groups can trace and retrace, mash and aggregate, geotag and share their trajectories via stories.

To only name a few examples from around the globe, the project Mapping Sexual Violence aims to provide a visual indicator of the prevalence of sexual violence by inviting survivors to share their stories. Through the website's "share your story" function, contributors can mark the location of their story, pinning it onto a world map. The numbers on the map indicate the number of incidents on each continent, and by zooming in, viewers can see the exact location and read each victim's story.[4] Other story maps focus more directly on the relationship between narrative and space, for instance by asking people to share their personal stories of certain geographic locales. Environmentalists often create such story maps to gather the stories of those living in the proximity of protected nature areas or areas of environmental disasters. These projects supplement science data by overlaying personal narratives onto crisis maps (like *Ushahidi*'s platform in Haiti) or risk maps (like those recording the stories of people threatened by rising sea levels).[5] Seeking to document conditions and to challenge the status quo, oral historians and activists also map urban neighborhoods. For instance, the project West Side Stories maps West Oakland's gentrification through the stories of its residents, while the Seven Families, Seven Journeys project explores the challenges of poverty in the lives of children in India. In addition, story maps are also being used to map displacement, migration routes, transnational lives, and cross-border living. For instance, the 1947 Partition Archive collects and maps stories of those affected by the Partition, and it uses dynamic arrows to visualize life trajectories and to tie personal stories to the cities that people migrated from and to. There are even attempts to bring time and space together by mapping people's stories in "real time," as they change locations. Migration Trail, for instance, is an interactive tool that uses maps, audio, and storytelling to visualize the real-time movements and communication of migrants.[6]

According to its proponents, this democratized, narrative remapping of our spaces and cities promises to be much more participatory and dynamic than our previous mapping practices. What is more, since maps are not just representations of space but means of (re)imagining and (re)producing space, collective story mapping promises to transform the very spaces we share. Ultimately, these narratively reimagined spaces are presented as a means to cultivate community. As the founders of one of these projects explain, "*Stories of Our City* collects and shares real stories from real people from around the world in an effort to cultivate community and global understanding. We produce these stories to reveal that our everyday experiences with family, love, religion, and culture are often similar to those of others living in cities and villages across the globe. We believe that when we share and celebrate a common humanity, we can begin to erase the boundaries and labels that divide us."[7] But what exactly does it mean to share a space by sharing personal stories about it? I argue that the emergence of what Becky Cooper describes as a "cartography of intimate narratives" presents, indeed, a positive alternative to the segregating dynamics of Cartesian geographic traditions, but only if we acknowledge its conflicting epistemologies.

New York Traditions

There is nothing new about engaging the city through stories: for as long as we have had cities, people have been telling stories in them and about them. Our personal stories reflect and constitute our experience of the city, and vice versa, our urban spaces shape our narratives about who we are. One could even argue that the city as a human habitat came about through storytelling, as a locus and nexus of storytelling. Folklorist Benjamin A. Botkin, author of *New York City Folklore* and editor of *Sidewalks of America*, was among the first to formulate a narrative definition of the city. In Botkin's words, "a city is 'we,' you and I and everybody else, what people say, especially what they have to say about themselves in their own way and their own words."[8] Such an autobiographical, performative understanding of space has long been promoted by urban folklorists and oral historians, but it has only recently gained popularity among the wider public.

The space I explore is one of the most mapped, if not *the* most mapped city in the world: New York City. I am aware of the ethical implications of

New York exceptionalism and realize that my analysis further skews the balance toward this over-studied space in the Global North. I can only justify my choice by the richness of examples offered by this metropolis. Story sharing and topophilia have a long tradition in New York, and "New York memoirs" form their own subgenre. From F. Scott Fitzgerald's *My Lost City* through Kazin's *A Walker in the City* to Pete Hamill's *Downtown: My Manhattan*, New York memoirists have always been nostalgic about the place they call home. The city also lures people with the promise of a uniquely voyeuristic, "optional" perspective. As E. B. White famously explained: "New York blends the gift of privacy with the excitement of participation . . . so that every event is, in a sense, optional, and the inhabitant is in the happy position of being able to choose his spectacle and so conserve his soul."[9]

New Yorkers have also been among the first to embrace the idea that *collections* of autobiographical stories can create a fuller representation of their colorful metropolis.[10] Over the last century, the paradoxical beauty of this urban space has inspired many to collect the stories of its inhabitants. Some focused on particular neighborhoods, groups, or social issues, others wanted to create an exhaustive catalog of the stories of every single person living in the city. According to city lore, Joe Gould (1889–1957), known as Professor Seagull, was among the first to be tempted by this idea of totality. A graduate of Harvard University and a regular patient at mental institutions, Gould most likely suffered from hypergraphia. He recorded everything he saw and heard, filling hundreds, if not thousands of notebooks. The stack of his notebooks was said to reach seven feet, but only a few of these have ever been recovered and published.[11] As we will see, Gould was neither the first nor the last to be seduced by the dream of an exhaustive catalog of every single New Yorker's story. In a sense, all the projects in this chapter were born on the wings of Gould's dream.

A Cartography of Intimate Narratives

A precursor of today's collective story mapping was a cartographic trend from the sixties and seventies called "mental mapping." To put it simply, "mental maps" (also called "psychological maps" or "imagined maps") are visual representations of the maps that people carry in their heads. Cognitive scientists realized that "the maps we carried in our heads" functioned not only as individual cognitive tools, but that they also had important social functions. As noted by Stanley Milgram: "The image of the city is not just extra mental baggage; it is the necessary accompaniment to living in a complex and highly variegated environment. . . . People make many important decisions based on their conception of a city, rather than the reality of it."[12] This realization led to a flurry of studies, and mental mapping became a popular way to illustrate the role of individual perception in evaluating space. Among others, Milgram and his team devised an experiment in which they asked New Yorkers to draw sketches of the city in order to measure the "recognizability" of certain neighborhoods and the general "imageability" of the city. Milgram and his team then aggregated these individual "mental representations of New York City held by its residents," producing "distorted" maps on which the size of each neighborhood depended on how well participants recognized them (not surprisingly, Manhattan was deemed to be the most recognizable borough).[13]

Today's collective story-maps build on this idea of mental maps to encourage people to imaginatively and narratively "seize" places, as Bachelard put it.[14] The project Map Your Memories is a whimsical variation of Stanley Milgram's experiment. Inspired by Italo Calvino's *Invisible Cities*, in 2009 Becky Cooper began distributing thousands of blank maps to New Yorkers, asking them to annotate them with personal associations. Cooper specifically asked people not to let the maps be defined by landmarks, but to focus on their own, personal impressions of this urban space, to map *their* Manhattan. The resulting blog has dozens of personalized sketch maps, some of which include complex narratives, others only images. The website offers a few illustrative samples, as shown in figure 1, such as maps marking romantic spots ("places where I've been kissed") and maps recording past and planned visits ("places I should go, shouldn't go, should I go? went"). Cooper describes her project as a "cartography of intimate narratives."[15]

Collective story-maps celebrate our capacity to "tame" spaces in the "urban jungle." As Gaston Bachelard explained in *Poetics of Space*, "space that has been seized upon by the imagination cannot remain indifferent space subject to the measures and estimates of the surveyor. It has been lived in, not in its positivity, but with all the partiality of the imagination."[16] Yi-Fu Tuan, in his influential *Space and Place: The Perspective of Experience* (1977), stressed the same point. Space is abstract and measurable, he argued, while place "incarnates the experiences and aspirations of a people."[17] In other words, place is space that has been given meaning and history through individual or collective actors: "Place is security and space is freedom: we are attached to the one and are longing for the other."[18] Personal stories are often seen as a way to "enliven" dead spaces by making them our own. This is how the mapping challenge called Love

Figure 1. "A Pedestrian's Guide to Leaving Manhattan and Exploring the Rest of the World." Matt Green's hand-drawn story map of Manhattan. (Courtesy of Becky Cooper)

This Place! (2015) invited people to add "their" places: "Make sure your home and places are added to the Story Map to show them your love! Your favorite place could be near a creek, where the sun glitters off the surface, mesmerizing your heart. . . . Don't let your home and places be left off the Story Map!"[19]

Collective story-maps illustrate beautifully the link between spatial imagination, storytelling, and embodied perception. To begin with, they draw on the rich semiotic tradition which defines urban spaces in terms of signifying practices. The advantage of this approach lies in its emphasis on the reciprocity of space "speaking to" people and people "speaking space." In the words of Roland Barthes, "The city is a discourse and this discourse is truly a language: the city speaks to its inhabitants, we speak our city, the city where we are, simply by living in it, by wandering through it, by looking at it."[20] Although in this study I am not looking at particular stories within these story maps, one of the advantages of collective story mapping is that it can tap into the rich dialectic between distantiation and belonging that is at the heart of all autobiographical stories. Autobiographical narratives had been long perceived as historical (if not always chronological) narratives of a person's life. Following the "spatial turn," however, storytellers and critics began to view the self in *spatial* terms also.[21] This then led to a more thorough examination of the role of autobiographical narratives in articulating hybrid and social spaces of belonging and displacement.[22]

Story maps also place a special emphasis on the role of experiential knowledge and physical embodiment. The website Map Your Memories, for instance, includes a brief video of Cooper walking around Manhattan distributing blank maps. This reference to the ambulatory nature of mapping underscores the physical aspects of the process, and it hints at the fact that the completed story maps will also be records of storytellers' physical movements around the city. The project called Creek Speak also stresses the value of embodied, experiential knowledge, by foregrounding sensory perception. The platform uses Google Maps and Habitat Map "to map true stories of life" around a specific natural environment within the city called Newtown Creek.[23] Newtown Creek, located in the heart of New York City and bordering Brooklyn and Queens, is an estuary that is reported to be one of the nation's most polluted waterways. The purpose of the project is to "document the experiential knowledge of individuals who are inside narrators of day-to-day life in these communities" and to better understand how people deal with such environmental challenges. According to its mission statement, "Creek Speak is an oral history project that uses online interactive maps to present the stories of people and places near Newtown Creek." The story map seeks to "document the *experiential* knowledge of individuals": "People who have a first-hand understanding of their neighborhood—who everyday use their eyes, ears, and noses—can provide essential contextual information that would otherwise be ignored or lost."

To further stress their subjective dimension, collective story-maps often promise emotional rewards of safety, love, and bonding. The project Map Your Memories, for instance, offers whimsical stories of "*past* loves, *lost* homes, childhood memories, *comical* moments, and *surprising* confessions," while City of Memory promises "some of the five boroughs' most *colorful* characters, *interesting* communities and *unusual* happenings."[24] The adjectives in these mission statements signal emotional intensities, guaranteed by glimpses into others' intimate spaces. Getting to know others' secret locales through personal story sharing is said to grow positive social bonds: "The maps were like passports into strangers' worlds."[25] Moreover, story maps not only produce affect but they circulate and intensify it, as seen in the social media echo of certain popular projects, such as Humans of New York (HONY).

At first glance, Humans of New York may not seem like a story map in the strict sense of the word, but it started out as such. When founder Brandon Stanton first conceived of Humans of New York, he was tempted by Professor Seagull's dream of totality: "I thought it would be really cool to create an exhaustive catalogue of New York City's inhabitants," he wrote, "so I set out to photograph 10,000 New Yorkers and plot their photos on a map."[26] Although Stanton referred to the first iteration of the project as an "interactive map," the word "interactive" had a rather limited meaning. It simply meant that one "could click on any neighborhood in New York and scroll through the faces of people who live there."[27] The map itself was static, and its pattern followed the traditional division of the city into neighborhoods.[28] Later, Stanton realized that the stories his subjects told about themselves were just as interesting as their photos, so he began to collect stories along with the pictures. Gradually, the photo blog expanded into a book with longer stories, and later it was also adapted into a film series.[29] While the project was initiated by a single person, it was soon adopted and adapted by millions of followers who eagerly liked, reposted, and commented on the pictures and stories. HONY soon attained international fame, with millions of followers on several social media platforms and hundreds of spinoffs worldwide (including "Humans of" blogs in many other cities such as Tehran and Bombay, as well as dozens of parodies such as Millennials of New York, Boring Humans of New York, etc.). With more than twenty million followers, one could argue that Stanton did attain his dream of totality by surpassing the city's population through the mediation of social media networks.[30]

Alternative Epistemologies

By contrasting their imaginative, narrative, embodied, and grassroots approach to the bureaucratic interests of official cartography, collective story-maps seek to promote alternative epistemologies. Just as mental maps were presented as alternatives to objective city maps, collective story-maps emphasize people's personal and collective ownership of space. They pride themselves on creating new knowledge by offering distinct perspectives. "What does the city look like when you're seeing it *not just through an official lens?*" asked designers of City of Memory (emphasis added). The story map City of Memory originated as a live performance at the 2001 Smithsonian Folklife Festival, where visitors were invited to record their memories onto acetate squares and then thumbtack them onto a giant Styrofoam map of New York City. The project defines itself as "an online community map of personal stories and memories organized on a physical geographical map of New York City."[31] According to its creators, "City of Memory creates a web of interlocking memories, chronicling the city's inner life. Place-based, it links stories and memories in ways that cut across chronology, sparking connections and enabling visitors to rediscover the city through the memories of others."[32]

"Rediscovering" the city implies that these memories have been forgotten or repressed. By promising access to the hitherto "invisible" corners of the city, organizers present their stories from the fringes as forms of unauthorized knowledge. They seek to reclaim physical and psychological territories—to put people back on the map, both metaphorically and literally. As Rebecca Solnit wrote in the Introduction to her stunning trilogy of story atlases, story mapping is a kind of counter-mapping which can result in forms of counter-knowledge: "any significant place is in some sense infinite, because its stories are inexhaustible and the few that are well known overshadow the many worth knowing."[33] Solnit's own atlas was described as an attempt to "reclaim New York's *untold* stories and *unseen* populations."[34] Narratives—temporal and tied to the specificity of individual speakers—have indeed a unique role in resisting the standardization inherent in mapping. Site-specificity and locational identity are often celebrated as "making room" for marginalized places and voices. Organizers encourage people to claim a parcel through their stories. In many cases, participants can literally plant a flag onto the story map to occupy a place.

These gestures of recovery are often framed as collective acts, since staking out a place through personal stories can be a way to claim community membership and to put entire communities back on the map. For instance, in 2013, the New York Public Library (NYPL) initiated the Community Oral History Project, which "aims to document, preserve, and celebrate the rich history of the city's unique neighborhoods by collecting the stories of people who have experienced it firsthand."[35] The project houses thousands of personal stories arranged into nineteen distinct "community projects," most of which are focused on particular neighborhoods (Greenwich Village, SOHO, Harlem, Washington Heights, Times Square, etc.).[36] While the site may not readily appear as a story map, the stories are all arranged behind clickable photos representing various neighborhoods, so the contours of the city do emerge. Organizers stress the community-based aspects of their project: hundreds of local volunteers were trained to conduct the interviews, interviewers asked specific questions about storytellers' community involvement, and NYPL called for volunteers to record and transcribe the interviews.[37]

In sum, creators often present their story maps as sites of resistance, as forms of engaged participation that produce less normative and more inclusive spaces by putting people on the same map, so to speak. Allowing people to claim their places through storytelling is said to improve solidarity by allowing people to visualize their connectedness in the form of a single map. The joyful exclamations about how "it only takes a few words to turn a stranger into a human being" are emblematic of this stance.[38] The enormous success of Humans of New York, among others, is built on this simple equation: "The more stories we read, the more the big city becomes a small community."[39] As one commentator noted: "This is exactly why the Humans of New York project works: We're let into a world of vulnerability that allows us to relate and empathize with each other, which leads us to not only think about, but to care for other people and their stories . . . Briana Cerezo, photographer of Humans of Portland, says her motivation stems from her desire to 'connect authentically' with people. In doing so, she hopes to build knowledge and a shared understanding of the city."[40] To return to the concept of collective intimacy, collective story-maps offer the same two ingredients: collective insights based on firsthand knowledge and the feeling of belonging to a "small community" within a "big city."

Illusions

Meanwhile, a growing number of critics are questioning these feel-good assumptions about remapping our spaces through collective story-sharing. Some argue that highlighting the relationship between stories and places leads to an unhealthy culture of nostalgia, which falsely promotes community as a source of a stable social and personal identity. Others caution that community mapping leads to an unhealthy sense of optimism, given the daunting task of resistance in the face of capitalist domination.[41] This warning is particularly timely these days, as companies use the unexamined spatial metaphors of our "networked" culture to celebrate community in the name of connectedness. Media artist Coco Fusco warned already in 2004 about the "technocratic fantasies" that take advantage of the spatial character of our networked modes of communication to reduce complex, historical, and embedded differences to a celebratory notion of "connectedness." He cautioned: "in the name of a politics of global connectedness, artists and activists too often substitute an abstract 'connectedness' for any real engagement with people in other places or even in their own locale."[42] More concretely, Daniel D'Addario criticized Humans of New York for emotionally manipulating users to believe that having thirteen thousand notes on Tumblr about a man who complained that "it's been a lifetime of loneliness" will somehow provide him with the sense of community he is longing for.[43]

Besides this critique of spatial-social connectedness, we should also reexamine the claim that these story maps offer alternative epistemologies. Humans have always sought to tame space, but as Henri Lefebvre pointed out, this process has been haunted by two conjoined illusions. The "realist" illusion creates the impression that space is like a "real" surface, something whole, neutral, measurable, decipherable, and ultimately ownable. Whether that ownership is material or ideological, the realist illusion suggests that increasingly precise descriptions of space will eventually lead us to a perfect understanding and/or ownership of it. Meanwhile, the "illusion of transparency" suggests that space is transparent, open to human imagination and that we can tame it through our personal thoughts, language, beliefs, movements, and desires. To simplify a bit, the former misleads us by overemphasizing the materiality of space while the latter highlights the subjective dimensions of space. Lefebvre's point is that these two illusions mutually nourish each other and that their harmful double effect downplays the important role of the *social* in producing space. Space is a social product, reminds Lefebvre, and there is no such thing as an empty space that later gets socialized. Space is continuously being "produced" and "reproduced" by the social, just as our social relations are constantly being shaped by space. Hence, neither the objective nor the subjective approaches can do justice to the role of the social in producing space. Instead, what we need is a model like a triad or a continuum that interlinks the objective, the subjective, and the social dimensions of space.[44]

Personal story maps are perfect illustrations of the dynamic triad described by Lefebvre, except that their organizers often fall prey to Lefebvre's illusions. The illusion of transparency is quite evident in the way story maps celebrate space as something subjective and expressible. Mental mapping in the 1970s was already criticized for wanting to mentally dominate space. Edward Soja objected that mental mapping could lead to the misleading impression that "the mental defined and indeed produced and explained the material and social worlds better than empirical explanations."[45] The same charge could also be raised against contemporary story maps, since they overemphasize the imaginative possession of space at expense of other (material or social) means of producing it. Materiality in this case need not refer to actual buildings; it can also refer to the materiality of databases and the infrastructure of social media, especially since the seemingly ethereal qualities of virtual and cloud technologies conceal the material culture on which they depend. Neither the belief that we can imaginatively possess places nor the idealism resulting from this illusion is therefore innocent at all, since they preempt critique.

The realist illusion, which privileges objectivity and describes space as a measurable and ownable grid-space, is a bit harder to detect, since story maps expressly deny their involvement with official cartographies. Nevertheless, many of them do rely on scale- and grid-oriented Cartesian cartography to map their stories. In fact, all the examples above follow the traditional division of New York City into boroughs. They either adopt traditional maps of the city, or they rely on geographic markers and names that delineate precise locations and subdivisions. They also rely on the geo-specific intertextual context of the history of mapping New York City, meaning they adopt general cartographic conventions and they presuppose users' familiarity with them. Evidently, the precision and interactivity of these maps varies, with some using GIS and others using hand-drawn maps. But they all rely on data and conventions inherited from bureaucrats, and none of their mission statements question the processes whereby norming insinuates itself into these received categories and data.[46]

The realist illusion also comes into play whenever story maps play up their documentary function. Since orientation is clearly not the primary purpose of these story maps, their informational value gets automatically inflated. In addition, organizers often explicitly state that their aim is "to document, preserve, and celebrate the rich history of the city's unique neighborhoods."[47] Their mission is of course more than just a passive reception of inherited data. By collecting personal stories, they aim to revise and/or supplement existing information about the city. Nevertheless, by treating collective story-maps as sources of spatial information, and by valuing stories for their contribution to ever more precise descriptions of neighborhoods, these story maps presume the possibility of epistemic completeness and neutrality. A telling example is the statement made by the founder of Humans of New York, according to which he wanted to simply "plot" the pictures and stories he gathered "*on* a map" (emphasis added). Stanton's statement evokes the Enlightenment legacy of a passive notion of space, as if space and maps were empty, neutral surfaces onto which stories and information could simply be inscribed. Story maps also evoke the fantasy of completeness by adding disclaimers about the limitations of their project. For instance, Creek Speak notes that "as with any qualitative study, its reliance on memory provides a rich tapestry of impressions and insights but historical and scientific accuracy is not guaranteed. It should also be noted that this project does not claim to represent all of the varied perspectives on Newtown Creek from the hundreds of thousands of people who have lived or now live in communities along Newtown Creek."[48] Stanton also emphasized that his map was "constantly evolving," meaning that through the continual addition of new portraits and stories, the "dot density" of his story map would improve. One could argue, however, that such disclaimers only reinforce the fantasy of totality and the idea that there *is* in fact such a thing as official, factual knowledge about the city or an "exhaustive catalog" of all the stories of all the inhabitants of a city.

The problem with this idea of neutrality is that it ignores story mapping's own entwinement with social control. This is particularly surprising since the field of cartography in the last half century has undergone a sort of ideological awakening. Following centuries of mapmaking practices that concealed who represented space and how, cartographers in the 1970s began to admit that maps were not, and never been, neutral artifacts, but rather they were socially and ideologically constructed, following the interest of those who commissioned them.[49] Moreover, cartographers also acknowledged that maps were not merely shaped by ideology, but themselves produced ideology: "In so far as mapping involves exploration, selection, definition, generalization and translation of data, it assumes a range of social *cum* representational powers, and as the military histories of geography and cartography suggest, the power to map can be closely entwined with the power of conquest and social control."[50]

In the last decade, however, as cartography became increasingly democratized, the ideological role of maps again became more veiled. Today, with the help of open-source mapping and citizen cartography, people without any special training can edit city maps that millions may then rely on. What is ironic about the popular appeal of this new cartography is that it once again conceals the fundamental connection between mapmaking and social control. Collective story-maps rarely, if ever, address either this conflict or their own entanglement with the authoritarian implications of the "norming fixity inherent in cartographic representation."[51] They tend to operate with a dual purpose: their primary audience is said to be the community from which the stories arise, but the story collection is often organized and funded by outside entities who rely on the stories to gain insight into the strengths and needs of these communities. Of course, to serve as effective tools of communication, story maps need to follow certain cartographic conventions, even as they seek to diversify them. These conflicts could in fact be productive—if only they were acknowledged. Instead, the majority of collective story-maps are symptomatic of how social control gets downplayed in mapping practices.

Segregated Stories

A case in point is their adoption of mental mapping's notion of recognizability. "Recognizability" was a key word in Milgram's experiments, and city planners consider recognizability (also called "imageability" or "legibility") a positive value, because more recognizable cities and neighborhoods are said to provide people with higher levels of individual and collective comfort. While most collective story-maps explicitly discourage storytellers from orienting themselves to these symbolic sites, they continue to operate with the same assumptions of territoriality. For instance, a commentary accompanying Humans of New York's 2012 map suggested that Stanton's story map "allow[s] us to visually understand the differences between places like the Upper West Side and Harlem, or the East Village and Washington Heights."[52] Note that to "visually understand the differences between neighborhoods" implies a very limited interpretation of difference: it suggests that these portraits and stories will confirm our existing preconceptions and stereotypes regarding the architectural style, economic development, and ethnic composition of these different boroughs. What is more, the same commentator suggests that this composite image of neighborhoods could eventually help marketing professionals identify their "target demographic": this "beautiful humanitarian effort... not only unites this New York community I adore, but also serves as a potentially groundbreaking way to view populations and markets. When companies begin exploring their target demographic, how significant could it be for them to see a face-by-face visual of their consumers."[53] The unfortunate consequence of this focus on recognizability is that it reduces the rich medium of stories to their denotative function. It uses people's personal stories to confirm existing patterns of recognition, as if the purpose of personal story mapping was to confirm that certain "neighborhood stories" do, indeed, belong to certain neighborhoods.

For instance, the very first story that pops up under "A People's History of Harlem" in the New York Public Library's story collection summarizes Abdou Karim Samb's story in the following words: "Abdou Karim Samb arrived in New York in 1991 and moved to Harlem, where he felt very much at home. There was an important African community in Harlem, and he quickly adapted to life in Harlem. Abdou bought a taxi business with some Senegalese friends. He goes to the various mosques and enjoys eating at the numerous Senegalese an [sic] Ghanaian restaurants in the area. Mr. Samb also talks about the numerous changes taking place as rents increase; the neighborhood is now being populated by Europeans while many Africans are moving out."[54] This recognizability and territoriality seems to be a shortcoming of most collective story-maps, for when a story map assigns a "Harlem story" a red dot on a city map within the boundaries of Harlem, and even when a collection places Abdou Karim Samb's personal story into a category under the heading "A People's History of Harlem," it thereby reduces the story's positive potential to transgress. Using traditional, fixed-point, plain-view maps means that each individual's story is represented by a dot on the map, as if that point in space were occupied by that particular storyteller and their story. The act of assigning stories to particular places on the map resembles the colonizer's gesture of planting a flag. The flag—whether it is on a digital map or on the soil—marks out a place by claiming some form of ownership or connection to that place. The problem with this recognizability and territoriality is that it segregates stories instead of liberating them.

Transgressive Stories and Maps

French philosopher Michel de Certeau argued beautifully for the spatially transgressive potential of all narratives. In "Spatial Stories," de Certeau studied the narrative operations on space that stories carry out. He examined a whole series of double-edged operations by which stories both fix place and move between places, delimiting borders and transgressing them by building bridges. He wrote: "Every story is a travel story—a spatial practice. . . . Every day [stories] traverse and organize places; they select and link them together; they make sentences and itineraries out of them. They are spatial trajectories."[55] I would add that through the constant negotiation of the multiple and shifting places in which they are being formed, our personal stories, too, are continuously reconstituting the boundaries of urban spaces. A new thread is being added to the urban fabric every time an immigrant recounts his or her memories of the places they left, when a storyteller recounts a daily commute that crosses limits, or when we share with each other our experiences of getting lost in strange places (such as our own house). Although de Certeau wrote this decades ago, his point about the power of stories to transgress cannot be overstated in the context of the contemporary trend of story mapping.

De Certeau notes that historically, the earliest maps served to record travelers' tours or itineraries. They were logs of journeys rather than bird's-eye-view representations. They were more like narratives. Over the centuries, the map "has slowly disengaged itself from the itineraries that were the condition of its possibility,"[56] and maps have become more abstract and more static. In contrast to the dynamic, traveling, transgressive perspective of narratives, modern maps presented a static, aerial perspective. To illustrate how narratives themselves can either retain their transgressive qualities or take on the perspective of a static map, de Certeau quotes a study about how New Yorkers talk about their apartments. He notes that their descriptions tend to oscillate between two types of narrations: the "tour," which describes an action, as if someone was moving through space ("you turn left to get to the kitchen"); and the "map," which describes a bird's-eye-view of space ("the bedroom is on the right of the kitchen"). Comparing these two types of narratives, de Certeau concludes that narratives that function as "tours" are more capable of marking out spaces "in between." The advantage of tour-like narratives is that they retain their capacity to trace alternative routes, to reimagine physical and social boundaries: "What the map cuts up, the story cuts across."[57]

While de Certeau's observations regarding the shifting boundaries created by narratives remain valid, maps have undergone such a fundamental transformation since he wrote his study that it may no longer make sense to contrast "maps" to "tours." As a result of recent technological developments, maps today can trace the physical movements of participants across space in real time, they can embed location-triggered audio components, and much more. Thanks to these locative technologies and participatory media, maps have returned to their original function as they become again more action-focused, serving as "logs" of journeys rather than mere "outlines."[58] Collective story mapping is uniquely situated to take advantage of the fact that maps are now becoming just as dynamic as tour-like narratives. Although locative media is still in its infancy, its advantage for story mapping is that it allows users to experience other people's stories in location, as they move through the city (for instance, an app may use push notifications to unlock the audio stories embedded at certain sites when users arrive at that site). To use a spatial image, this would mean that whoever crosses a point in space could contribute to the ongoing conversation that is building up in that locale. Imagine the future of story mapping as a circular process in which the internal and external processes of mapping enfold into a single loop. In this scenario we could trace the events of our autobiographical story on a map at the same time as we create that map by geotagging events in our story to the map. To return to de Certeau, this means that we can now think of maps, too, as spatially transgressive stories.

Responding to this shift in technologies, theorists of cartography in the last decade began to emphasize the personal, embodied, and located processes whereby people generate, use, and reuse maps. The thing to recognize, they argue, is that all maps are designed to perform specific tasks through a series of practices, which means that maps are never ontologically stable objects. This represents a shift away from the epistemological valorization of maps as sources of knowledge towards a phenomenological emphasis on the involvement of both mapmakers and map-users in the process of mapping. The new approach accentuates the spatially and temporally located, singular moment when the map is being created and re-created through each individual use. Note that locality in this definition is not fixed but moveable, marked out by transportable boundaries that shift not only with each user but with each moment that the map is being used. In the words of Rob Kitchin, maps are never stable but rather "always of-the-moment, brought into being by practices (embodied, social, technical, political) . . . transitory and fleeting, being relational and context-dependent; their history and development contingent and non-progressive."[59]

The project Invisible Cities illustrates well this new generation of spatially transgressive, dynamic story maps.[60] Invisible Cities was created by Christian Marc Schmidt and Liangjie Xia to trace the emergence of social urban networks in New York City by visualizing and geographically mapping Twitter and Instagram data as well as Flickr photos in real time. The original intention of the programmers was to "visualize the collective memory of a city."[61] As they explain, "Our memories are often linked to places, and places become aggregators of memories"[62]; "Invisible Cities reveals social networks in the urban environment. It displays geocoded data from online services such as Twitter and Instagram in real-time and in aggregate. Real-time activity is represented as individual markers that appear whenever a Tweet or image is posted. Aggregate activity is reflected in the underlying terrain—the landscape warps as data is accrued, creating hills and valleys representing areas with high and low densities of data."[63] In other words, instead of using narratives to map the city, this locative project creates a narrative out of story data that is being captured at sites. The experimental project promises a "new kind of geography in which the urban landscape is reframed through narrative (a sequence of events in space and time). In this case, however, the story is told not by a single person, but by groups of individuals."[64]

Figure 2. A view of a topic path amid an extruded Manhattan basemap. Invisible Cities mapping project, created by Christian Mark Schmidt and Liangjie Xia. (Courtesy of Christian Mark Schmidt)

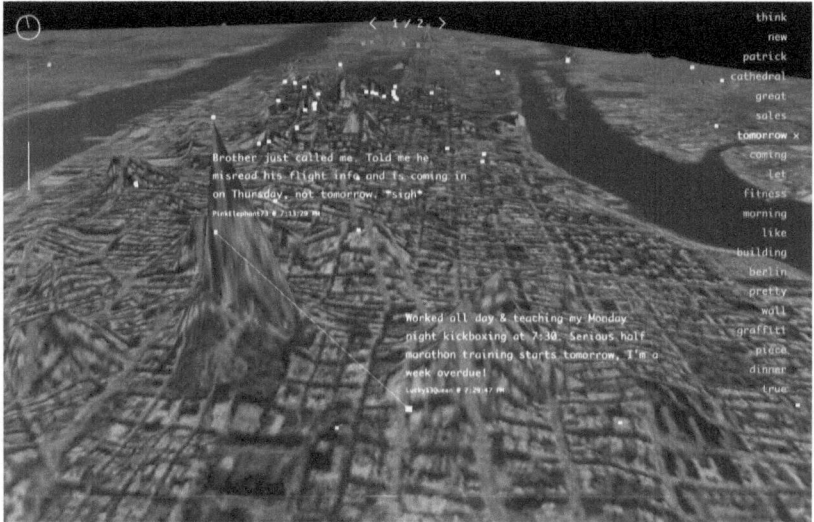

Figure 3. An image demonstrating how data records are linked based on shared keywords. Invisible Cities, Christian Mark Schmidt and Liangjie Xia. (Courtesy of Christian Mark Schmidt)

Note that while the Invisible Cities map is produced and used by groups of individuals, its creators wanted to first and foremost optimize the experience of the single user. They therefore turned the visualization into an immersive three-dimensional space that users can experience from a first-person vantage point. They also built in some self-reflexivity through the feedback mechanism whereby users can experience the reshaping of space triggered by their own data contribution. According to Schmidt and Xia this is a distinguishing feature of Invisible Cities. Since the three-dimensional map is closer to how we normally experience the physical world, the first-person perspective of users "encourages continuous discovery" and a "sense of presence, of 'being there,'" which is particularly important if such story maps are to become means of solidifying collective bonds. Of course, once these experimental story maps leave beta testing and enter the real world, the difficult question of who uses the data gets magnified, since all map-users get access to storytellers' real-life location data.[65] In the last decade, geospatial analysis has become a profitable industry, and apps such as Foursquare have managed to convince people to share their location data in exchange for personalized push notifications, promotional offers, and so on. In addition, companies such as Map Your City are made to look like collective story-maps by using a marketing language rich in references to community values to bring together those who upload their stories about places and those who use that data for commercial purposes: "It's a new kind of map that's connected to the communities you love and the world"; "A Map Your City Community is simply a group of people mapping places and telling stories together."[66] As such, it becomes increasingly difficult for collective story-maps to maintain even a semblance of independence.

Maintaining the Tension

To conclude, I want to reiterate the need to uphold the productive tension of these conflicting drives and epistemologies. Collective story-maps, just like the other forms of story sharing in this book, support the idea of a hybrid model of circulation where top-down efforts to map and control a city's spaces intersect with inhabitants' bottom-up initiatives to "reclaim" urban places through storytelling. To return to Lefebvre, we need to remember to carefully balance our subjective desire to imaginatively remap space with our objective reliance on official networks of information as well as the social drive needed to renew our shared spaces. One way to maintain this productive tension is to recognize that mapping practices affect participants' subjectivities and vice versa.[67] To avoid positing an overly immediate relationship between our lives and the places on the map, we should keep in mind the role that narratives and intertextuality play in mediating this relationship. As noted above, mapping and storytelling have been brought into very close proximity, as geographers increasingly rely on discursive genres to create and interpret maps while storytellers seek to spatially represent their narratives. Despite this unprecedented proximity, many rightly fear that our understanding of space is again regressing to the idea of a flat surface that can be subdivided and neutrally represented through scale values (as in visualizations like Google Earth), which conceals the fact that space is always produced through relations.[68]

One way to acknowledge the ties between narrative imagination and our modes of inhabiting space is by foregrounding the role of intertextuality in collective story mapping. By intertextuality I mean both the way in which stories within these maps talk to each other, as well as the cartographic conventions and past mapping practices that inform each new, current use of these story maps. With respect to intertextuality, I would like to conclude by pointing to a promising new concept worked out recently by literary cartographers. Cartographic theory in recent years seems to have shifted back and forth between the phenomenological concern with the process of mapmaking and the hermeneutic concern with the (inter)textuality of maps. The former emphasizes the importance of the temporal, spatial, and social situatedness of the individual mapmaker and map-user, as well as the immediacy that comes from this specificity, while the latter stresses the distance created by the mapping process and the need for interpretation that arises from this distance. David Cooper and Gary Priestnall propose a hybrid concept called "processual intertextuality" to bring these two positions closer to each other. They argue that the two concerns can actually reinforce each other in that "an awareness of the intertextuality of cartography . . . reinforces the open-endedness and intrinsic subjectivity of mapping practices: each use constitutes a remaking of the map; and each map use unfolds within a series of interrelated and individuated intertextual contexts."[69] According to the authors, the processual (phenomenological) and the intertextual (hermeneutic) perspectives are not merely supplementary but rather mutually dependent on one another to produce their effects. While the intertextual layers add depth to each map, their successful functioning depends on each individual user's subjective and located actualization of those references. The advantage of such a double-pronged approach is that it can account both for the ideological functions of mapmaking and for its transformative potential.

This mediation between individual map usage and communal sense-making should be key to how we interpret collective story-maps as well, for only with the help of such a double-pronged approach can we acknowledge the transformative effects of mapmaking on individuals and communities while also tempering overly enthusiastic and naïve celebrations of the imaginative remaking of our urban spaces. Collective story mapping belongs to the field of participatory mapping, which balances the autobiographical aspects of mapmaking and map usage with the task of collective sense-making. Those committed to participatory mapping recognize that our sense of community and belonging is politically charged precisely because it develops from the many conflictual ways of imagining our personal and collective relations to space. In participatory mapping, the process whereby maps are created is as valuable as the maps themselves, meaning that the fact that community members have to work out a spatial representation *together* is of value by itself. According to the website Mapping for Rights, "Participatory mapping—also called community-based mapping—is a general term used to define a set of approaches and techniques that combines the tools of modern cartography with participatory methods to represent the spatial knowledge of local communities. It is based on the premise that local inhabitants possess expert knowledge of their local environments which can be expressed in a geographical framework which is easily understandable and universally recognized."[70] Note the conflict in this last sentence between "universally recognizable" mapping conventions and personal knowledge about local environments. The promise of collective, participatory story-maps lies in this productive tension. The promise, however, can only be put to work if we can resist the sense of determinism that comes with the "flattening effect" of our Cartesian heritage, as well as the illusion that we can "reclaim" our spaces by the sheer force of our personal or collective imagination.

6 STORIES AND STATISTICS

Numbers tell stories.
Numbers don't tell stories, people do.
   —GINA NEFF AND DAWN NAFUS

All the projects in the previous chapters assembled or aggregated stories into collections. But what does it mean to bring many individual stories into a single whole? How have statistical ideas shaped our story collections historically, and how do current technologies of aggregation structure and pattern them? And most importantly, what is the role of aggregation in creating a sense of community? The word "aggregation" describes the process whereby we arrange things into clusters. In statistics, aggregation refers to a process in which numbers are gathered for statistical purposes and expressed as one number. In the twenty-first century, however, we use the word in a much wider sense to mean the formation of a number of things into a cluster. In our data-driven world, algorithmic aggregation has become an immensely powerful strategy. Data aggregation shapes the content and services we rely on so that we can get better, personalized access, representation, and care. Aggregating people's data, however, also enables institutions to identify people who meet or do not meet certain criteria, which leads to greater discrimination.

Data bias is an urgent topic. What data we use, how we collect and process it, who uses the data, and what we do with the data are all important factors to consider, since bias in any of these domains will lead to biased models and outcomes. Those promoting data justice argue that once data becomes capital, the system follows an extractive logic which operates on multiple levels to drive profit and to justify surveillance. Once our attributes are extracted from our physical bodies and context and reassembled into datasets and algorithmic profiles, these "data doubles" become derived assets.[1] Ethicists worry about the systemic distortions and inequalities resulting from this "function creep" of data mining, because it reduces our autonomy, privacy, and rights. As ethicist Michael McFarland explains, "the capability the computer gives of being able to assemble these seemingly innocent and insignificant facts into a comprehensive personal profile and to make it widely available gives that information a different significance. . . . Apart from the obvious potential for error and prejudice, [the] use of profiling is objectionable because it dehumanizes those being judged, as well as those making the judgments. It substitutes calculation for human judgment on what should be very sensitive human issues, and thus treats those profiled as objects, as collections of facts, rather than as persons."[2]

Some seek to correct this data bias by producing counter-data and counter-narratives, often through autobiographical storytelling. While statistics is said to reduce people to data, personal storytelling is said to liberate them by making them masters of their own story. Personal stories are often presented as antidotes to dehumanizing statistics. "I am not a number, I am a free man!" shouts Number 6, the central character in the 1960s television series, *The Prisoner,* as he tries to escape his prison. The words of Number 6 are iconic because they evoke our deep fear of "being reduced to numbers." Western cultures tend to associate numbers with totalitarian regimes and social control. Our deep aversion to quantification and aggregation is of course well founded, since—as the root of the word "statistics" also signals—statistics was first developed to assist states and rulers to keep track of their assets and people. The capacity to tell one's own story is therefore taken as the ultimate proof of freedom. As Neil Gaiman put it in *American Gods,* "we need individual stories. Without individuals, we see only numbers: a thousand dead, a hundred thousand dead, 'casualties may rise up to a million.' With individual stories, the statistics become people."[3]

Today, as citizens feel increasingly powerless in the face of corporate and political datafication, many engage in personal storytelling to try to counterbalance data profiling. Somewhat paradoxically, they do not just share single stories but also seek to counter algorithmic profiling by creating alternative databases of personal stories. Just as data miners use massive datasets, organizers of autobiographical story collections seek to aggregate large numbers of personal stories to derive insights and to mobilize. For instance, the organization Narrative Nation aims to "champion health equity by democratizing how the story of health disparities is told."[4] The project grew out of journalist Kimberly Seals Allers's own personal experience. Seals Allers had her first child as an "unwed black woman with basic insurance and [she] always wondered why a hospital that had treated others so well, treated [her] so poorly." Four years later, married and with better insurance from a corporate employer, she delivered her second child at the same hospital, and her treatment was shockingly different. The impact of bias on her care prompted Seals Allers to found Narrative Nation, which "co-create[s] culturally relevant, narrative-centered, multi-media communication, by people of color for people of color, to foster systemic change, transform current health messaging and communication practices and catalyze behavioral shifts to eradicate health disparities. [They] also educate, train and mentor the youth to become the next generation of health story-tellers."[5] Seals Allers also launched a mobile app called Irth ("irth" is "birth" with the "b" for "bias" removed) where people can share their own experiences of bias in maternal care.[6]

The three buttons on the Irth app encourage women to "find an experience," "share your story," and "connect with the community"—each of which highlights a reason for why such projects have the potential to resist data profiling. First, the call to "find an experience" draws attention to the importance of embodied experiences and emotions, as opposed to abstract, disembodied data. One of the fundamental causes of data bias is the false assumption regarding the neutrality of data, hence we need to phenomenologically reorient our data practices to stress the partial and situated experience of every single data provider and user. One way to do that is to tell stories about our embodied experiences. Second, the call to "share your story" highlights another common cause of data bias, namely the prevalence of deficit narratives that only point up the negative. Even those who seek to produce counter-data often fall into the trap of only focusing on "problem areas" in certain communities, so that inviting mothers to share the full story of their birthing experience can be seen as a way to frame their experience as an asset. Third, the call to "connect with the community" reminds users of the importance of who collects, processes, and uses what I call their "story data." As opposed to commercial and surveillance data extraction, Irth prides itself on its "by us for us approach," which aims at "democratizing access to developing and disseminating the narratives that shape our understanding of the world around us."

While initiatives such as Irth present crucial modes of resistance, we have to be careful not to set up a false opposition between stories and statistics. As my expression "story data" also signals, our stories can also be thought of and handled as data. It is not just bank account numbers, shopping preferences, or medical data that are being aggregated in today's data economy; our personal stories are also being analyzed and assembled into clusters. Every post, blog, and story we share can be mined and analyzed for data points, which are then bought and sold, used and misused, often without our knowledge. And there are other fundamental connections between stories and statistics as well. First, the success of infographics and data-driven storytelling suggests that combining statistics with individual stories might well be the most powerful way to relay a message. However, we have to remember that numbers do not speak for themselves and that data bias is just as harmful in the case of story collections as it is with other data sets. Second, presenting stories as an antidote to statistics conceals the fact that autobiographical storytelling itself is deeply rooted in calculation and statistics. Even when not doing so explicitly, storytellers and diarists quantify their existence in statistical terms, wondering how their life compares to those of others, how they fit into statistical categories, how "average" or "normal" their life is. Autobiographical storytelling is literally a way to ac-*count* for one's life, whether through words, images, or numbers.

In the following analysis, therefore, I promote a complementary view of the relationship between personal stories and statistics. There are a number of false binaries to dismantle here: stories versus numbers, qualitative versus quantitative, small data versus big data, privacy versus surveillance, autonomy versus discipline, and liberation versus exploitation. To underscore the inseparability of stories and statistics, I show both how personal stories are aggregated through statistical approaches and how personal storytelling itself implies statistical calculation. Cases will include historical examples from the early twentieth century as well as contemporary digital humanities and social media projects. My objective is to show not only that statistics and personal stories are complementary, but that there is a special value in aggregating our stories, in that databases of personal stories can push us towards more open-ended definitions of collectives. Statistics, of course, will always shape the grand narratives about society as well as our own stories about who we are, but the opposite is also true: when people think about their own lives as data points, their self-quantification can reflect back on and transform the definition of what constitutes a statistical category.

Statistical Studies of Memoirs from the Early Twentieth Century

Throughout the ages, editors have often compiled people's stories into thematic collections, hoping to reveal themes or truths that monographs of single authors alone could not. Plutarch's *Parallel Lives* (officially entitled

Lives of the Noble Greeks and Romans) is a famous early example of aggregated life stories. Plutarch's aim was to uncover common virtues and patterns in the lives of those he compared. In the Middle Ages, similar anthologies of lives of saints became popular, later followed by collections of lives of statesmen. Starting in the eighteenth century, these anthologies became increasingly colorful as editors began to also include the lives of deviants and ordinary citizens. By the mid-nineteenth century, biographical story collections were so popular that several dozen appeared each year in English alone.[7] With the nineteenth-century rise of the science of statistics, the purpose of these "collected lives" shifted. No longer mere illustrations of general trends or truths, they became the source of scientific data. Historians even developed a special methodology called prosopography to study the "the common characteristics of a group of historical actors by means of a collective study of their lives."[8] According to *A Short Manual to the Art of Prosopography,* "Prosopography is not interested in the unique but in the average, the general and the 'commonness' in the life histories of more or less large numbers of individuals. The individual and exceptional is important only insofar as it provides information on the collective and the 'normal.'"[9]

Biographies have long been aggregated, but it was not until the beginning of the twentieth century that statistically minded scholars turned their attention to *auto*-biographies. Inspired by the results of statistics in the fields of the natural and social sciences, literary scholars at the turn of the last century began to apply statistical methods to autobiographies and memoirs as well. Their choice to rely on an ego-focused genre to study groups or types of people may seem counterintuitive, for how could stories of individual, idiosyncratic lives reveal statistically relevant information? Yet, as literary critic Elizabeth Bruss explained, precisely because autobiographies seem to deal with "real life," readers tend to assume that these texts "stand for" people in a more referential sense, which means they are more likely to view them as sources of factual knowledge. Thus, "if it is tempting to classify any literature into A B C, it is even more so with autobiography, where texts 'stand for' people."[10]

Lured by the promise of statistical data gained directly from people's self-reflections, early scholars set out to study autobiographies and memoirs with a "Linnean lust to ... categorize."[11] *The Autobiography: A Critical and Comparative Study* (1909) by Anna Robeson Burr was among the first systematic studies of the genre.[12] Burr, an American writer and essayist, opens her book with the following optimistic statement: "If it is true, as [Adolphe] Quetelet asserts, that man is tending toward a common type;

that the oscillation of his elements is becoming less and less extreme, then the comparative study of individuals in the past furnishes us with an immense illumination on the subject of character. Into this unmapped field of autobiography we are about to enter. If we would not wander aimlessly, the material must submit itself to an attempt at classification."[13] Like an explorer about to enter an "unmapped field," Burr glorifies the nature of the fieldwork: "Our concern lies with that mass of heterogeneous subjective data up to the present ungathered, unclassified, and unregarded."[14] She cautions her fellow critics not to "wander aimlessly,"[15] but to select, sift, and judge. One must study individual details, she urges, but always with an eye on general tendencies, since the aim of statistical study is to reveal commonalities. The idiosyncrasies found in each story should ultimately help reveal those traits that are most representative of the particular autobiographer's community: "Although the study of autobiography repays us most richly where it is most personal, yet there is a sense in which we gain most by detaching ourselves from the examination of particular cases, in order to try for some generality, and then to see what comment these cases make upon our thought. General attitudes, rather than special information, become interesting to seek."[16] Burr summarizes the advantages of aggregation as follows:

> The personal record has an effect on literature far wider than can be conveyed by describing detached individual cases . . . As nuclei of certain past social energies, regarded not individually but in groups, they show the prevailing tones and predominating influences of their time. . . . it is not the special instance which should be considered, but the weight of aggregate instances. One statement here, one impression there, means nothing; but the body of likeness or unlikeness contained in a contemporaneous group of autobiographies must show the main tendencies of the society by which the group was surrounded.[17]

According to Burr, grouping must always precede individual analysis: "The first thing to be determined of any individual *mémoire* . . . is its relation to its group."[18] She maintains that "the most hasty purview of the main autobiographical groups shows their participation in certain common attitudes, views, and feelings, which must be realized before we can separate those attitudes, views, and feelings peculiar to the individual himself."[19] Following this principle, she classifies autobiographies based on their author's "Nationality and Profession," "Religion," "Humor," "Work and Aims," and so forth. This normative and typological stance leads Burr to exclude authors she considers "pathological," on the grounds that they are not sufficiently representative of "common attitudes, views, and feelings."[20] Pathological memoirists are "not to be regarded as representative of countless unwritten cases, not to be regarded as representative of common experience, but rather the reverse."[21] Her statistical analysis also leads her to conclude that Italian autobiographers are the best, French second, English third, and so on.[22] Burr's case against French *mémoires* is based on the argument that "they fail to relate their group to the world of humanity in general":[23] "whereas Cardan and Alfieri are, first of all, men, and secondly, creative intelligences and Italians, the French *mémoiriste* is, first of all, a French person, secondly, soldier, poet, or *grande dame*, moving quite serenely in a little world apart."[24] In other words, French autobiographers fail to reveal what is universally human about their existence.

Burr was not alone in her views; many of her contemporaries were similarly enthusiastic about the statistical insights provided by memoirs. As an example, in his 1908 study *Great Autobiographies: Types and Problems of Manhood and Womanhood*, E. H. Griggs relied on a similar statistical and typological framework to aggregate memoirs; and in 1937 E. Stuart Bates classified 410 autobiographies based on their authors' professions, such as "Soldier, Sailor," "Tinker, Tailor," "Beggerman, Thief," "Womenfolk," and "Businessmen."[25] There is, however, an important difference between Burr's views and those of her colleagues. Whereas other editors resorted apologetically to classification (I can't think of a better way to arrange these stories), Burr argues that classification is inherent in the very act of storytelling. It is autobiographers themselves who reveal (or fail to reveal) "the general character" of their group by highlighting certain experiences of their lives; hence, the aggregation done by the literary critic or editor is not an external imposition but a mere continuation of the storyteller's gesture. To make her point she quotes the founder of crowd psychology, Gustave Le Bon from *The Crowd: A Study of the Popular Mind* (*Psychologie des Foules*, literally *Psychology of Crowds*). Focusing on "the psychological law of the mental unity of crowds," Le Bon argued that individuals do not constitute a crowd until all the different individualities are at least temporarily submerged by the pressure of a common energy: "The crowd, therefore, partakes of a single general character, very different from that produced by its separate units."[26] Burr applies Le Bon's thesis to "the autobiographical group" and concludes: "When carefully observed, this fact . . . will be found equally true of the autobiographical group, and explanatory of certain apparently contradictory elements in the individual documents forming that group."[27] In other words, storytellers themselves can tend towards unity and create crowds by focusing on what is generalizable in their experience.

Historical Examples of Memoirists Quantifying and Generalizing Their Own Experience

Burr's observation raises the question of to what extent autobiographers themselves participate in their "deindividualization" by submitting themselves to certain common pressures and calculations. Burr is right in that memoirists have long been concerned with their place in groups, and many have used storytelling as a way to situate themselves vis-à-vis their fellow humans. One way to measure oneself to others is to count one's years, connections, possessions, or achievements and to compare it to those of others. In the earliest forms of autobiographical writing, accounting for one's life literally meant counting or taking stock of one's possessions. It is easy to trace the connection between self-reflection and calculation by following the epistemology of the word "account," from the Latin *computare* (to calculate, to count), through the Old French *acont* (reckoning), to the mid-fourteenth-century meaning of "statement answering for conduct," and finally to the more general sense of "narration, recital of facts" (attested by 1610s).[28] In her study of the evolution of the genre of diary, Jill Walker Rettberg uses the example of medieval annals to show how recording "quantities of grain or other valuables can be a form of self-representation, or at least representation of what belongs to the self."[29] Tallying involves more than counting, she notes, since every list of numbers tells a story and that story reflects a certain valorization.[30] Indeed, the earliest diaries took the form of logs before evolving into increasingly complex narratives about the self. For example, Japanese diaries (*nikki bungaku*) from the eighth century served as daily records of public events before they were expanded to include personal details. Similarly, the accounting books kept by fourteenth-century Florentine merchants (*ricordanze*) contained a special mélange of business transactions and autobiographical stories before evolving into more narrative forms of journaling.

Later, as self-reflection took on increasingly complex narrative forms, authors continued to rely on quantification to assess their lives. Scientifically minded memoirists in particular, such as Gerolamo Cardano or Benjamin Franklin, studied their lives in the aggregate, pondering its value for the statistical study of humankind. Franklin, for instance, quantified his life down to its minute details, hoping to extract generalizable rules of exemplary behavior.³¹ The rise of statistics in the early nineteenth century pushed memoirists to be even more precise about what exactly they meant by an exemplary or "sample" human life. Challenged by Adolphe Quetelet's statistical concept of the "average man" (*homme moyen*), which combined the social and physical characteristics of populations, nineteenth-century authors began to ponder the question of statistical representativeness: Can my life be described as "average" or "normal"? How does it compare to that of others? Could my autobiographical study contribute to the statistical investigation of humankind? Victorian autobiographers like Beatrice Webb, T. H. Huxley, Charles Darwin, and John Stuart Mill delighted in statistical interpretations of their autobiographical selves. Drawing heavily on scientific vocabulary, they wondered to what extent they could be considered representative samples of generalized human types. Herbert Spencer, the founder of social Darwinism, became so fascinated by the "sample value" of his own life that he fantasized about living in a glass case at the British Museum.³²

Another autobiographer who took this fascination with statistics to an extreme was the science fiction writer H. G. Wells. Inspired by the possibilities of statistical self-investigation, Wells spent more than seven hundred pages trying to explain what an "average" life he had lived. Aptly titled *Experiment in Autobiography: Discoveries and Conclusions of a Very Ordinary Brain (Since 1866)*, Wells's book is an extended meditation on his status as a sample human being. As Wells put it, an autobiography should not be "an apology for a life but a research into its nature."³³ He insists that "the dead rabbit of his former self" is only worth displaying if it is sufficiently representative of its species: "Naturally, in my autobiography, my mind must occupy the central position of this story of disillusionment, as a rabbit on the table represents its species."³⁴ Wells begins by comparing the brain of historical and contemporary figures to his own and concludes that his mental instrument is rather mediocre. His description borders on the grotesque when he suggests that perhaps he should commit suicide in a fixative solution so that his sample brain could serve as a scientific specimen: "I do not know whether it would be of any service after I am dead to prepare sections of my brain."³⁵

Beside his physical characteristics, Wells also frames his emotional and mental experiences as "average" and "common." He admits that he has never been "easily carried away by immediate things and made to forget the general in the particular."³⁶ In analyzing his life, he is only interested in delineating the "normal developmental phases."³⁷ As an adolescent, for example, he was put to trade, "like nearly every boy in the British lower and lower middle classes of that time,"[38] so he adds: "If this had been the case only with my brothers and myself, then this aspect of my story would hardly have been worth discussing. It would have been an individual misfortune."[39] Throughout the text, Wells claims that "[his] experience was the general experience" of those who lived around him. He describes his autobiography as "an attempt to put my case in the character of Everyman."[40] He even develops a special method to "de-individualize" his and others' personal experiences. As he puts it, personal stories are only worth recording if "we can *de-individualize* what happened."[41]

To demonstrate his method, Wells presents the life of his own mother in strictly generalizing terms: "She was born on October 10th, 1822, in the days when King George IV was King, and three days before the opening of the first steam railway";[42] she lived in a "world much more like Jane Austen's than Fanny Burney's . . . Still more was it like the English countryside of Dickens's *Bleak House*."[43] As the text progresses, Wells's mother becomes literally one in a million: "Against the background of such generalizations my little mother, you see, becomes the symbol of the blind and groping parental solicitude of that age. . . . My mother becomes a million mothers."[44] While Wells's case may seem somewhat extreme, the point is that storytellers have always positioned themselves as one of many, even when not specifically in numerical terms. Memoirists have always measured their lives with a view on the statistical whole, well before scholars and programmers began to aggregate their stories to extract information from them. And the trend of self-quantification continues today, as the following examples demonstrate.

The Quantified and Qualified Self

Nothing illustrates the interconnectedness of autobiographical storytelling and statistical calculation better than the contemporary practices of the Quantified and Qualified Self. A couple of years ago, whenever I would mention the concept of the Quantified Self, I knew I was in for a long explanation. Even at the conference of the Society for Utopian Studies, where I presented on this topic in 2014, people were baffled to hear about weirdly narcissistic "uber geeks" who quantified themselves by measuring their bodily functions. Since then, the trend of self-tracking has gone mainstream. People today keep track of everything: the steps they take, the things they own, the people they meet, the breaths they draw. Store shelves are full of tools and sensors that monitor and measure biological functions, behaviors, environmental conditions, and even sentiments. Market researchers predict that the number of wearable sensors will grow to over 1.1 billion in 2022.[45] The websites Quantified Self and Personal Informatics offer impressive inventories of all the things people quantify, including drinking habits, productivity, glucose levels, migraine triggers, time management, reading habits, calories, and finances. There is no limit on what can be quantified: people wear acoustic monitors to quantify their social interactions, parents monitor the development of their unborn baby, and women insert motion sensors into their vaginas to learn to strengthen their pelvic floor muscles. The Ancient Greeks, who carved the maxim "know thyself" (*gnothi seauton*) into the Temple of Apollo at Delphi, would surely be impressed by our creativity in this domain.

At first, the Quantified Self does not seem to have much to do with storytelling, but looking closer it becomes clear that all self-trackers are storytellers. They hope that the revelations afforded by their quantitative analyses will allow them to tell new and different stories about their lives. For example, self-tracker Ellis Bartholomeus decided to track her physical scars (date of injury, scar size, healing time, etc.) in order "to learn to deal with life more playfully and appreciate it more." She emphasized the potential of numbers to tell a different story about her life. "While most 'quantified scar' studies and articles on the web focus on how to get rid of scars as effectively as possible," Bartholomeus said she was more interested in "the *narrative* scars tell us about our bodies and our activities— from fun childhood games to recovery from car accidents."[46] Indeed, to assess, contextualize, and interpret any form of data, we need to engage reflexively with the results. In the words of Davis: "If self-quantifiers are seeking self-knowledge through numbers, then narratives and subjective interpretations are the mechanisms by which data morphs into selves. Self-quantifiers don't just use data to learn about themselves, but rather, use data to construct the stories that they tell about themselves."[47]

Recently, scholars coined the term "Qualified Self" to describe the complementary relation between self-quantification and self-qualification: "Where the *quantified* self gives us raw numbers, the *qualified* self completes our understanding of those numbers."[48] Those promoting the concept of the Qualified Self argue that by contextualizing and narrativizing data "we can better understand the quality of these quantities," since "context humanizes the numbers and places them back into our lives in meaningful ways."[49] The point here is not to contrast the statistics-driven Quantified Self to the narrative, contextualized Qualified Self but to explore how they can together lead to richer insights about our lives. In an interesting twist, in the last few years developers began to contemplate the possibility of automating the Qualified Self as well. Built upon AI, the most recent experiments in Qualified Self use a digital version of the age-old tradition of journaling and supplement it with the interpretive capabilities of machine learning. For instance, the journaling app Scribe encourages people to "get their thoughts out" as a means of gaining control of their lives, and it does so by providing instant feedback about users' emotions using IBM's Watson. Based on the input of daily journal entries, the algorithm analyzes users' moods and thought patterns through word analysis, and while at this stage the feedback is limited to revealing potential emotions, users already praise the app for helping them track mood states and practice mindfulness. Developers of the app argue that machine learning enhances the interpretation of personal data because "it can be difficult for people to accurately pull findings from their writings since they might be biased or dishonest with themselves."[50] These emergent, AI-assisted practices of self-reflection raise crucial questions about who interprets the data that we produce through self-reflection. For once we offload the task of interpretation to machines that are trained on massive datasets gained from others' self-reflections, we essentially create a closed loop of automated collective self-reflection.

The Quantified and Qualified Us

The Quantified and the Qualified Self are supposed to be all about the single individual, and participants agree that quantitative and qualitative self-reflection is about individual growth and self-knowledge. The original motto of the Quantified Self was "self-knowledge through numbers." This navel-gazing attitude, however, soon attracted criticism, as demonstrated by the following snide remark heard at a Quantified Self presentation: "Does [your project] measure your narcissism too?" to which self-trackers responded with humor by designing a project to measure their level of narcissism.[51] Critics question not just the motivation but also the scientific validity of self-trackers' n-of-1 studies.[52] To put it simply, the term refers to single subject research with a sample size of one, which in this case means that the data is generated by the same individual who is doing the observation by means of self-quantification. In self-defense, one self-tracker embraced self-knowledge unapologetically:

> I am not running an $n = 1$ study. I am not the sample, I am the population. I'm doing a $P = 1$ study. I am taking samples from

myself, such as my mood and what I am doing, and comparing that with population data such as the food I'm taking in. Even if those "quants" who are criticizing us still think I'm doing a n = 1 study, what's the problem with that? The problem is that n = 1 studies are not transferable to other n's. I'm not trying to transfer it to other n's, I'm just trying to understand myself. Problem solved.[53]

The problem is, in the age of data mining it is becoming increasingly difficult to maintain this separation of individual self-knowledge. Although some self-trackers hold on tight to their dream of independence, most acknowledge that the idea of strictly personal, individual data is now an illusion. We can no longer ignore that our data and stories can be accessed and mined by others. In theory, we can distinguish between recording and sharing data, but in practice, the moment we use digital devices to track any of our functions, we make that data available, even if not readily publicly accessible. Contemporary self-trackers and storytellers are all haunted by the specter of Big Data Brother. Quantified and Qualified Self data stored on cloud computing databases are no longer safe from prying eyes, since cybercriminals, government agencies, software developers, data mining companies, and their clients can all access them legally. Our numbers and stories are aggregated by others, for purposes that we have no control over. Questions about privacy and security are particularly pressing in the case of Quantified and Qualified Self data, since they tend to contain highly sensitive information about our bodily functions and life choices. In short, self-trackers' private attempts to use numbers and AI to tell new stories about their lives are compromised by dataveillance.[54]

As a response to this challenge, self-trackers began to create *collective* practices that aim to aggregate individual findings, but not for third-party purposes. Explaining why he launched Quantified Self in 2007, Gary Wolf expressed a strong hope that "outside" efforts at surveillance could be successfully co-opted by self-trackers for "inside" purposes of sousveillance:

> In 2007 we began looking at some new practices that seemed, loosely, to belong together: life logging, personal genomics, location tracking, biometrics. These new tools were being developed for many different reasons, but all of them had something in common: they added a computational dimension to ordinary existence. Some of this was coming from "outside," as marketers and planners tried to find new ways to understand and influence us. But some of it was coming from "inside" as our friends and acquaintances tried to learn new things about themselves. We saw a parallel to the way

computers, originally developed to serve military and corporate requirements, became a tool of communication. Could something similar happen with personal data? We hoped so.[55]

The Quantified Self is seen here as a form of "soft resistance" to big data practices. Dawn Nafus and Jamie Sherman consider this resistance particularly urgent in fields such as the health technology industry. As they argue, self-quantification "practices constitute an important modality of resistance to dominant modes of living with data, an approach that we call 'soft resistance.' Soft resistance happens when participants assume multiple roles as project designers, data collectors, and critical sensemakers who rapidly shift priorities. This constant shifting keeps data sets fragmented and thus creates material resistance to traditional modes of data aggregation. It also breaks the categories that make traditional aggregations appear authoritative. This enables participants to partially yet significantly escape the frames created by the biopolitics of the health technology industry."[56] Those who believe in the possibility of maintaining this distinction stress the voluntary nature of their data collection. They insist on the need to distinguish between big data, which refers to the datasets mined by business and governmental organizations in order to study entire populations and trends, from the grassroots efforts of self-trackers who voluntarily pool their data or stories in order to gain a better understanding of their own lives. Martijn de Groot argues that instead of adhering to a simplistic "me" versus "them" model, we should distinguish between four different modes of self-quantification: the Quantified Self, the Quantified Us, the Quantified Other, and Citizen Science, as shown in figure 4. According to de Groot, "the crucial question you should ask yourself to figure out if it is in fact Quantified Self is: 'Who wants to learn something?' When the answer is 'I,' you are good."[57]

Adherents also stress the benefits of collective self-reflection. If we combine many n = 1 studies, then everyone can compare their own data to those of others, thereby gaining further useful insights. The emphasis here is on self-trackers doing their own aggregation in the interest of the common good. As Alexandra Carmichael explained already back in 2012, "this will require a concerted and collaborative effort by the QS community that will involve developing a system where QSers can post their data to the cloud and have the data aggregated and analyzed across individuals (e.g. curetogether)."[58] Carmichael's projection has since become reality. The self-aggregated n = 1 data even has a name now: it's called the Quantified Us (to distinguish it from the Quantified Self and the Quantified

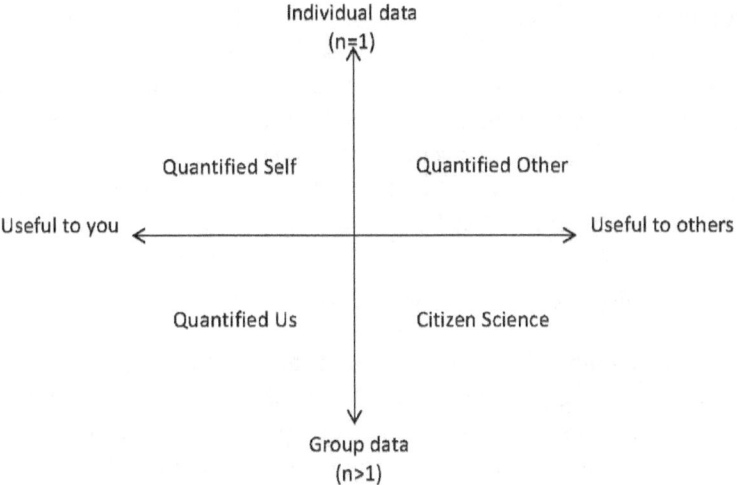

Figure 4. Diagram illustrating the difference between Quantified Self, Quantified Other, Quantified Us, and Citizen Science. Quantified Self Institute, Martijn de Groot. (Courtesy of Martijn de Groot)

Other). Analysts describe the Quantified Us as a collaborative space where "small data meets big data."[59] According to its proponents, the Quantified Us promises to bridge these two kinds of data: "Imagine a future where self-tracking harnesses the power of a whole population's data to identify patterns and make meaningful recommendations about what we should do next. Imagine a future where we can fluidly move between our own data and the data of the collective to gain insights on how best to live the life we desire, and where we decide what privacy we give up because we control the benefit it brings us."[60]

Autobiographers have often entertained this dream of merging their personal data with the data of the collective. Wells's radical socialism led him to project an ideal planetary community in which "the story of [his] father and mother and all [his] family [was] just the story of so many individual particles in the great mass of humanity,"[61] and the same vision inspires all those who create and participate in bottom-up initiatives to share personal stories in large numbers. As the app Irth or the #metoo movement demonstrate, the age of datafication is giving a new boost to the old democratic ideal of "power in numbers"—more specifically, to the idea of power in numbers of stories. The dream of a Qualified Us, where each member's self-reflection is supported by insights gained from machine-assisted analyses of their own as well as others' data, is based on the observation that statistical analyses can affect people's subjectivities through positive feedback mechanisms. With the rapid expansion of IoT (Internet of Things), the Quantified and Qualified Us will offer ever new possibilities of crowdsourced self-aggregation and self-reflection. However, the same question of agency that troubled the rosy prognostications about the Quantified and Qualified Self also challenges this optimistic notion of a democratic Quantified and Qualified Us.

The Double Face of Aggregation

To contrast bottom-up self-aggregation to top-down aggregation is to ignore the willing participation of storytellers in their own datafication. The etymology of the word "aggregation" gives us some clues regarding the deep complicity between bottom-up, democratic self-aggregation and top-down, exploitative aggregation. "Aggregation" is a strange word in that it has two seemingly opposite meanings. The verb "to aggregate" refers to the act of *bringing* things or people together, as if from outside, and it is in this sense that we mostly use it today. But the verb "to aggregate" also refers to things or people *coming* together, as if from inside, by themselves.[62] The first meaning expresses a top-down action whereby outsiders bring things together, whereas the second meaning suggests a bottom-up action of people coming together. In fact, the English word "together," from the Proto-Germanic *gaduron*, carries the exact same duality, meaning both "to bring together" and "to come together" (together = to gather). This underscores that aggregation and self-aggregation, us being collected and us gathering ourselves into collectives, are deeply interwoven, inseparable processes.

German philosopher Friedrich Nietzsche was among the first to point out this catch-22. According to Nietzsche, the problem starts the very moment we try to distinguish "objective" numbers from "subjective" values.[63] Measuring and valuing things are not as distinct as we would like them to believe, warns Nietzsche, for there is no objective reality that has not already been colored by our prior (e)valuation and vice versa, and there are no values that cannot be calculated and quantified. The seemingly objective act of measuring and the seemingly subjective act of valuing (or evaluating in the sense of bestowing esteem) are inseparable. Nietzsche's statement undermines the basic argument that contemporary ethicists use against the datafication of human life, namely that aggregation "substitutes calculation for human judgment on what should be very sensitive human issues."[64] According to Nietzsche's view, it is useless to complain about how datafication substitutes calculation for human judgment, since human judgment already entails calculation. Instead, we should explore their dynamic interconnectedness.

Michel Foucault built on Nietzsche's insight to further explain how we become complicit in our own subjectivation. According to Foucault's famous admonition, "he who is subjected to a field of visibility, and who knows it, assumes responsibility for the constraints of power."[65] In other words, when we internalize the logic of disciplinary observation by observing ourselves through the eyes of those observing us, we "become the principle of [our] own subjection."[66] Foucault argued that, in contrast to the coercive measures associated with "hard power," "soft power" makes people behave in the interest of the state by convincing them that certain behaviors are better for their own health and happiness. For example, people who self-track develop self-management practices with the purpose of acquiring deeper self-knowledge, but in the process, they also become better, meaning more manageable, citizens. In other words, the rationale for surveillance or dataveillance can be internalized to such a degree that surveillance and self-surveillance collapse into each other until they are no longer distinguishable. People self-manage (for instance through Quantified and Qualified Self technologies) not because they are being told or because they are worried that someone else is watching them, but because they are genuinely convinced that it is in their best interest to do so. Foucault's theory applies particularly well to autobiographical storytelling, because subjectivation (the process of self-inscription that seems to guarantee subjecthood) becomes here the very means of subjection.

While critics mostly cite Foucault to dismantle the false binary between big data and small data, discipline and autonomy, it is worth noting that the logic also works on the collective level of the Quantified or Qualified Us. Increasingly, people are called on to observe and reflect on their lives so as to contribute to a better understanding of not just themselves but also their communities. The scenario is familiar from contemporary dystopias such as Dave Eggers's bestseller *The Circle*, in which people convince themselves that they should share all aspects of their lives so as to become better citizens and humans. *The Circle* is founded on the principle that humanity as a community can only reach "its full potential" if people pool their resources, including information about their personal lives. This social vortex siphons people in until they are all fully convinced that everyone needs to participate, just as people today feel the urge to contribute their stories to large databases in the interest of the common good. To illustrate the double bind between accounting for ourselves and being counted, telling stories and having our stories mined for information, we could cite a recent speech by the UN Secretary-General Ban Ki-moon. In his opening remarks at the 2016 session of the Commission on Population and Development, Ban Ki-moon argued for the necessity of counting people in their own interest: "We all understand that people can never be reduced to mere numbers. At the same time, statistics are essential for tracking progress. When people are not counted, they are excluded. To live up to the commitment to leave no one behind, we have to make sure everyone is counted."[67] In other words, everyone needs to be counted to make sure that they count, and everyone needs to share their stories to make sure their storylines are included. And there is no escaping this double bind.

The Advantages of Story Data and Story Statistics

While some activists prefer to ignore this deep complicity between statistics and personal stories so as to celebrate the act of us coming together through storytelling, others draw pessimistic conclusions regarding the impossibility of resistance in the face of corporate and governmental datafication. My view is that it is precisely *because* of this complicity between aggregation and self-aggregation that collective storytelling has a chance to become a transformative praxis, one that is distinct from data mining. To conclude, I will argue that the specific kind of data we call personal stories can teach valuable lessons about our attitude to data and statistics in general, as well as about how we construct our definitions of collectives in particular. In their book, *Data Feminism*, Catherine D'Ignazio and Lauren F. Klein lay out the guiding principles of data justice, which include: examining and challenging power and rejecting the idea that data are neutral or objective; elevating embodied knowledge; rethinking systems of classification; embracing multiple perspectives and uncertainty; and considering context and making data labor visible.[68] This is a tall order, but autobiographical story collections are uniquely situated to embody these principles and even to serve as models in how to handle data. In connection with the app Irth mentioned above, I already noted three advantages of story-based platforms: they elevate embodied experiences as opposed to the abstraction of statistical data; they counter deficit narratives with a more holistic perspective; and their "by us for us" approach claims agency for those whose stories become data. To this, we should add two more advantages: first, story collections underscore how data is always already "cooked";[69] second, by their open-ended framing, stories can push us to question statistical classifications. Both of these points are relevant to the larger question pursued in this book about how collections of personal stories may reframe the boundaries of communities.

First, as critics of the Quantified Self and Quantified Other have often underscored, numbers do not speak for themselves. As Lisa Gitelman stated forcefully in the title of her book *"Raw Data" Is an Oxymoron* (2013), data is always the result of cultural production, so there is no such thing as "uncooked" data. Autobiographical stories illustrate this point well, since even when a statistically inclined author chooses to quantify their experiences in terms of numbers, it is clear that the narrated events undergo multiple processes of interpretation and curation. If anything, autobiography is the antithesis of "raw" data understood as information free of human judgment: autobiographers are famed manipulators, and readers know to take their truths with a pinch of salt. And yet, the moment we subject autobiographical texts to statistical analysis, critics seem to forget the agency of authors in handling their autobiographical data. We saw this already in statistical studies from the early twentieth century, and we also see it in today's digital humanities projects. Computational analyses of autobiographical material are still in their infancy, but the existing studies illustrate well the challenges of dealing with previously cooked material. For example, Esmeralda Kleinreesink's 2016 book, *On Military Memoirs: A Quantitative Comparison of International Afghanistan War Autobiographies, 2001–2010*, compares fifty-four memoirs and their soldier-authors to seek a deeper understanding of who writes such books and why.[70] Kleinreesink argues that mixed-method projects combining qualitative and quantitative analyses of memoirs, such as hers, are becoming increasingly attractive to humanities scholars.[71] As the author explains, "with the advent of computer technology, it became viable to search much more data and to find new connections that are also more complex than before, even the kind of complex data that the humanities research. This brought a renewed interest in finding patterns even in the humanities (Bod, 2012:11)."[72] Kleinreesink employs the arguments of data science to underscore the utility of her research. She promises "reliable, quantifiable insight into 21st century soldier-authors . . . that is not only academically useful, but also to a number of different practitioners, from psychologists and social workers who work with veterans, to publishers who (wish to) publish military autobiographies, to defense policy makers in the fields of public relations, operational security, and international relations."[73] To make good on her promise, Kleinreesink draws several broad conclusions. For instance, she offers statistical data about the identity of memoirists, their motivation, and their writerly strategies. In the conclusion she even offers an aggregated "Profile of the Soldier-Author":

> The average soldier-author who writes about his or her Afghanistan experiences is an average soldier when it comes to branch of service and gender: most of the writers are male and are army personnel, in exactly the same ratios as their country's armed forces. Apart from these two variables they are not representative of the normal military population. The average soldier-author is an officer who is over 40 years of age, who is either a combat soldier (a foot soldier or a fighter pilot), a doctor, works in the intelligence gathering community and/or does work that is specific to the Afghanistan mission.[74]

The European Research Group on Military and Society must have found the book's conclusions useful and applicable, since it awarded Kleinreesink a prize. Yet, the pattern-seeking and profiling techniques used in this study highlight again the "raw data" fallacy: they suggest that algorithms provide neutral information, when in fact potential bias has been introduced through the very choice of algorithms and in the process of translating texts into machine-readable data. The accuracy and ethical implications of the group profile drawn from these memoirs is also questionable, since most group profiles generated through computer techniques are non-distributive, meaning that the profile does not necessarily apply to all the members of the group, which becomes an ethical issue when it leads to inaccurate individual profiling based on data matching with the non-distributive group profile.[75]

One way to avoid this fallacy is to consider the "cooking process that produces 'raw' data" by "interrogating the context, limitations, and validity of the data under use."[76] In the case of autobiographical story collections, we can do this on two levels: "inside" each individual story, as we consider the lacunae and emphases in the story, the cultural and sociopolitical conditions that skew the author's perception and selection of experiences, the circumstances of publication that shape the writing, and so on; and on the meta-level of the collection, in looking at what is missing from the dataset, who is doing the text collection and why, the method of sampling and the limitations of the algorithms, and the like. The point is not to develop "unbiased" analyses or applications, but to acknowledge that all data is always already cooked, and what better way to underscore this than through databases of pre-digested personal reflections. Because authors have already "measured" their lives as data points in relation to other lives, if critics and other data-users can take their own data ethics into consideration when aggregating these data points, then autobiographical story collections could even serve as models as we fine-tune our methods of text analysis through machine learning and as we strive to set boundaries to the exploitative datafication of our lives.

Second, autobiographical story collections, whether top-down or bottom-up initiatives, also teach useful lessons regarding the statistical aggregates that we operate with. When we ignore the complicity of aggregation and self-aggregation, we risk limiting our capacity to reimagine our communities. For instance, when we create archives in which we separate Latine voices from other immigrant groups' stories, the very structure of our archive will solidify those lines of division between various groups of migrants. The same is true for the gender categories of #metoo, which elicited many passionate calls for diversifying gender categories. Even though these projects pride themselves on self-aggregation, they end up pigeonholing stories in the name of solidarity, which only reinforces preexisting statistical categories instead of allowing stories to question them.

It seems to me that the greatest potential of story-sharing projects lies not in bringing people together in solidarity, as many would claim. That would only mean reinforcing prior conceptions about who belongs to a certain group and who does not, which is exactly the danger of automated, algorithmic aggregations, which silo us into prefabricated communities. Instead, the greatest promise of self-aggregated stories lies in the power of stories to renegotiate our statistical definitions of collectives. Over the last few centuries we have internalized the pressure to "ac-count" for our lives by learning to view ourselves as statistical samples. One key advantage of today's crowdsourced aggregating technologies is that knowledge production has become circular in that people who contribute their stories can also became the consumers of their own information. The fact that we can access each other's personal stories on a large scale and can begin to compare our own behaviors and data to those of others means that we can also begin to question our preconceptions about the statistical wholes or collectives to which we belong.

On the one hand, such aggregations risk solidifying existing categories and instrumentalizing the "common good." On the other hand, and this is where we can be hopeful, sharing stories on a large scale may also prompt people to question existing social categories. Once people begin to challenge the principles that justify inclusion and/or exclusion in certain groups, they can begin to imagine themselves into new kinds of communities. Seen from this perspective, the practice of self-aggregating personal stories gives people a chance to imagine themselves into new collectives, because when people think about their own lives in terms of belonging to a statistical category, their self-aggregation can reflect back on the definition of what constitutes that statistical collective. The culture of surveys provides a great example of the potential of such a feedback mechanism.

In *The Averaged American*, Sarah E. Igo presents a compelling account of how twentieth century statistical surveys, such as the famous Middletown Studies or the Kinsey Reports, came to shape Americans' understanding not just of themselves but also of their collectives.[77] Igo argues that as knowledge production became circular and the people who were surveyed became the consumers of their own information, people learned to view themselves in terms of statistical samples, but they were never just passive recipients of their data. To the contrary, fascinated by what the surveys revealed, Americans began to compare their own behaviors and data to those of others and to question the very categories used to construct the emerging portrait of the "average American." As a result, they began to question existing social categories and the principles that justified inclusion and/or exclusion in certain groups, which in turn made it possible for them to imagine new kinds of communities. As Igo explains: "Survey technologies never worked simply to normalize their subjects in the service of a consensus society, however. This would not account for their widespread appeal. Surveys could also encourage and give new weight, through numbers, to nonnormative habits, beliefs, and identities. Social statistics, highlighting both inclusion and exclusion, prompted some to imagine themselves into new collectives or to forge new minority consciousness. . . . In such ways, social scientific data created novel possibilities for community and self-assertion even as they placed new constraints on self-fashioning."[78]

Similarly, aggregating quantities of personal stories has the potential to transform not only people's own self-understanding but also their understanding of the categories and communities to which they belong. To preserve this positive potential of aggregated personal stories, we need to remember what makes stories a unique kind of data: namely, narratives are productively open-ended, not just in their refusal to offer a single valid answer (which is often acknowledged) but also in their reluctance to be constrained by a single question. This is particularly important as we consider the effects of aggregation on our definition of collectives. How can we maintain the flexibility of our definitions of who belongs and who does not belong to certain communities? Database technologies relying on numbers are always limited by the definitive formulation of the question to which they seek the answer. Those developing our newest deep-learning algorithms are painfully aware of this limitation. By contrast, stories have the freedom *to not know to which question they seek the answer*. As Gary Wolf, founder of the Quantified Self movement, put it: "For many self-trackers, the goal is unknown. Although they may take up tracking with a specific question in mind, they continue because they believe their numbers hold secrets that they can't afford to ignore, *including answers to questions they have not yet thought to ask*."[79] Not having a preformulated question may seem like a waste of an effort, yet that is precisely the advantage that storytelling brings to our thinking, both when we reflect about ourselves and about our communities. Not knowing which statistical populations we belong to while pondering our place as one of many, opens up the possibility of new collective formations. Self-aggregating ourselves via stories is promising not because it is an alternative to aggregation, and not because it reinforces solidarity along existing lines of division, as many claim today. Rather, self-aggregating ourselves via storytelling is promising because it allows us to imagine ourselves into new communities that have *not been thought yet*.

POSTSCRIPT
Toward Algorithmic Collectives

> *We can't put it together. It is together.*
> —WHOLE EARTH CATALOG

Sharing Our Pandemic Experiences

This volume has showcased a wide range of autobiographical story collections from the Enlightenment to digital platforms in order to study the epistemic and political role of aggregated personal stories. These final pages are being drafted in the midst of the 2020 pandemic, which supplies ample support for the ideas I have presented. Covid-19 is the first worldwide pandemic to be documented live on social and other media, often through personal storytelling.[1] When comparing it to the 1918 "Spanish" flu, the most striking difference is our zealousness to document the 2020 pandemic, not just privately but also publicly and collectively. The trauma of pandemics often elicits a double reaction: on the one hand, the experience of isolation occasions an inward turn which often takes the form of intensive autobiographical reflection; on the other hand, isolation may spark a renewed interest in social relationships, and a desire to participate in deeper, richer forms of community life. The 1918 flu has often been characterized in terms of a collective amnesia. Historians describe it as the "forgotten pandemic," because there was no collective will to remember it.[2] This does not mean that people were not documenting it privately: family attics and the archives of local historical societies are full of private diaries describing the personal experiences of those who lived through the Spanish flu. I personally grew up with the memory of the pandemic because my grandmother often talked about it. She was eleven when she lost her mother and two older siblings within a few months. This family tragedy, however, existed in a vacuum. As Thomas Mullen put it, there was "a wall of silence surrounding survivors' memories of the 1918 flu," which was "quickly leading to the very erasure of those memories."[3]

By contrast, the 2020 pandemic was characterized by intense *collective* story-sharing. Technology enabled people to share their personal Covid stories instantaneously, and it also allowed for collective projects where people could crowdsource their stories into shared collections. In the spring of 2020, within weeks of the first news announcements about the virus, a new subgenre popped up on the internet. The "quarantine diary" or "Covid diary" is a visual or narrative documentation of day-to-day life during the pandemic. Social media sites, of course, had an unbeatable advantage in terms of distribution and participatory engagement, so the largest, most dynamic projects were created on social media. Hashtags such as #IStayHome, #QuarantineLife, or #afterlockdown attracted millions and became literal lifelines to people in isolation. In addition, there were thousands of other story projects, organized by traditional media, national and local archives, various community organizations, and individuals. Some of these collections targeted specific groups, but most emphasized their inclusiveness and democratic intentions. As the Pandemic Journaling Project urged: "Usually, history is written only by the powerful. When the history of COVID-19 is written, let's make sure that doesn't happen."[4]

In addition to archives, experimental and artistic projects also proliferated. For example, the film *Covid Diaries NYC* chronicled the lives of five young filmmakers, ages seventeen to twenty-one, "who turn[ed] their cameras on themselves and [told] the stories of their families during the first wave of the COVID-19 pandemic in New York City."[5] Many sites employed transmedia storytelling, taking advantage of multiple platforms and formats. For instance, *#AfterLockdown* is an animated film based on the personal stories of people in various corners of the world. People "recorded themselves narrating their personal experiences with lockdown [and] travel-restrictions" and these were "grouped together and illustrated, to form a collective scrapbook."[6] Some took the idea of collaborative writing to a whole new level by creating a single plotline out of the Covid stories of many. Russian artist and user experience designer Maria Fedorova, for example, collected personal anecdotes about coping with the pandemic and then combined digital 3D animation with traditional Russian fairytale tropes and illustrations to create "a magic space of collective writing."[7]

As I have argued in this book, and as demonstrated by these Covid projects, people tend to share their personal stories collectively because they want to document a particular historical moment and because they seek social connections. I used the expression "collective intimacy" to designate this double function and to show that story-sharing sites circulate information and affect, in conjunction. As organizers of one of the collective Covid diaries announced: "We not only hope to preserve experiences through a memory archive, but also through personal narration, bring comfort, peace, reflection and healing to participating individuals."[8] To highlight their epistemic, documentary function, organizers evoked the idea of future historians using these collective diaries to write the story of life during coronavirus. They also praised the unique value of personal storytelling over other kinds of narratives: "The story it tells . . . is a deeper one than the many one-off surveys . . . which reported predictable increasing levels of distress. The thoughts [in the diaries] are a messy, ever-shifting chronicle of psychological adaptation over months of imposed isolation, together documenting a landscape of everyday concerns, emotions, and expectations."[9] In addition, pandemic story projects also had a strong "campfire effect." Unlike the static print archives of the 1918 flu, the digital platforms of 2020 gave people instant access to each other's personal stories, often as they were unfolding, day to day, which created a powerful sense of belonging and a spectacle of unity. As one commentator noted: "Social media has transformed into a *space of unity* during the coronavirus crisis."[10]

Unity is of course deeply interwoven with the concept of "comm-unity," as seen in the popular etymology of the word "community" as *com-unus* ("together-one").[11] Previous chapters showed how the unity of community can be imagined in various ways. Whether they project unity as a public forum (like Herder and Moritz), as a global community of storytellers (like social media companies), as a database of all of us (as in visions of a Quantified Us), or as a single globe, map, or date, all story collections ritualize togetherness. For instance, just like the one-day diaries presented in chapter 4, organizers of these pandemic diaries appealed to the idea that all of humanity was sharing a single "global present." As one commentator noted: "Around the world, the history of our present moment is taking shape in journal entries and drawings."[12] There was a sense of solidarity among those who lived through this historical moment, and aggregated stories, especially when shared "in the moment," helped create this sense of a single, shared time. Pandemic mood surveys illustrate well the aggregate effect of this sense of simultaneity and unity. For instance, the German daily *Süddeutsche Zeitung* created a "Corona Crisis Collective Diary" by compiling written, audio, and video stories as well as mood surveys into a single online archive. The mood surveys literally only took a single click a day, but with more than a million clicks, over the months, their aggregation resulted in collective mood visualizations. Like in the one-day diaries presented earlier, these mood visualizations and daily check-ins created a composite portrait and a sense of community.[13]

Visual collections, such as the project Coronamaison, provided particularly poignant examples of these scenes of unity. The challenge #Coronamaison was launched on Twitter in March 2020 by a group of cartoonists and illustrators, inviting people to imagine their dream home where they would like to spend their pandemic isolation.[14] Organizers provided a template (fig. 5), which people illustrated with astounding imagination. Some transformed the room into jungles or swimming pools and painted windows with endless vistas, others expressed their claustrophobia by adding zoom screens and towers of toilet paper. And cats. Lots of cats.

The submissions were then collected onto a single website, which organizers described as a "shared apartment complex" with 1470 stories (pun intended).[15] Note the significance of the staircase, which connects the stories of this giant imaginary building into a single, infinite community (on the website each drawing is immediately below the previous one, so the aggregate image does look like a single apartment building with many residents). I chose this example because visual collections representing shared spaces (like the story maps from New York in chapter 5) make our

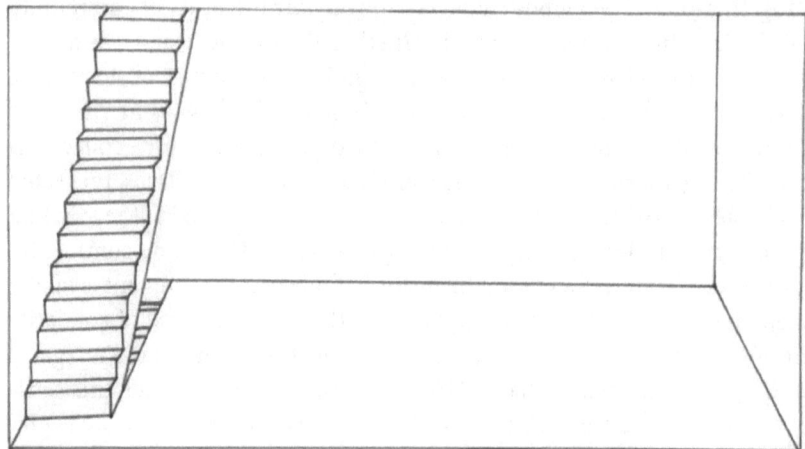

Figure 5. Template of empty room posted on Twitter to be illustrated by people in Covid-19 isolation. #CoronaMaison, Timothy Hannem. (Courtesy of Timothy Hannem)

sense of unity more tangible. My point, however, throughout this book has been that all story collections, including narrative ones, function as *spectacles of unity.*

Performing Unity

I started out with the observation that community, more precisely the way we imagine and talk about community, is a crucial form of social and political imagination. The dream of being in community is what attracts most people to these story-sharing sites, and by assembling our stories into collections we create spectacles of unity. On the one hand, these sites have a significant pro-social, productive potential in that they help people discover connections between their own stories and those of others, which in turn can help reimagine collectives. On the other hand, aggregating personal stories has many harmful and even dangerous downsides, as demonstrated by contemporary data-extraction and surveillance practices. As I argued, the idea of a single time or a single shared space, or the concept of objective statistical categories and all-inclusive "human libraries," are all misleading and even harmful in that they homogenize valuable heterogeneity and preempt critique. Moreover, nostalgic and fuzzy feelings of belonging delude us into schemes where we freely provide our story data to companies and governments that then resell them.[16] As a result, we get trapped in a catch-22: we want to connect to others by sharing our stories, but those stories become the sources of our own entrapment. This double bind is particularly dangerous for democracy, since democracy depends on the active and reflexive participation of citizens, but when large numbers of personal stories are being aggregated and harvested, the ideal of "power in numbers" can easily be corrupted.

Pandemic story collections also raise urgent questions about the role of market forces and universalizing concepts in creating community. They illustrate how rosy pronouncements about how "we are all in this together" can conceal other motives and deep disparities in the pandemic's impact. It is clear that the racial, social, economic, ethnic, and geographic disparities that characterized the pandemic were also reflected in the story archives themselves. The question of who owns the stories people posted is up for debate, and documenting the pandemic through private stories was a risky business in many corners of the world (see the case of diarists like Fang Fang, whose Wuhan diary chronicling life under lockdown was deemed unpatriotic by the authorities).[17] Also, wealthy countries from the Global North were heavily overrepresented in these story archives, a phenomenon that has both cultural and economic causes. Moreover, one could argue that these story collections not only reflect inequities but contribute to them in that the distribution of funds is often driven by storytelling. In *Narrative Economics: How Stories Go Viral and Drive Major Economic Events,* Nobel prize–winning economist Robert Shiller argues that the stories people tell have far-reaching consequences for economic decisions—a statement that also applies to story collections such as these Covid projects. Whose stories are captured and whose are forgotten is clearly not just a matter of willingness on the part of storytellers, but the result of access, censure, structural inequalities, and systemic blind spots. How else could we explain the fact that even in the richest countries, some communities' pandemic stories remain untold, and that many Covid stories remain hidden behind paywalls?

Visions of community have clear material implications. What makes political imagination such a potent force is precisely that it is not just ideal but also material. Materially, the spectacles of unity that we offer ourselves through these story platforms are tied to consumerist phantasmagorias about belonging. Story collections, not unlike nostalgic housing communities or utopian social media communities, generate endless desire for belonging. Situations such as the pandemic naturally reinforce this desire, but consumer capitalism is always built on the insatiability of our dreams of community. In the words of Keally D. McBride, "Consumptive desire allows us to act according to our desire for community, yet never especially want or expect that desire to be gratified. Instead, the mirage of community continually works to draw us into the future or daydream into a mythical past—it is a repository of our desires for another life, but without the danger to the status quo that such social dissatisfaction might provide."[18] The greatest danger in this commodification of community is of course complacency, since the temporary satisfaction with the idea of "one world together" may thwart community action.[19]

This is not to say that community is corrupted by its consumerist aspects. Rather, as I have argued throughout the book, the ideal of community and its commodification mutually reinforce each other. As "producers" of the media where we exchange our stories, we are both passive consumers and active agents in creating these visions of togetherness. Most critics and story activists react to this dilemma of participatory democracy by contrasting top-down exploitation to bottom-up liberation. They oppose the interests of the state and the market to grassroots "community projects." Instead of this binary, I proposed that the two groups pursue complementary interests in complex, morally messy ways.[20]

Some argue that by giving ourselves these spectacles of unity and community we engage in a "bottomless reflexivity," meaning we get trapped in participatory, "repetitive loops" of "reflexive communication."[21] We cannot get out of these performances of story sharing because the illusion of intimacy feels good, and because we need to legitimate our democracy by giving ourselves the image of a democratically public forum of deliberation. Guy Debord was among the first to offer a critique of the "the society of the spectacle."[22] According to Debord, mass media and consumer society offer constant entertainment or "spectacles" of social life to individuals, as a result of which they become passive consumers and spectators of these images instead of directly participating or actively producing their own lives. In *Blog Theory* (2010), Jodi Dean updated Debord's critique to reflect the changing media landscape of the twenty-first century. According to Dean, people today experience a different form of passivity, since in principle at least, they are actively contributing to the participatory culture of the internet and social media. In reality, however, the constant urge to communicate, to post and to respond, leads to pervasive voyeurism and self-disclosure, where everyone willingly reports on their own lives and on those of others, so that we end up performing the spectacle of our own entrapment: "Networked, participatory spectacles let us stage and perform our own entrapment."[23] We don't "need spectacles staged by politicians and the mass media. We can make and be our own spectacles—and this is much more entertaining. . . . Corporate and state power need not go to the expense and trouble to keep people entertained, passive, and diverted. We prefer to do that ourselves."[24]

The advantage of Dean's reformulation of the "society of the spectacle" is that by emphasizing citizens' participation, she underscores the active process of staging community as a performance. Dean's participatory society enacts their togetherness self-reflexively, through constant communication. And while Dean does not single out autobiographical stories as part of this self-reflexive spectacle, our personal stories clearly play just as important a role as the cute cat videos we share. I would even argue that autobiographical story collections redouble, so to speak, the idea of reflexive democracy: if the notion of a public sphere suggests the *reflexivity* of power (since in democracy power is distributed and the emphasis is on communicative exchange), then collections of personal stories, understood as forums of citizen voices, redouble this reflexivity by adding a further layer of self-reflexivity through autobiographical reflection. This added layer of self-reflexivity is what renders these projects so lively, since the ongoing process of citizens' self-reflection promises to keep their communicative exchanges more open-ended. Story collections are not mirrors that reflect the geometries of sociality but spectacles where we perform our togetherness and enact our boundaries.[25]

The disadvantage of Dean's theory is that it treats the spectacle of being-in-community as a secondary act, as if there was something more "real" compared to which our performance was "just acting." Jean-Luc Nancy has cautioned against treating community as a spectacle. According to Nancy, thinking about community as a spectacle leads to the misleading assumption that there exists something outside the spectacle, that the spectacle is the representation of something else, of something more "real" than the spectacle. He also acknowledges that these spectacles of togetherness are indispensable. As noted earlier, philosophers often describe our social being as specular in the sense that community is about how we appear to ourselves and to each other. They imagine the world as a stage on which each "self" plays their unique role while also being "one of us," one of "each and every one."[26] It is as if the world was a stage and "the stage is the space of a co-appearing,"[27] where each one presents itself to itself and to others while also presenting the "we" to each other. Some have described this as a game of mirrors, in which each one sees oneself as already seen by an other as an other, as a result of which we also all appear to each other at once as a collective.[28] That is why, as Jean-Luc Nancy acknowledges, "there is no society without spectacle, or more precisely, there is no society without the spectacle of society" because "society is the spectacle of itself."[29]

As Nancy explains, in Western thought, the archetype of the "good" spectacle is the Greek theater, where the community gathers to give itself a spectacle of its own foundation. For the Ancient Greeks, "being together is defined by being-together-at-the-spectacle, and this being-together understands itself as an inversion of the representation of itself, which it believes to be capable of giving itself as originary (and lost): the Greek city assembled in community at the theater of its own myths."[30] In contrast to this Greek unity of *logos* and *mythos*, the archetypical "bad" Roman spectacle had a negative split between appearance and reality, resulting in a "self-consuming spectacle."[31] "In the bad spectacle, the social being imagines (*se représente*) the exteriority of interests and appetites, of egoistic passions and the false glory of ostentation,"[32] which explains the vulgarity and popularity of Roman spectacles. Political philosophers have often built their theories on this supposed contrast between a "good" and a "bad" kind of communal self-representation.[33] Nancy, however, is skeptical about this binary opposition between a full and empty spectacle, as well as the attendant separation of good and bad communities. The problem is that by highlighting the disconnect between appearance and original togetherness, we imply that communities appear from somewhere, from some prior depth, as if there ever was a Being that is not always already collective. The division wrongly suggests that there is a distinction between presentation and re-presentation, between presence and being-present to each other. Instead, Nancy proposes that we think of the two as intertwined, that we move beyond this Greek-Roman division: "Maybe we have to begin by taking some distance from this double spectacle, by no longer wishing to be Greeks, by no longer fearing that we are Romans..."[34]

With-nessing Each Other

Nancy's intervention makes me reconsider the idea of these story collections being spectacles of community. Community, in Nancy's redefinition, is neither something that we have lost nor something that we can build for the future. The problem with our traditional interpretations of community is that they all posit community as an essence.[35] Organicist theories define community as a shared origin and appeal to a lost community in the past, while contractual theories view community as a shared obligation and appeal to the future promise of community.[36] They both start out with the concept of human as an immanent being that is only later marked by difference. Organizers of story collections tend to follow the same pattern, either talking about the need to reconstitute old communities or a desire to build new ones. Instead, Nancy posits that multiplicity "belongs to Being as its constitution,"[37] meaning there is no such thing as "not being together," because we are always already together. Togetherness is the nature of Being, so it does not make sense to talk about how we were once in community or how we will be in community in the future. Community is not a deeper or more meaningful mode of being together. Instead, community is a kind of *co-exposure,* a condition in which we are all together in being alone.

The pandemic isolation, us all sitting at home, together alone, is a fitting illustration of Nancy's notion of community. Sharing the situation of isolation means acknowledging our co-presence without insisting on a more authentic form of being-together. Nancy "preferred to concentrate [his] work around the 'with': almost indistinguishable from the co- of community, yet it carries with it a clearer indication of the spacing at the heart of proximity and intimacy. 'With' is plain and neutral: neither communion nor atomization; just the sharing/dividing [partage] of a place, at the most, contact: a being-together without assemblage."[38] To continue his line of thought, I propose that by sharing our stories we simply *with-ness* each other.[39] In life writing studies and in studies of collective memory, scholars often discuss personal stories as acts of witnessing, as in "we all witnessed this global pandemic." The notion of witnessing stresses shared ground and solidarity, but in doing so it subsumes individual experiences under collective, representational ideas. By contrast, my notion of *with-nessing* acknowledges the spacing at the heart of collective intimacy. At first, this may seem like a limitation since it calls for disidentification: "We do not have to identify ourselves as 'we,' as a 'we.' Rather, we have to disidentify ourselves *from* every sort of 'we' that would be the subject of its own representation."[40] Yet, renouncing our attempts to represent community is exactly what creates the positive opportunity to ethically co-appear with others and to find new meanings. In Nancy's words, "the 'thought' of 'us' is not a representational thought (not an idea, or notion, or concept). It is, instead, a *praxis* and an *ethos*: the staging of co-appearance."[41] Building on Nancy, I propose that story sharing is not about representing a past or building a future community, but it *is* one of the most essential practices of being with others. By sharing our stories, we *practice* togetherness.[42]

Algorithmic Collectives

To conclude, I want to expand this notion of *with-nessing* to also include machines and non-human agents into our story-sharing collectives. In my earlier discussions I already emphasized how new technologies make new imaginings of community possible. I also underscored that media are never mere carriers of content; it is not that we use technologies simply to express a preformed vision. Rather, in our engagement with these new tools we "co-emerge" with media.[43] This view is also in line with my argument that our spectacles or performances of community are not secondary manifestations of some preformed reality. Instead, in sharing our stories we co-appear with each other and with our media. To illustrate this idea, I will point to some recent experiments with algorithmic autobiography and their implications for our notions of collectivity. For as algorithms and machines join us as authors of our life stories, they also expand the meanings of "we."

The question of authorship is a hot topic in auto/biography studies, mostly because of its consequences for human rights and social justice issues.[44] But given the vast scale of digital, aggregated life narration, we should also investigate the meaning of authorship in the world of hyperconnected, technologically mediated autobiography. As noted in chapter 1, our stories are now increasingly engineered by algorithms. In what Alison Booth termed "extreme collective narration,"[45] programs such as Facebook's Timeline engineer our biographies by linking events, tags, names, and appearances in our profile. To add a touch of personalization and to downplay the role of automation, Facebook invites users to edit their own machine-created life stories: "What will you create? We can't wait to find out."[46] Yet, as Booth rightly notes, the "you" and the "we" in this question should make us uneasy, since they treat the corporation as a person and the person as part of the corporation. The results are collaboratively produced "piecemeal ghosted memoirs"[47] that blur the boundaries of autobiographical storytelling, not just between people but also between people and machines.

In "Algorithmic Autobiography: The Uncertain Boundaries of the 'I' and the 'Self' in the Age of Hyperconnectivity," Salvatore Iaconesi and Oriana Persico reflect on the effects of "non-human and algorithmic subjects/entities" on the construction and perception of the self.[48] Iaconesi and Persico treat the self as a "membrane" that "acts simultaneously as the separation and meeting point between the subject and the outside world," they describe the author as a data "curator" and the autobiographical process as a "remix." In doing so, they stress the opacity and unpredictability of co-creating life stories with machines: "A new space exists in which we are confronted with unprecedented actors and materials: the software and the algorithmic matter. Most of the time their logic is opaque and inaccessible to us, from the ways in which algorithms watch and classify us; to the simple knowledge and perception of all the data we produce; to the algorithmic influence on our perceptions which comes about as software agents become able to shape our media environment around us, according to logics which are beyond our grasp and understandings."[49]

To demonstrate the results of such a machine-human collaboration, Iaconesi and Persico created GhostWriter, which uses machine learning, natural language analysis, emotion analysis, and network analysis to observe, analyze, and interpret the digital traces we leave behind in our daily lives. The program extracts patterns from the "non-structured data flow" of our lives and structures them using a model of autobiographical memory. The authors stress that the algorithm does not simply repost the data but "recomposes it with different logics," resulting in new autobiographical stories. They also underscore the circular process whereby technologically mediated memories reflect back on and influence autobiographical memory. Iaconesi and Persico exhibited the AI-generated autobiography at a public installation in traditional book format (with a digital screen inside a paper book), to stress that algorithmic autobiographies can become interactive objects that can be collectively circulated, interpreted, and manipulated.[50] In this way, what Canevacci calls "multividuals" can also become authors, since "a couple, a class of students, a group of friends, a collective of artists, a company, an institution and so on, could decide to feed the GhostWriter, collecting and using their data sources: the result would be an 'autobiography' attributable to and directly written by the couple, the class, the group, the collective, the company and the institution itself, here respectively recognised as the 'authors' and as single defined identities." Thus, algorithmic autobiographies distribute authorship, both among people and among people and machines. Moreover, the Internet of Things is turning inanimate objects, too, into sentient agents, and GhostWriter does not distinguish between our personal data and the data fed by non-human agents. Hence, an "apartment building, a square, a wood, a river, a fridge, our dog can now write their own autobiography and tell us their own life story, just like we do."[51]

Such projects become relevant to the questions posed in this book when we begin to ask about the ramifications of these machine-human interactions, not just for private individuals but also for collectives. While Iaconesi and Persico focus mostly on the tricky question of authorship, transmedia artist Stephanie Dinkins expands this conversation to also ask about the consequences of distributed authorship on community relations and remembering. Dinkins's projects explore the possibilities of AI-assisted autobiographical community stories. For example, *Not the Only One* (*N'TOO*) is "an experiment in making a multigenerational memoir of a black American family told from the perspective of a custom deep-learning artificial intelligence."[52] *N'TOO* is based on Dinkins's own family history, which she chose both because she wanted a subject that she deeply cared about and because she wanted it to reflect "the concerns and ideals of people who are underrepresented in the tech sector."[53] Dinkins began the project by recording conversations between three members of her family ("data contributors") and she fed this data to a deep-learning chatbot. Originally, Dinkins imagined *N'TOO* as an entity that could answer simple questions such as "where is your family from?" As the project evolved, however, Dinkins realized that the algorithm had its own unique and unpredictable logic, which meant that it was not just repeating information but was becoming like "the fourth member of the

Figure 6. *Not the Only One* avatar, Stephanie Dinkins. (Courtesy of Stephanie Dinkins)

lineage of people informing our family going into the future."[54] Dinkins stresses that the algorithm is not a passive archiving tool but an active "co-creator of living repositories for the memories, written and oral histories, myths, values and dreams of specific communities." The fact that *N'TOO* answers in first-"person" and that it is represented by a "face" helps imagine the algorithm as a family or community member (in one version it is an abstract sculpture with reliefs of faces; in another one it is a computer-generated composite image of the women whose stories inform it—see fig. 6).

In describing this new "member of the lineage," Dinkins emphasizes several priorities: (1) the fact that it was created through small data (personal interviews infused with care), (2) that it is stored on local computers to highlight data sovereignty, privacy, and transparency, and (3) that it only uses easily accessible technologies to encourage people to experiment and to have a stake in the algorithmic systems that shape their lives. In Dinkins's words: "Here, storytelling, art, technology, and social engagement combine to create a new kind of artificially intelligent narrative form. This project works toward the creation of culturally-specific, natural language-based AI that reflects the goals of the communities making them. By centering oral history and creative storytelling methods, such as interactivity and verbal ingenuity, this project hopes to spark crucial conversations about AI and its impact on society, now and in the future."[55] The result is a "a new kind of conversant archive,"[56] a futuristic story collection that not only gathers and archives people's stories but *thinks alongside members of the community* about the preservation and meaning of their shared memories.

Such "conversant archives" take the idea of *with-nessing* to a whole new level, and by doing so, they help highlight the main points I have argued throughout this book. First, storytelling is not an alternative to datafication because database and narrative, big data and small data, aggregation and self-aggregation intersect on many levels. On the one hand, this has a positive implication: story collections can transform social reality, because when people reflect about their own lives in the context of other lives, their self-reflection will also reflect back on the definition of statistical categories. On the other hand, if statistics and stories are complementary, then promoting personal storytelling will not suffice to counter data bias. Second, Dinkins's emphasis on situated knowledges and embodied engagement help counterbalance the fallacy of "raw" data and the "view from nowhere" that characterizes some story projects. The challenge here is to balance the phenomenological valorization of each person's lived experience with the need to continue to collectively interpret the larger historical, cultural, and discursive context that shapes those experiences. Third, the unpredictability of these artificially intelligent narrative forms underscores the value of the open-ended dynamism of narratives, which can avoid simplistic questions about who belongs and who does not.[57] Finally, by introducing non-human agents into our story-sharing collectives, these AI projects underscore that we cannot have a perspective *on* community quite simply because we are together in it. My posthumanist notion of *with-nessing* is simultaneously limiting and liberating. It is limiting in that it renounces the affective offerings that accompany romanticized notions of community, and it is liberating in that it keeps the borderlands of the idea of community more open. The question is: are we willing to accept the former for the sake of the latter?

NOTES

Introduction

1. Garcia, "#MeToo Long before Hashtags."
2. Park, "#MeToo Reaches 85 Countries."
3. According to organizers, #metoo aims to provide empathy and resources to victims and to raise awareness about sexual violence. Meanwhile, the movement has been criticized for not being inclusive enough and for celebrating victimhood. Since it began, the movement has galvanized millions more, and it has spread to other countries as well. #metoo has also given rise to secondary campaigns such as #HimToo, #ChurchToo, #MeTooMilitary, etc.
4. Pflum, "Conversation about #MeToo."
5. Alyssa Milano (@Alyssa_Milano), "One Tweet Has Brought Together 1.7 Million Voices from 85 Countries. Standing Side by Side, Together, Our Movement Will Only Grow. #MeToo," Twitter, October 24, 2017, https://twitter.com/Alyssa_Milano/status/922826342890131456.
6. Ohlheiser, "The Woman behind 'Me Too.'"
7. Holmes, "Succeed with Stories."
8. Constine, "Stories Are About to Surpass Feed Sharing."
9. Throughout the book, I use the term "personal story" to refer to autobiographical narratives about experiences that people have personally lived through. Most scholars use the terms "life writing," "autobiography," and "memoir," but I fear that the rich history of these terms may prevent us from embracing the growing variety of self-expressions in the digital age, including "small stories" (Bamberg, "Small Stories," 139–47) and episodic modes of self-narration (Strawson, "Against Narrativity"; Simanowski, *Facebook Society*). Autobiography studies (also referred to as life writing studies) is a rich and dynamic scholarly field with its own journals, conferences, and associations. See the journals *a/b: Auto/Biography Studies, Biography, Life Writing*, and other regional journals, as well as the International AutoBiography Association and its regional chapters. The systematic study of autobiographical material began in the first decade of the twentieth century, and the field has gradually expanded from the study of literature and textual interpretations towards cultural studies, sociology, philosophy, anthropology,

memory studies, human rights studies, and digital media studies. For an overview of the terminology and developments in the field, see Smith and Watson, *Reading Autobiography*; and Chansky and Hipchen, *Routledge Auto Biography Studies Reader*.

10. For an excellent overview and in-depth reflection on recent developments in story sharing in online environments, see the two special issues of *Biography* edited by Laurie McNeill and John Zuern: *Online Lives* (2003) and *Online Lives 2.0* (2015).

11. For a general discussion of the role of personal storytelling, see Maguire, *The Power of Personal Storytelling*; Niles, *Homo Narrans*; and Gottschall, *The Storytelling Animal*. For insightful analyses of the connections between narrative and identity, see books by Philippe Lejeune and Paul Ricoeur, as well as Eakin, *Writing Life Writing*. For more specific studies of the collective aspects of personal storytelling, see Poletti, *Stories of the Self*; Smith and Schaffer, *Human Rights and Narrated Lives*; and Popkin's notion of "coordinated lives."

12. "About StoryCorps," https://storycorps.org/about/.

13. See, for example, Lambert, *Digital Storytelling*; Van Dijck, *The Culture of Connectivity*; Jasper, *Protest*; Keren, *Politics and Literature*; and Lingel, *Digital Countercultures*.

14. Alsaleh, *Voices of the Arab Spring*, 1.

15. Rothfeld, "Crowd-Sourced Storytelling."

16. Maier, "Creating Community." See also Stephen Bradley, "The Power of Community Storytelling." *WIRED*, January 2014, https://www.wired.com/insights/2014/01/power-community-storytelling/; and Polletta, *It Was Like a Fever*.

17. Bauman, *Individualized Society*, 9.

18. Zygmunt Bauman described this phenomenon in several books, including *The Individualized Society* and *Community: Seeking Safety in an Insecure World*. Bauman described the relationship between individual identity and community in terms of a complex relationship of surrogacy. He argued that since neither community nor identity are available as "safe havens" in our rapidly changing world, a curious surrogate relationship has developed between them. As Bauman explains, "'Identity,' today's talk of the town and the most commonly played game in town, owes the attention it attracts and the passions it begets to being a surrogate of community: of that allegedly 'natural home' or that circle that stays warm however cold the winds outside." Bauman, *Community*, 15. The paradox is that "in order to offer even a modicum of security and so to perform any kind of healing or pain-soothing role, identity must belie its origin; it must deny being 'just a surrogate'—it needs to conjure up a phantom of the self-same community which it has come to replace." Bauman, *Community*, 16.

19. For a useful analysis of the contemporary ethos of sharing, see John, *Age of Sharing*.

20. Bauman, Individualized Society, 14.

21. Eakin, *How Our Lives Become Stories*.

22. See *Oxford English Dictionary*. The word "community" is in Frequency Band 7 (Band 8 contains the most frequently used English words).

23. Farrar, *Struggle for "Community,"* 80, 111, cited in Day, *Community and Everyday Life*, 25.

24. For a comprehensive overview of the idea of community as well as the development of community studies, see Day, *Community and Everyday Life*. See also Delanty, *Community*; and Bessant, *The Relational Fabric of Community*.

25. See Devisch, *Jean-Luc Nancy*; Derrida, *Politics of Friendship*; Nancy, *The Inoperative Community*; Nichols, *The End(s) of Community*; and Esposito, *Communitas*.

26. See Derrida, *Rogues*, 35.

27. As Ignaas Devisch aptly put it, "There can be no reflection on community from a position outside community," meaning that we cannot have a perspective on community because we are always already part of some kind of community (Devisch, *Jean-Luc Nancy*, 73).

28. Moretti, *Distant Reading*.

29. Limiting myself to these three eras and to Western culture means that I ignore other important examples, such as the rich Latin American tradition of testimonio. The genre of testimonio in Latin American literature fosters collective efforts to remember, using eyewitness accounts and other forms of personal storytelling to document socially significant events while also building solidarity among community members. As a native speaker of a non-Indo-European language, I find it important to acknowledge the extent to which Western paradigms have shaped my own thinking about concepts of community, time, space, knowledge, and identity.

30. See Cyca, "Snapchat, Instagram Stories, or Facebook Stories?" Social media companies' "story products" have rendered most of these companies obsolete, although some resist the trend. See José Van Dijck, *Culture of Connectivity*, on the move from "channels for networked communication" (5) to "two-way vehicles for networked sociality" (5). More in chapter 1.

31. See Barney et al., *Participatory Condition*, which seeks to reassess the meaning of participation in the digital age.

32. Miranda, *Against the Romance of Community*, 1.

33. Miranda, *Against the Romance of Community*, 1.

34. Miranda, *Against the Romance of Community*, 2.

35. Nancy, *Inoperative Community*, xxxviii.

36. Nancy, *Inoperative Community*, 35.

1. Towards Collective Intimacy

1. Allex, "Vaughn Allex and Denise Allex," https://storycorps.org/stories/vaughn-allex-and-denise-allex-160909/.

2. As of 2019, "more than 600,000 Americans had participated in recording Story-Corps interviews about their lives." Isay and Sparkman, "Letter from Leadership," StoryCorps website.

3. Persico, "This is my Story."

4. StoryCorps, "Discover StoryCorps," https://storycorps.org/discover/.

5. StoryCorps, "About," https://storycorps.org/about/.

6. StoryCorps, "About."

7. Montaigne, *Complete Essays*, 908.

8. Bretonne, *Monsieur Nicolas*, 24.

9. Gide, *Œuvres complètes*, 453–54, cited in Lejeune, *L'autobiographie en France*, 153.

10. Menchú, *I, Rigoberta Menchú*, 1.

11. Angelou, "Interview with Claudia Tate," 105–6.

12. [Hillers], *Eine Frau in Berlin*, foreword.

13. Miller, *Getting Personal*, x.

14. Miller, *Getting Personal*, xi.

15. Nussbaum, *Autobiographical Subject*, 34.

16. Miller, *Getting Personal*, xiv.

17. Eakin, *How Our Lives Become Stories*, 43–44.

18. McHugh and Komisaruk, "Something Other than Autobiography," viii–ix. See also Monica Orlando ("Double Voicing and Personhood"), who studied double voicing in collaborative life writing about autism, or G. Thomas Couser's study of the ethics of collaborative life writing, "Making, Taking, and Faking Lives," 334–50. See also studies of women's collaborative forms of life writing, such as Culley, *British Women's Life Writing*.

19. Frank, "'Steller Stories.'" The most recent version is available at: https://steller.co/explore.

20. Ha, "Storylane Combats Social Media Glibness."

21. "Storylane Is a Recently Launched Social Media Platform," *StartUp Beat*, https://startupbeat.com/qa-with-storylane-founder-and-ceo-id2023/2812/. Similarly, Steller Stories defined itself in contrast to social media companies and promised "to enable real world communities." Frank, "'Steller Stories.'"

22. Fiegerman, "Facebook Acquires Storytelling Site."

23. The company Storify illustrates this process of integration well. Originally, the service was mostly used by media organizations to generate news stories. With the expansion of social media the range of Storify users also expanded, and the service became popular because users could import content from various social media into their own storylines. By December 2017, however, the company announced that it was shutting down after a series of acquisitions. Digital Rhetoric Collaborative, "Storify," http://webservices.itcs.umich.edu/mediawiki/DigitalRhetoricCollaborative/index.php/Storify.

24. "Instagram Stories Statistics," 99firms blog, https://99firms.com/blog/instagram-stories-statistics.

25. Morrison, "Autobiography in Real Time."

26. Lockshin, "Measure the Effectiveness of Stories."

27. Landwehr and Carley, "Social Media in Disaster Relief," 240.

28. For definitions of "small stories," see Bamberg and Georgakopoulou, "Small Stories."

29. "About," Collective Biographies of Women, University of Virginia, http://cbw.iath.virginia.edu/about.php.

30. Booth, "Prosopography and Crowded Attention," 87.

31. Booth, "Prosopography and Crowded Attention," 88.

32. Booth, "Prosopography and Crowded Attention," 97.

33. Booth, "Prosopography and Crowded Attention," 88

34. Booth, "Prosopography and Crowded Attention," 73. Emphasis added.

35. See Poletti and Rak, *Identity Technologies*, and Lindgren, *Digital Media and Society*.

36. Smith and Watson, *Reading Autobiography*, 168.

37. Poletti, *Stories of the Self*, 58.

38. Poletti, *Stories of the Self*, 19.

39. Wittel, "Toward a Network Sociality."

40. Berlant and Prosser, "Life Writing."

41. Berlant, *Female Complaint*, viii.

42. Berlant, *Female Complaint*, 5.

43. Berlant, *Female Complaint*, vii.

44. In Berlant's definition, "A certain circularity structures an intimate public, therefore: its consumer participants are perceived to be marked by a commonly lived history;

its narratives and things are deemed expressive of that history while also shaping its conventions of belonging; and, expressing the sensational, embodied experience of living as a certain kind of being in the world, it promises also to provide a better experience of social belonging—partly through participation in the relevant commodity culture, and partly because of its revelations about how people can live" (Berlant, *Female Complaint*, viii.). Berlant discusses more specifically the relationship between personal storytelling and intimate publics in Berlant and Prosser, "Life Writing and Intimate Publics."

45. There are a few notable exceptions, including Anna Poletti in *Stories of the Self*; Jeremy Popkin, who studies collections of academics' life stories (Popkin, *Coordinated Lives*); Emma Maguire, who studies self-presentation by girls in digital environments (Maguire, *Girls, Autobiography, Media*); Ioana Luca's work on post-socialist life writing and secret police files (Luca, "Secret Police Files"); studies on collaborative, relational, and serial autobiographies (James and North, *Writing Lives Together*; Chansky, *Auto/Biography in the Americas*); and recent work on collections of migrants' and immigrants' stories (Lenart-Cheng, "Personal Stories in Migration Museums"). See also Gillian Whitlock's work on databases of oral testimony by indigenous Australians (Whitlock, "In the Second Person").

46. Weinman, "How Customer Intimacy Is Evolving."

47. Weinman, *Digital Disciplines*, 181. Weinman goes on to explain: "To derive these insights requires applying sophisticated, processing-intensive algorithms against massive datasets acquired from customers on characteristics, preferences, behaviors, and contexts, such as genetic sequences, movie and music preferences, electric power consumption, and, well, just about anything."

48. Jeff Goldby, "Intimacy in the Age of Everything All at Once," *Fast Company*, https://www.fastcompany.com/3068094/intimacy-in-the-age-of-everything-all-at-once. Emphasis added.

49. Fiegerman, "Share Your Life Story," https://www.ibtimes.com/facebook-acquires-storylane-get-more-personal-1118835. Emphasis added.

50. Harris, "Cowbird," *Number 27* (blog), http://number27.org.

51. "About StoryCorps," https://storycorps.org/about/.

52. Jeffery, "Ushahidi."

53. "About Ushahidi," https://www.ushahidi.com/about.

54. Kurtz, "About participatory narrative inquiry," https://www.workingwithstories.org/aboutpni.html. "PNI focuses on the profound consideration of values, beliefs, feelings, and perspectives through the recounting and interpretation of lived experience. Elements of fact, truth, evidence, opinion, argument, and proof may be used as material for sensemaking in PNI, but they are always used from a perspective and to gain perspective. This focus defines, shapes, and limits the approach." See also Kurtz, "Participatory Narrative Inquiry."

55. Lambert, *Digital Storytelling*.

56. The two are of course related, but there is a difference in emphasis and I will mostly focus here on the latter. In his recent book, Nobel Prize–winning economist Robert Shiller stresses the former when he discusses the role of stories in shaping our understanding of larger economic issues. See Shiller, *Narrative Economics*.

57. Zak, "How Stories Change the Brain." Though Zak's research focuses on the brain and on how "stories bring brains together," his point is that stories engage people on a much more elemental level than just the intellect. He argues that the emotional

connections we form through storytelling are fundamental to the social functioning of our species. This has also been proposed by those who study the evolutionary development of communication. As narratologists point out, the social functions of storytelling are amazingly versatile: stories help build empathy, affirm shared cultural values, co-construct shared identities, enact family relationships, negotiate social positions, socialize younger generations, etc. Due to the interactive nature of storytelling—and on an even more fundamental level, due to the dialogic nature of language—stories allow communities to reason together, to address controversial issues, and to perform collective memory. See Dessalles, *Why We Talk*.

58. Zak, "Good Storytelling," https://hbr.org/2014/10/why-your-brain-loves-good-storytelling.

59. Zak, "Good Storytelling."

60. Zak, "How Stories Change the Brain," https://greatergood.berkeley.edu/article/item/how_stories_change_brain.

61. Terre des hommes (aka Marion Darcissac), "'My Story Is Not Just My Own Story. It's about Thousands of Other Lives,'" Thomas Reuters Foundation News, June 24, 2014, https://news.trust.org/item/20140624125954-hcqwj/.

62. love, rose. "Not Just My Story, My Life (Rape, Sexual Abuse, Ptsd)." YouTube, July 14, 2014. https://www.youtube.com/watch?v=SCgKzRQZh8o.

63. U.S. Mission to the UN (@USUN). "'My story is not just my own . . . it is the story of so many North Korean women & children." Twitter. March 18, 2016, 4:05 p.m. https://twitter.com/USUN/status/710935132312440835.

64. Moth, "The Story Behind the Stories," http://themoth.org/about. Emphasis added. See also the donation prompt on the website of The Moth: "Do you believe in the power of Moth stories to connect us as humans and foster mutual understanding?" See also Moth, "Become a Partner," http://themoth.org/community/get-involved.

65. Moth, "History," https://themoth.org/history.

66. Moth, "Membership Levels," https://themoth.org/support-the-moth/membership-levels /. Emphasis added. See also CBC Radio, "The Moth at 20: How It Helped Spark a Modern Storytelling Movement," June 9, 2017. https://www.cbc.ca/radio/day6/episode-341-comey-s-testimony-things-arab-men-say-the-moth-at-20-come-from-away-at-the-tonys-and-more-1.4151513/the-moth-at-20-how-it-helped-spark-a-modern-storytelling-movement-1.4151663.

67. Moth, "Community," https://themoth.org/community. Emphasis added.

68. Moth, "Community."

69. Storycorps, "About," https://storycorps.org/about/. Emphasis added.

70. Storycorps, "StoryCorps Archive Communities," https://archive.storycorps.org. Emphasis added. The description goes on to explain that "StoryCorps communities are the perfect place to preserve and share your community's voices." StoryCorps is also described as a "new place to spark conversations and share stories with family, friends, neighbors, colleagues and more."

71. StoryCorps, "Storycorps for Hire," https://storycorps.org/participate/host/.

72. Lambert and Faleiros, "International Day." Emphasis added.

73. Valle, "Silence Speaks."

74. "Why Are Personal and Collective Stories Important for Social Transformation?" https://learn.saylor.org/mod/page/view.php?id=28086&forceview=1. Emphasis added.

75. John, *Age of Sharing*.

76. Zuckerberg, "Power to Share," Facebook, https://www.facebook.com/notes/10160195698976729/.

77. Facebook, "Sharing on Facebook," https://developers.facebook.com/docs/sharing/overview/.

78. Constine, "Facebook Changes Mission Statement to 'Bring the World Closer Together,'" *TechCrunch* (blog), June 22, 2017, https://techcrunch.com/2017/06/22/bring-the-world-closer-together/.

79. Zuckerberg, "Building Global Community," Facebook, May 5, 2021. https://www.facebook.com/notes/3707971095882612/. Emphasis added.

80. Constine, "Facebook Changes Mission Statement."

81. Zuckerberg also rewrote the company's mission statement. As seen in the various subtle changes in the company's mission statements made over the years, Facebook has gradually expanded the scope of connections, from classmates (2004 and 2005) to "people around you" (2006), to "people in your life" (2008) and "the world" (2009), before finally embracing the "global community" (2017).

82. Constine, "Stories Are About to Surpass Feed Sharing. Now What?" *TechCrunch*, May 2, 2018. https://social.techcrunch.com/2018/05/02/stories-are-about-to-surpass-feed-sharing-now-what/.

83. Kozlowska, "Facebook Is Pinning Its Future." See also "5 Facebook Stories Statistics For Marketers To Know," June 12, 2018. https://mediakix.com/blog/facebook-stories-statistics-changing-social/. For an insightful analysis of how social media's stories products are changing user engagement and autobiographical self-presentation, see Cardell, Douglas, and Maguire, "'Stories.'"

84. Stampler, "Snapchat," https://time.com/2890073/snapchat-new-feature/.

85. "Snapchat Support," https://support.snapchat.com/en-US/a/our-story. Snapchat was the first.

86. Stampler, "Snapchat." I focus here on Snapchat because it is the most integrated version of collective storytelling, but versions of "community voices" are ubiquitous. See the hundreds of online sites entitled "Community Voices," such as Multicultural Resource Center, "Community Voices," http://www.multiculturalresourcecenter.org/stories; or "Snapchat Enlists 20 Partners to Curate Our Stories from Submissions," *TechCrunch* (blog), September 13, 2018, https://social.techcrunch.com/2018/09/13/snapchat-curated-our-stories/. Oral historians have long embraced the notion of "community voices" and they have developed important ethical guidelines for collective story sharing: "in artistic collaborations with local communities, we should strive that people should speak for themselves, and as often as possible that gatherings of storytellers should be facilitated within the community, by community members, for the general benefit of the community (as opposed to an outside audience)." Lambert, *Digital Storytelling*, 117.

87. "Community Voices' Facebook Page," https://m.facebook.com/CommunityVoices/posts/facebook-stories-is-now-community-voices-welcome-to-our-new-page-facebooks-missi/1595474033824835/. There are many other variations of the "our story" function. For instance, some storytelling platforms use technologies such as SenseMaker (Sensemaker, "Get Sensemaker," https://sensemaker.cognitive-edge.com/), which allows people to relate their personal stories to those of others by tagging them. This is how Globalgiving describes the process: "Using the SenseMaker® methodology of capturing people's stories and asking those people to 'tag' their own stories, we are able to see how thousands of stories relate to each other. We can visualize patterns in the stories that

help us understand how people see organizations working in their communities." Hecklinger, "Globalgiving's Storytelling Project."

88. Danny Kaplan defines "public intimacy" on social network sites in a social sense "as a staged performance of interpersonal ties in front of a third party." He compares users of social media to audience members in an interactive theater and concludes that by displaying their ties to intimate others, the inner circle can draw others into the conversation. As a result, "social media do not necessarily entail a reduction in intimacy but rather a concretization of social relations." I agree with Kaplan that it is useful to "move away from the current focus on the presentation of self in social media to the performance of relationships," although I am more skeptical about the resulting public intimacy. See Kaplan, "Architecture of Collective Intimacy"; "Public Intimacy in Social Media."

89. Simanowski, *Facebook Society*, 51.

90. Bauman, foreword to Beck and Beck-Gernsheim, *Individualization*, xviii. In his criticism in general, Bauman does not single out story-sharing platforms, but he does apply his concept of "peg communities" to communities formed through aesthetic experiences (Bauman, "On Mass, Individuals, and Peg Communities," 111). See also Richard Sennett's critique of vague proposals of "community building" and his views on the "tyranny of intimacy." Sennett, *Fall of Public Man*.

91. Freund, "Under Storytelling's Spell?" See also Simanowski, *Facebook Society*. Simanowski raises similar questions to mine but approaches them from a different angle. Simanowski takes Facebook as a starting point to investigate our social media society, but he is mostly concerned with the consequences of social networking for our understanding of personal identity, whereas I am more interested in its effects on our collective imaginings. For a critique of manipulative uses of storytelling, see Frank, *Letting Stories Breathe*.

92. See also Klein, *Compañeras*.

93. See Zuboff, *Age of Surveillance Capitalism*.

94. For insightful analyses of the circulation, commercialization, and politicization of memoirs, see Rak, *Boom!*, Whitlock, *Soft Weapons*, and Gilmore, *Tainted Witness*.

95. Van Dijck, *Culture of Connectivity*, 10.

96. According to Van Dijck, traditional accounts tend to describe the evolution of the web as a series of conflicts between corporate domination and a communitarian spirit. The problem with this popular version of the history of online sociality is that it pits commerce against community, as if the two were neatly separable domains. Instead, urges Van Dijck, we should pay attention to the complex interaction between the communitarian and the corporate messages. In the chapter "Engineering Sociality in a Culture of Connectivity," Van Dijck explains how the meaning of the term "connectivity" has shifted from its original association with "automated computer transmissions" to the "social capital that people accumulate by being online" (3–23).

97. Van Dijck, *Culture of Connectivity*, 12.

98. Van Dijck, *Culture of Connectivity*, 11.

99. Van Dijck, *Culture of Connectivity*, 16. In 2019, Zuckerberg announced yet another shift, this time from the openness of the "town square" towards the intimacy of the "living room": "For the last 15 years we've built Facebook and Instagram into digital equivalents of the town square, where you can interact with lots of people at once. Now we're focused on building the digital equivalent of the living room, where you can interact in

all the ways you want privately." Note that this new focus on "living rooms" and privacy does not mean that Facebook rescinded its commitment to "building community." The idea is that by now, communities have become like friends in the sense that they, too, have a place in our personal lives: "We have redesigned Facebook to make communities as central as friends." Zuckerberg, "Today at F8," https://www.facebook.com/zuck/posts/10107278677803131.

100. In *Blog Theory*, Dean focused mostly on the blogosphere, but her arguments are also applicable to my wider category of personal story sharing.

101. Dean, *Publicity's Secret*, 151.

102. Dean, *Blog Theory*, 21.

103. Dean, *Blog Theory*, 22.

104. Dean, *Blog Theory*, 3-4.

105. Dean, *Blog Theory*, 95.

106. Dean, *Blog Theory*, 96.

107. Dean, *Blog Theory*, 114.

108. Van Dijck and Nieborg, "Wikinomics and Its Discontents," 856.

109. Dean, *Blog Theory*, 125.

110. Andrejevic, "Watching Television without Pity," 43.

111. McNeill and Zuern, "*Online Lives 2.0*," xx.

112. Jenkins, Ford, and Green, *Spreadable Media*, 174. See also Zizi Papacharissi, ed., *A Networked Self* (Routledge: 2011), as well as Poletti and Rak, eds., *Identity Technologies*, for substantial contributions to the discussion about emerging technologies and the construction of the self.

113. Webber, Johnson, and Lessard, *Storied Communities*, 14. Emphasis added.

114. Webber, Johnson, and Lessard, *Storied Communities*, 13-14. See also Hannah Arendt's views on political theory as storytelling.

115. Manovich, *Language of New Media*, 225.

116. Hayles, *How We Think*, 176.

2. Early Story Collections

1. Cox, *Recovering Literature's Lost Ground*, 11. In *Altered Egos: Authority in American Autobiography*, G. Thomas Couser argues that "autobiography is the literary form, and democracy the political form, most congruent with this idea of a unique and autonomous self." Couser, *Altered Egos*, 13. For a more recent argument tying autobiography to democracy, see Bennett, *Claims of Experience*. Although Bennett introduces the book with a collective act of storytelling, the rest of the book deals with single texts.

2. This questionable dichotomy originated in the work of Ferdinand Tönnies (1887), but the distinction between a more organic community based on immediate relationships and a more abstract kind of sociality based on impersonal ties goes back much further.

3. Thompson, *Voice of the Past*, vi.

4. The full title was *Gnothi Sauton; oder, Magazin zur Erfahrungsseelenkunde als ein Lesebuch für Gelehrte und Ungelehrte* (Know thyself, or, a journal of empirical psychology and a reader for the educated and the uneducated). The original periodical was published by Mylius in Berlin and edited by K. P. Moritz (with K. F. Pockels, 1787-88, and S. Maimon, 1792-93). The collection was reprinted in ten volumes in 1978, with an afterword by Anke Bennholdt-Thomsen and Alfredo Guzzoni. Available in digital format:

https://catalog.hathitrust.org/Record/102455649. Hereafter *Magazin*. The magazine was also republished in 1986 as *Karl Philipp Moritz: Lesebuch. Die Schriften in dreißig Bänden*. Moritz himself published several articles outlining his project. The version that appeared in the journal *Deutsches Museum* is available through the Digital Library of the University of Bielefeld (http://ds.ub.uni-bielefeld.de/viewer/image/1923976_013/501/LOG_0081/). See also Moritz, *Reisen eines Deutschen in England im Jahre 1782*. Hereafter *Reisen*. For insightful analyses of the journal's material, see Gailus, "A Case of Individuality;" Köhnen, "Selbstschrift mit Beobachter"; Davies, "Karl Philipp Moritz's Erfahrrungsseelenkunde;" and Boulby.

5. Moritz, "Vorschlag zu einem Magazin einer Erfahrungsseelenkunde," 489. Author's translations unless otherwise noted.
6. Moritz, "Vorschlag zu einem Magazin einer Erfahrungsseelenkunde," 490.
7. See the table of contents of all ten volumes in *Magazin*, vol. 10, 147–65.
8. Moritz, "Vorschlag zu einem Magazin einer Erfahrungsseelenkunde," 489.
9. Moritz, "Vorschlag zu einem Magazin einer Erfahrungsseelenkunde," 489.
10. Moritz, "Vorschlag zu einem Magazin einer Erfahrungsseelenkunde," 488.
11. Moritz, "Vorschlag zu einem Magazin einer Erfahrungsseelenkunde," 488.
12. Moritz, "Vorschlag zu einem Magazin einer Erfahrungsseelenkunde," 489.
13. Förstl, Angermeyer, and Howard, "Karl Philipp Moritz's Journal."
14. Rousseau, *Reveries of the Solitary Walker*, 33.
15. Köhnen, "Selbstschrift mit Beobachter," 115.
16. Moritz, "Vorschlag zu einem Magazin einer Erfahrungsseelenkunde," 496.
17. This historicizing account contrasting the self-care of ancient traditions to the disciplinary measures of the modern state is arguable. See the section on Foucault and Nietzsche in chapter 6.
18. Franklin, *Autobiography*.
19. Moritz, "Vorschlag zu einem Magazin einer Erfahrungsseelenkunde," 489.
20. Moritz, "Vorschlag zu einem Magazin einer Erfahrungsseelenkunde," 486.
21. Moritz, "Vorschlag zu einem Magazin einer Erfahrungsseelenkunde," 486.
22. Foucault, *Discipline and Punish*, 189–191.
23. *Magazin*, vol. 1, part 1, 2.
24. Moritz, "Vorschlag zu einem Magazin einer Erfahrungsseelenkunde," 489. In volume 4, Moritz began to add brief interpretive essays, and in later years other editors introduced even more analysis.
25. Müller, *Die kranke Seele*, 77, cited in Gailus, "Case of Individuality," 78.
26. Davies, "Karl Philipp Moritz's *Erfahrungsseelenkunde*," 7.
27. Moritz, *Reisen eines Deutschen in England im Jahre 1782*, 98.
28. *Magazin*, vol. 10, *Nachwort* (Afterword), 1.
29. Moritz, "Vorschlag zu einem Magazin einer Erfahrungsseelenkunde," 496.
30. Gailus, "Case of Individuality," 69.
31. Moritz, "Vorschlag zu einem Magazin einer Erfahrungsseelenkunde," 485.
32. *Magazin*, 10, *Nachwort* (Afterword), 42.
33. Herder laid out his views regarding autobiographies in his early "Vom Erkennen und Empfinden der menschlichen Seele: Bemerkungen und Träume" (1778), in his introduction to Müller's "Bekenntnisse merkwürdiger Männer von sich selbst" (1791), in his "Briefen zur Beförderung der Humanität" (1793), and in "Adrastea" (1801–2). See also Herder, *Sämmtliche Werke*, in particular vols. 17, 18, and 23. See also Goodman,

"Autobiographie und deutsche Nation"; and Nübel, "Menschliche Selbstbilder als Seelen- und Gesellschaftsinkarnat: Herder in zivilisationstheoretischer Perspektive."
   34. Goodman, "Autobiographie und deutsche Nation," 261.
   35. In German: *Selbstbiographien berühmter Männer* (David Christoph Seybold, 1796), and *Bekenntnisse merkwürdiger Männer von sich selbst* (Johann Georg Müller, 1793). To my knowledge, the books have not been translated into English.
   36. Herder, *Sämmtliche Werke*, 17:22.
   37. Herder, *Sämmtliche Werke*, 23:224.
   38. Herder, *Sämmtliche Werke*, 24:225.
   39. See Schubart, *Leben und Gesinnungen*.
   40. Herder, *Sämmtliche Werke*, 17:21.
   41. Herder, *Sämmtliche Werke*, 23:229.
   42. Herder also cites Tacitus about history's objective: "This I regard as history's highest function, to let no worthy action be uncommemorated, and to hold out the reprobation of posterity as a terror to evil words and deeds." Herder, *Sämmtliche Werke*, 17:27.
   43. Whitton, "Herder's Critique of the Enlightenment."
   44. Herder, *Sämmtliche Werke*, 4:361.
   45. Weintraub, *Value of the Individual*, 334.
   46. Manuel, Introduction, xv. According to Manuel, Herder saw "the particular as impregnated with the universal, but still [sought] the particular in all its uniqueness" (xi).
   47. Manuel, Introduction, xvii.
   48. Weintraub, *Value of the Individual*, 368.
   49. Hallberg, "The Nature of Collective Individuals," 293. See also Herder's extensive writings on language and his concept of "public of language" (*Publikum der Sprache*).
   50. Herder showed great admiration for Benjamin Franklin's autobiography, and he agreed with the American polymath that life writing was a collective duty. Herder, *Sämmtliche Werke*, 23:231–32. Herder was so inspired by Franklin's community-oriented self-presentation that he set it as a "model" (*Exempel*) to follow. He argued that autobiography should affect the reason by offering an "instructive model" (*lehrendes Exempel*). Herder, *Sämmtliche Werke*, 8:181. Autobiography should become a matter of "practical accountability" (*praktische Rechenschaft*) for both the individual and their community, argued Herder.
   51. Herder, *Sämmtliche Werke*, 17:22.
   52. Herder, *Sämmtliche Werke*, 24:226.
   53. Herder, *Sämmtliche Werke*, 24:226.
   54. Herder, *Sämmtliche Werke*, 23:221–26.
   55. Herder, *Sämmtliche Werke*, 23:226.
   56. Herder, *Sämmtliche Werke*, 17:25.
   57. Herder, *Sämmtliche Werke*, 24:227. Herder's references to national stereotypes in these passages are slightly misleading; for example, he calls French autobiographers "vain", the English "glitzy" (Herder, *Sämmtliche Werke*, 18:17.), since his other remarks make it clear that he is less interested in how autobiographers reflect national stereotypes than in how they shape them.
   58. Herder, *Sämmtliche Werke*, 23:229.
   59. Many have commented on Herder's complex and paradoxical views on nationalism, for while he hated Prussian nationalism he actively promoted the idea of cultural nationalism and a German *Volk*.

60. Barnard, *Herder's Social and Political Thought*, xix.

61. Herder, *Sämmtliche Werke*, 17:27.

62. For a more in-depth discussion of Herder's understanding of the *Publikum* see La Vopa, "Herder's Publikum."

63. The idea itself was not new, as French kings had relied on various forms of popular consultation since the thirteenth century. The first surveys were conducted by Louis IX in 1247–70, and by the sixteenth century, it was common practice to collect such *cahiers* in preparation for the Estates General. The extent in which these *cahiers* contributed to the downfall of the regime is of course debatable, and it would be wrong to insist on a direct correlation.

64. Zaretsky, "Old Regime."

65. The tradition of *cahiers de doléances* continues today. In 2018, in response to the growing dissatisfaction expressed by the movement of the *gilets jaunes* (yellow vests), French president Emmanuel Macron asked for a compilation of *cahiers* from across the country. More precisely, it was local leaders who issued the call for putting together lists of grievances, and Macron responded by addressing them in what he called a "great national debate." Citizens in about five thousand communities used this opportunity to express their private and shared concerns, which were compiled and made public. Association des Maires Ruraux de France, "Doléances et propositions collectées." https://www.amrf.fr/wp-content/uploads/sites/46/2019/01/Synth%C3%A8se-Globale-V2.pdf.

66. Moritz, "Vorschlag zu einem Magazin einer Erfahrungsseelenkunde," 490.

67. Herder, *Sämmtliche Werke*, 18:375.

68. Latour, "Search for Political Heteronomy," 2.

69. Latour, "Search for Political Heteronomy," 2–3.

70. Latour, "Search for Political Heteronomy," 2.

71. See Derrida on the undecidability created by the rhetorical "we" in "we the people," which is simultaneously both performative, in the sense that the community comes into being by making a promise, and constative, in that it draws on the authority of a preexisting community that can vouch for those who make the promise. Derrida, "Declarations of Independence."

72. See Meijers, "Collective Speech Acts," 93–112.

73. Habermas, *Structural Transformation*, 27.

74. Dean, *Publicity's Secret*, 151. Dean is critical of this fantasy.

75. La Vopa, "Herder's *Publikum*," 15. The flourishing publishing industry of the eighteenth century created a paradoxical situation. On the one hand, print offered a means of emancipation, a tool to lift people out of specific contexts and power relationships, allowing them to form independent opinions and to connect to each other more freely, outside traditional hierarchies. On the other hand, mass circulation turned books into standardized commodities which created abstract, self-referential worlds that isolated people from each other. Print isolated and connected people at the same time, and this was also true in the case of memoirs.

76. Habermas, "Further Reflections." Habermas has been heavily critiqued for focusing only on the male, bourgeois public and for positing a single, exclusionary, homogenizing "public sphere." Later, in "Further Reflections on the Public Sphere" (1992) Habermas conceded that at any given time, multiple public spheres coexist, but the role of publics in political emancipation remains a contested issue.

77. Culley, *British Women's Life Writing*, 204. See also Nussbaum, *The Autobiographical Subject;* Coleman, *Women's Life Writing.* Similarly, abolitionists in the nineteenth century used autobiographies by former slaves to counter sceptics (in the years following the Civil War, at least fifty full-length memoirs were published), and although the individual narratives of Harriet Jacobs or Solomon Northup were convincing enough in their own right, one could argue that it was the aggregate effect of their collective autobiographical efforts that made the difference.

3. Libraries of Human Experience

1. StoryCorps, "About StoryCorps."
2. Jimenez, "Is Your Organization Losing."
3. "StoryCorps Archive," https://archive.storycorps.org. The full collection is housed at the American Folklife Center at the Library of Congress, and StoryCorps partners with local institutions to ensure local access to its collections. The company also developed an online archiving platform, The StoryCorps Archive, which serves as a resource for people wishing to access or research the stories.
4. Cowbird, "About," http://cowbird.com/about/.
5. Cowbird, "FAQ," http://cowbird.com/faq/.
6. Preston, "Pull Up a Mouse."
7. Memory of Mankind, "Home," https://www.memory-of-mankind.com/.
8. Gray, "World's Knowledge."
9. September 11 Digital Archive, "Home," https://911digitalarchive.org/.; Statue of Liberty & Ellis Island, "A Record of Living Memory," https://www.statueofliberty.org/discover/stories-and-oral-histories/; Memory Project, "Compilations," http://memoryproject.online/installation/. I selected these examples at random from thousands of story collections available online.
10. Personal History, "Personal History," http://www.personalhistory.org/.
11. Wende, King, and Schwabe, "Exploring Storytelling."
12. Dilthey, *Gesammelte Schriften,* 107. See also Lenart-Cheng, "Wilhelm Dilthey's Views on Autobiography."
13. Niglas, "Combining Quantitative and Qualitative Approaches."
14. Oral History Association, "Oral History" https://www.oralhistory.org/about/do-oral-history/.
15. As Paul Thompson argues, oral history was in fact "the *first* kind of history" (emphasis added). Thompson, *Voice of the Past,* 23. The irony is that the professionalization of the science of history in the nineteenth century led to oral history being temporarily devalued. Oral sources were dismissed for their lack of objectivity, while written documents were celebrated for their scientific value. The field developed rapidly in the twentieth century.
16. Born in Slavery: Slave Narratives from the Federal Writers' Project, 1936 to 1938, Library of Congress Digital Collection, https://www.loc.gov/collections/slave-narratives-from-the-federal-writers-project-1936-to-1938/about-this-collection/. See also Federal Writers' Project and Regional Staff, *These Are Our Lives.*
17. Thomas and Znaniecki, "Introduction," 6–7. Emphasis added.
18. Lebow, "Autobiography as Complaint," 14.
19. Lebow, "Autobiography as Complaint," 17.
20. Warkentin, "Writing Competitions."

21. Bohman, "Formal Pragmatics and Social Criticism."
22. Gullestad, "The Intimacy of Anonymity," 51. Contests usually involved a prize, a jury, and a possibility of publication. Organizers published two volumes from the material of this particular contest. For a list of other initiatives in various countries, see Thompson, *Voice of the Past*, 66–76.
23. Abel himself was a Polish immigrant and published a review of Znaniecki's *The Polish Peasant in Europe and America*.
24. Abel, *Nazi Movement*, 2.
25. Abel, *Nazi Movement*. The 1934 call may be viewed at: https://oac.cdlib.org/findaid/ark:/13030/tf3489n5vz/.
26. Abel's collection can be found in the Hoover Institution Library & Archives, "Newly Digitized Nazi Biograms," https://www.hoover.org/news/newly-digitized-nazi-biograms-now-available. Hereafter cited as Hoover. The Hoover Institution has digitized most of the materials related to Abel's contest, including the submissions and Abel's notes on the contest. The text of the call for contributions in the Hoover Archive is missing the first line and the last paragraph; I added those lines from Abel, *Nazi Movement*, 3, where the whole text is included. The 1966 edition contains two introductions, the original introduction that appeared in the first edition in 1938 (cited below as "old introduction") and a new introduction (cited as "new introduction"). The new introduction has no pagination, so I simply counted the pages.
27. Abel, new introduction, *Nazi Movement*, 4.
28. Abel, new introduction *Nazi Movement*, 5.
29. Parts I and II of Abel's book discuss the history of the Nazi movement and the factors that contributed to its growth. He also published six of the stories in full in Part III, adding that "their reproduction in full [was] intended to supplement the illustrative material used in the historical and analytical parts." Abel, old introduction, *Nazi Movement*, 9.
30. Abel, new introduction, *Nazi Movement*, 5.
31. Abel, new introduction, *Nazi Movement*, 5.
32. Allport et al., "Personality under Social Catastrophe" includes the English version of the call. Here, however, I have provided my own translation.
33. The call appeared in the *New York Times, Pariser Tageblatt, Gelbe Post Shanghai*, etc. Although Allport et al.'s project had several coauthors, I tend to refer to the contest as Allport et al.'s because he was the most active proponent of this project and method.
34. Allport et al., "Personality under Social Catastrophe," 1.
35. For a guide to the manuscript collection, see Liebersohn and Schneider, "My Life in Germany."
36. Despite the striking similarities, to my knowledge the two contests have never been studied together, nor has their connection been traced to Znaniecki's Polish contests or to other similar initiatives.
37. Hesse-Biber, "Qualitative Approaches to Mixed Methods," 1.
38. Abel, call for papers, Hoover.
39. Allport et al., call for papers.
40. Allport et al. were more demanding: "No manuscript will be accepted if it does not state clearly on the first page the following information," whereas Abel only asked that "special attention should be given to . . ." and then he himself collected that data.

41. Abel, call for papers. "Style, spelling, or dramatic story value will not be considered.... so that even the simplest and most undramatic story will receive full consideration"; "Even if you have never written before, . . . you should try."

42. Abel, *Nazi Movement*, 7.

43. "He is male, in his early thirties, a town resident of lower middle-class origin, without high school education; married and Protestant; . . . His economic status was secure, for not once did he have to change his occupation, job, or residence, nor was he ever unemployed." Abel, old introduction, *Nazi Movement*, 6. Abel gathered data on "education, employment, membership in various associations, place of residence, marital status, wartime service, participation in military activities after the war [World War I], first contacts with the [National Socialist] movement, the main reason for joining it, expressions of anti-Semitism, and so forth." Abel, *Nazi Movement*, 5.

44. It is one thing to anonymize the findings (Abel, call for papers) and another thing to accept anonymous submissions (Allport et al., call for papers).

45. In the 1966 edition, Abel began to stress the public utility of his findings. In the new introduction, he generalized his results to argue that the three key factors he identified in the rise of Nazism would also be applicable to other sociopolitical movements: the "interpretive framework [used to analyze the rise of Nazism] can be used in evaluating the chances of success of an incipient or ongoing social movement." Abel, new introduction, *Nazi Movement*, 1. He even mentioned "the current Civil Rights Movement in the United States" to highlight how his study of biograms could be "of considerable practical value." Abel, new introduction, *Nazi Movement*, 2.

46. Soyer, "Documenting Immigrant Lives," 226.

47. Soyer, "Documenting Immigrant Lives," 227.

48. Soyer, "Documenting Immigrant Lives," 227. For a statistical analysis of the contestants' gender, nationality, language, age, etc., see Soyer, "Documenting Immigrant Lives," 227. For more information about the contest see also Cohen and Soyer, *My Future Is in America*, which includes nine stories, chosen from over two hundred entries, translated from Yiddish into English.

49. YIVO was an Eastern European institute that relocated to New York. Already in the 1930s, YIVO had sponsored several memoir contests in Poland, and later it organized several others in the US. See, for instance, "Autobiographies of Polish-Jewish Youth in the 1930s." http://epyc.yivo.org/content/6_1.php.

50. Soyer, "Documenting Immigrant Lives," 220.

51. Soyer, "Documenting Immigrant Lives," 221.

52. Weinreich, *Der YIVO in a Yor Fun Umkum*, 9–10. Cited in Soyer, "Documenting Immigrant Lives," 222.

53. Soyer, "Documenting Immigrant Lives," 221.

54. Harrisson, Jennings, and Madge, "Anthropology at Home," cited in Sheridan, *Writing Ourselves*, 24.

55. Harrisson, Jennings, and Madge, "Anthropology at Home."

56. Harrisson, Jennings, and Madge, "Anthropology at Home."

57. Sheridan, Street, and Bloome, *Writing Ourselves*, 33.

58. Sheridan, Street, and Bloome, *Writing Ourselves*, 35.

59. Mass Observation, "Collaborating on Research," http://www.massobs.org.uk/the-archive/collaborating-on-research.

60. Mass Observation, "Mass Observation, 1937–1950s," http://www.massobs.org.uk/mass-observation-1937-1950s. See also MOA's *May the 12th Diary* project, chapter 4, http://www.massobs.org.uk/write-for-us/12th-may.

61. Harrisson, "The Future of Sociology," 24.

62. Sheridan, Street, and Bloome, *Writing Ourselves*, 34. The founders of MOA were committed to a hybrid approach, insisting that the observers were both objects and subjects. As Charles Madge and Tom Harrisson explained: "We did not regard these people as being themselves scientists studying the mass, nor did we consider them as being a random sample of public opinion. Their position was something different. They were observers, untrained but shrewd, placed at vantage points for seeing and describing in their own simple language what life looks like in the various environments which go to make up England" (cited in Sheridan, Street, and Bloome, *Writing Ourselves*, 34). The original purpose of MOA was to bring anthropology home (Sheridan, Street, and Bloome, *Writing Ourselves*, 79) by developing an "anthropology of our own people" (Geoffrey Pyke, cited in Sheridan, Street, and Bloome, *Writing Ourselves*, 25).

63. Madge, "The Birth of Mass-Observation," 1356.

64. Sheridan, Street, and Bloome, *Writing Ourselves*.

65. Elborough, *Our History of the 20th Century;* "Publisher Description: Our History as Told in Diaries." https://books.apple.com/us/book/our-history-of-the-20th-century/id1287962393.

66. Harrisson, Jennings, and Madge, "Anthropology at Home," 155.

67. *Memoir,* "2018 #METOO Nonfiction Essay Contest," April 16, 2018, https://memoirmag.com/nonfiction/the-2019-metoo-trigger-warning-nonfiction-essay-contest-win-500-publication/. Some contemporary memoir contests are open to all and aim at discovering new writing talents; others address themselves to certain segments of society (such as immigrants, women, or seniors).

68. This measure of protection is important in all of these cases, because storytellers are invited to discuss experiences that are taboo, censured, or repressed. See Poletti, "Intimate Economies," for a useful discussion of contemporary practices of anonymous confession, including the project Postsecret.

69. One could argue that this is a return to the approach in the original Polish contests, many of which had a strong social justice element.

70. "Being able to put that out into the world was a powerful experience. You've created an amazing, almost sacred, space." Evan T., "Cowbird Press," http://cowbird.com/press/.

71. Mark K., "Cowbird Press," http://cowbird.com/press/.

72. "Experience Project was a free social networking website consisting of various online communities. It operated from 2007 until 2016, when it announced it would suspend new registrations indefinitely. Members submitted 'experiences'—their personal, first-person stories about various life experiences they had. Users could then form or join communities based on these experiences and/or interests, and interact with other members who shared them. As of May 2016, the site had over sixty-seven million of these 'experiences.'" "Experience Project," last Modified January 29, 2021, https://en.wikipedia.org/wiki/Experience_Project.

73. To add a few more examples, the story project of the US Holocaust Memorial Museum encourages "all survivors to share their unique *experiences* to ensure their preservation for future generations," while the Archive of Immigrant Voices underscores

the priority of each individual migrant's personal understanding of their own experience. They collect "stories of the *experience* of migration . . . as immigrants, asylum-seekers, refugees, and other newcomers themselves understood it" (emphasis added). The emerging genre of "body story," promoted by the body positivity movement, illustrates in a literal fashion the centrality of the notion of experience and embodiment in story collections. As the website Be Nourished explains, a body story is "the story of your body as you experience it. It is the story about what it has meant to live in your body.... Create the story you want to tell. We'd love to hear your body story in your own words, or images, or however you want to tell it." Be Nourished, "Explore Your Body Story," https://benourished.org/body-story-archive/.

74. Experience Project, "Until We Meet Again . . . ," March 21, 2016, https://web.archive.org/web/20180217102800/www.experienceproject.com/until-we-meet-again.

75. "Immigrant Women Storytelling Group With The Moth," https://www.nywomenimmigrants.org/immigrant-women-storytelling-group-with-the-moth/.

76. Suicide Call Back Service, "Lived Experience Storytelling Can Help"; Crazy Wild Film, "Stories of Lived Experience," https://www.suicidecallbackservice.org.au/mental-health/understand-how-lived-experience-storytelling-can-help-your-mental-health/; Prevent. Support. Heal., "Lived Experiences," http://preventsupportheal.org.au/lived-experiences/.

77. marmello, "The Coronavirus Days: Archive Your Story," August 24, 2020, https://libraries.indiana.edu/coronavirus-days-archive-story.

78. Walsh, "Filmmaker Claudia Stack."

79. Empathy Museum, "A Mile in My Shoes," https://www.empathymuseum.com/a-mile-in-my-shoes/.

80. "Empathy museums" offering immersive encounters with others' stories are increasingly popular. See, for example, The Empathy Museum (https://www.empathymuseum.com) or the Virtual Empathy Museum (https://theempathyinitiative.org/virtual-empathy-museum).

81. Humanity House, "Museum," https://www.empathymuseum.com/a-mile-in-my-shoes/. As libraries, archives, and museums converge, they are referred to as LAMs.

82. Weller, "Libraries of the Future."

83. Empathy Museum, "Human Library," https://www.empathymuseum.com/human-library/.

84. Empathy Museum, "Human Library." Historians sometimes talk about people as "living documents." The celebrated nineteenth-century historian Jules Michelet, for instance, called people "personal documents." Thompson, *Voice of the Past*, 23.

85. Human Library, "About the Human Library," https://humanlibrary.org/about/.

86. Human Library, "Get Published," https://humanlibrary.org/meet-our-human-books/get-published/.

87. Lorentzen, "Deafblind."

88. Human Library, "Welcome to the Human Library," https://humanlibrary.org/.

89. Nakamura, "Feeling Good about Feeling Bad."

90. Nakamura, "Feeling Good about Feeling Bad," 49.

91. Nakamura, "Feeling Good about Feeling Bad," 51.

92. Nakamura, "Feeling Good about Feeling Bad," 53.

93. "Her Story: Our Story," *Seattle Times*, https://projects.seattletimes.com/2019/her-story-our-story/.

94. Nakamura, "Feeling Good about Feeling Bad," 53.
95. Nakamura, "Feeling Good about Feeling Bad," 53.
96. Harris, "Back to Life."
97. Cowbird, "About."
98. "Interview with Vincent Mosco about His New Book," by Rory Litwin. Litwin Books & Library Juice Press, June 14, 2014, https://litwinbooks.com/interview-with-vincent-mosco-about-his-new-book/.
99. *Stanford Encyclopedia of Philosophy*, s.v. "Scientific Research and Big Data," by Sabina Leonelli, https://plato.stanford.edu/archives/sum2020/entries/science-big-data/. See the difference between representational versus relational views of data. The advantage of the relational view, in the context of story data, is that highlights the history of data, including questions of curation, interpretation and impact.
100. Mosco, "Interview with Vincent Mosco."
101. See also Fuchs, *Social Media*.

4. To-Gather in Time

1. For an excellent discussion of the changing, contemporary uses of diary-writing, see Cardell, *Dear World*.
2. Daniel M. Gold, "Movie Review; One Day on Earth," *New York Times*, June 1, 2012, https://query.nytimes.com/gst/fullpage.html?res=9E00E5DF1631F932A35755C0A9649D8B63.
3. Ruddick, "One Day on Earth."
4. BBC, *Britain in a Day*, https://www.bbc.co.uk/programmes/p00kqz5p.
5. Reilly and Wrenn, "Just One Day"; "Global Photo Exhibit Captures a Day in Life of World," *Reuters* (blog), October 9, 2012, https://www.reuters.com/article/us-exhibition-aday-photographs-idUSBRE8970ZW20121009.
6. Fabricius, Klaus, Red Saunders, Wanda Coleman, and Jeff Spurrier, eds. *24 Hours in the Life of Los Angeles*. New York: Alfred van der Marck Editions, 1984.
7. On July 25, 2020, in the midst of the global pandemic, 324,000 people sent in videos from 192 countries in 65 languages. By *Life in a Day* I will be mostly referring to the 2010 version (https://www.youtube.com/watch?v=JaFVr_cJJIY), but many of my comments are equally relevant to the 2020 version. For the 2020 sequel, see *Life in a Day 2020*, https://www.youtube.com/watch?v=vcsSc2iksCo. In addition, both films and the archives are available at https://www.youtube.com/user/lifeinaday/experience. *Life in a Day 2020* premiered at the Sundance Film Festival in February 2021, and the film had more than fifteen million views in the first three months. Viewers continue to access the 2010 film and the archive as well.
8. Partridge, "Life in a Day."
9. Angela Watercutter, "*Life in a Day* Distills Forty-Five Hundred Hours of Intimate Video into Urgent Documentary," *Underwire* (blog), *Wired*, July 29, 2011, https://www.wired.com/2011/07/life-in-a-day-interviews/. Includes an interview with Kevin Macdonald and Joe Walker.
10. Christopher Brian, "One Year Later," accessed November 18, 2012, www.youtube.com/user/lifeinaday/experience.
11. Ian Buckwalter, "'Another Earth,' 'Life in a Day,' and 'Cowboys and Aliens': Movie Tickets." *After Hours* (blog), *Washingtonian*, August 3, 2011, www.washingtonian.com

/blogs/afterhours/film/another-earth-life-in-a-day-and-cowboys-aliens-movie-tickets.php.

12. Liz Braun, "'Life in a Day' a Free Wheeling Look at Human Events," *Toronto Sun*, July 29, 2011, www.torontosun.com/2011/07/28/life-in-a-day-a-free-wheeling-look-at-human-events.

13. *The Cozyhunter* (blog), "Life in a Day," July 19, 2011, cozyhunter.com/musings/life-in-a-day.

14. Watercutter, "Life in a Day."

15. Betsy Sharkey. Review of *Life in a Day*. *Los Angeles Times*, July 29, 2011, articles.latimes.com/2011/jul/29/entertainment/la-et-life-in-a-day-20110729.

16. "Life in a Day Trailer," *National Geographic*, 2011, https://www.youtube.com/watch?v=bT_UmBHMYzg.

17. "Film Review: Life in a Day (2011)," *Thoughts of a SteelMonster* (blog), November 6, 2011, https://thoughtsofasteelmonster.blogspot.com/2011/11/film-review-life-in-day-2011.html.

18. MacDonald, quoted in "Life in a Day: About the Production. A Discussion with the Director and the Editor," *National Geographic Online*, accessed February 3, 2017, http://movies.nationalgeographic.com/movies/life-in-a-day/about-the-production/.

19. Dodes, "'Life in a Day' Director." Macdonald credited Jennings's Mass Observation Archive with providing him the inspiration.

20. Gorky, cited in Chernikova, "September 27—A Day of the World." I am grateful to Mary Rees for helping me translate parts of *Den Mira*.

21. Cited in Chernikova, Chernikova, "September 27—A Day of the World."

22. Gorky, Introduction, *Den Mira*, 5. My translation.

23. Published on September 15, 1936. For more information about the project, see Sung-chiao, "One Day in China." I am grateful to Caly Wei for translating this article for me. See also Laughlin, *Chinese Reportage*, 158–59.

24. Cochran, Hsieh, and Cochran, *One Day in China*, App. A. 266–67.

25. Cochran, Hsieh, and Cochran, 272.

26. Cochran, Hsieh, and Cochran, 276. The editors of the English edition also celebrated the value of diverse perspectives and personal reflections: "in our judgment [the project's] ultimate significance lies in the perspectives provided not by scholars but by the contributors and their subjects." Cochran, Hsieh, and Cochran, xxi. "As insiders writing or speaking for insiders [participants] provide views from the inside: not abstract analyses, but personal reactions and intimate insights. They express themselves in a variety of styles—formal and casual, elegant and crude, flowery and straightforward, pretentious and earthy—but almost all seem to base what they say on their own direct observations of daily life in China." Cochran, Hsieh, and Cochran, xxii.

27. Cochran, Hsieh, and Cochran, *One Day in China*, 276.

28. Cochran, Hsieh, and Cochran, xvii. Charles A. Laughlin calls them "collectively written piece[s] of reportage."

29. Jennings and Madge, *May the Twelfth*. Preface. First sentence.

30. Compiled from the stories of "over two hundred" observers, the crowdsourced diary vividly portrays the story of a single day in Britain. Like Gorky and Mao Dun, the organizers of *May the Twelfth* prized the experience of the "man in the street." See chapter 3 for more information on the Mass Observation Archive.

31. The idea also resonated with individual writers. Inspired by Gorky's call, French writer André Gide contributed his own reminiscences about September 27, 1935. Also, East Germany's celebrated writer, Christa Wolf, was so inspired by the second Soviet call that she recorded every single 27th of September for fifty years in a longitudinal diary (*One Day a Year 1960–2000* and *One Day a Year: 2001–2011*). And poet Thomas Brasch dedicated an entire poem to the beauty of the 27th of September: "Der schöne 27. September." Planet Lyrik, January 12, 2011, http://www.planetlyrik.de/thomas-brasch-der-schone-27-september/2011/01/. Despite the clear connections between these various one-day projects, they have never been studied in relation to each other.

32. Mass Observation, "Wednesday 12th May 2021: Would you like to keep a one-day diary for Mass Observation?" http://www.massobs.org.uk/write-for-us/12th-may.

33. See also Wolfe, *Governing Soviet Journalism*, 49–50. As Yulia Chernikova observed, in the 1935 version "there is room for uncertainty and surprise in the face of the ordinary and mundane even in one's own country (in 1960 the world was totally reduced to the leading articles of Soviet newspapers)." Chernikova, "Uroki Istorii," http://urokiistorii.ru/en/taxonomy/term/1295/2805. The 1961 editors also added an interview with the Soviet leader Nikita Khrushchev about his own 27th of September.

34. Gorky, quoted by Koltsov, in Cochran, Hsieh, and Cochran, *One Day in China*, xv.

35. Cochran, Hsieh, and Cochran, *One Day in China*, 266. As Mao Dun noted, *One Day in China* may represent a single day only, but the validity of its truths and observations "is not confined only to this one day!" (Cochran, Hsieh, and Cochran, *One Day in China*, 276.) According to the director of *Life in a Day*, they, too, purposely chose a historically insignificant, random day: "The date was chosen fairly quickly. It was a date that fell after the FIFA World Cup and early enough in the summer not to lose too many contributors to their holidays. The date, July 24, was also a Saturday—a day when it was felt many people could devote more time to the project."

36. Whitrow, *Natural Philosophy of Time*, 224. My understanding of the concept of simultaneity is based on Whitrow and Jammer.

37. In Greek, the word *hama* means "togetherness" in several different senses. Aristotle, for instance, uses it to refer to logical, natural, spatial, and temporal togetherness. See Jammer, *Concepts of Simultaneity*, 35.

38. Whitrow, *Natural Philosophy of Time*, 224.

39. CBS News, "Study: 'Time' Is Most Often Used Noun," June 22, 2006, https://www.cbsnews.com/news/study-time-is-most-often-used-noun/. See also Burdick, *Why Time Flies*, and Campbell, O'Rourke, and Silverstein, eds., *Time and Identity*.

40. The connection between time and identity counts among the most perplexing philosophical problems, and the apparent familiarity of these two words only makes them more difficult to work with. Narratologists and philosophers have developed rich theories to explain the connection between time and narratives. See, among others, Ricoeur, *Time and Narrative*.

41. Greenhouse, "Moment's Notice," 19–48.

42. Newton, cited in Scheffel, Weixler, and Werner, "Time."

43. Fabian, *Time and the Other*, 144.

44. Fabian, *Time and the Other*, xii.

45. Einstein and Bergson did debate the concept of simultaneity, though not directly. Bergson's reflections on Einstein were published under the title *Duration and Simultaneity*, but apparently Bergson did not authorize any new editions of the book because he

was worried that his limited understanding of mathematics may have prevented him from fully grasping Einstein's arguments. Meanwhile, Einstein conceded that while physics had no use for the idea of "now," "the experience of the Now meant something special for man." Einstein, cited in Jammer, *Concepts of Simultaneity*, 14.

46. Bergson, *Duration and Simultaneity*, 52.
47. Anderson, *Imagined Communities*, 24.
48. Anderson, *Imagined Communities*, 26.
49. Macdonald and Walker both used the expression "time-capsule" to describe their project.
50. Partridge, "Life in a Day."
51. Cochran, Hsieh, and Cochran, *One Day in China*, 274.
52. Editors also used this image for ideological purposes, to contrast the communist and the capitalist worldviews.
53. Watercutter, "Life in a Day." To record their experiences, some contributors used their cellphones, while others used professional quality HD cameras.
54. One could argue that video as a temporal medium is inherently incapable of projecting synchronicity. Still, there are techniques to mitigate this condition.
55. Parallel editing—a form of crosscutting technique that creates a parallel narrative—is effective in creating a sense of simultaneity. However, editors of *Life in a Day* had to use it sparingly, since too much parallel editing would have suggested a storyline and narrative continuity, which they sought to avoid.
56. Eisenstein, *Film Form*, 49.
57. Bergson, *Duration and Simultaneity*, 52.
58. Bergson was concerned with the extension of the present into a continuous duration. As Wittgenstein clarified, "the function of the word 'now' is entirely different from that of a specification of time" (Jammer, *Concepts of Simultaneity*, 14.), since the adverb "now" (just like the pronoun "I") is inseparable from the concrete, situated speaker who utters it.
59. The only section to referentially anchor the film *Life in a Day* is a three-minute section focusing on the tragedy of the stampede at the 2010 Love Parade in Germany. This brief passage is significant in that it is the only instance in the film where the official news–version of an event is allowed to momentarily overwrite the individual views.
60. Cochran, Hsieh, and Cochran, *One Day in China*, 266.
61. I focus here mostly on the 2010 film version of *Life in a Day*, but organizers also made the collection available in the form of an online archive. Since the structure of the online archive allows for individual, non-synchronized access, this mode of access automatically disperses the homogenous time of the edited film. Organizers also added a special editing tool to the archive, which allows viewers to remix footage from the original trailer and some of the best clips into new, individualized sequences.
62. Bergson, *Duration and Simultaneity*.
63. Whitrow, *Natural Philosophy of Time*, 35.
64. Fink, Eugen. *Zur ontologischen Frühgeschichte*.
65. Fink, *Zur ontologischen Frühgeschichte von Raum*, 138. My translation. Einstein rejected the idea of a universal simultaneity. He argued that distant simultaneity was a relative (or frame-dependent) concept, because "two events that are simultaneous when observed from some particular coordinate system can no longer be considered simultaneous when observed form a system that is moving relative to that system." Einstein,

cited in Jammer, *Concepts of Simultaneity*, 118. Bergson, on the other hand, maintained that Einstein's thesis was actually anti-relativistic, because Einstein's observer does not know, but only assumes, that the other observer experiences a different simultaneity. Yet, although Bergson did promote "mankind's natural belief in a unique and universal time" (Bergson, *Duration and Simultaneity*, 107), he did not posit the idea of a universal simultaneity. Bergson's preoccupation with multiplicity would clearly undermine Fink's notion of a unified Here and Now. See Boven, "Review of Simultaneity and Delay."

66. Harootunian, *History's Disquiet*, 4.

67. "The individual being attains his or her present presence ('here and now'—hic et nunc), therefore, from the society he or she belongs to, as a result of that society's temporalizing the individual being, giving to him or her a temporal structure which ensures a presence in the world now (in the present)." Scott, *Gilbert Simondon's Psychic and Collective Individuation*, 126.

68. Joe Walker: "They're all gems, and I'd have loved that to have been in the film but the truth is, and Kevin is right, his view on it was that it wasn't representative of the world enough, and there wasn't enough material from the third world to be able to kind of like, take it out there, it felt like it resolutely wanted to say a thing about white middle class teenage boys playing drums, which is what it sort of was!" Bradley, Porter, "Interview Joe Walker: Life in a Day Editor," *Eat Sleep Live Film* (blog), June 28, 2011, http://www.eatsleeplivefilm.com/interview-joe-walker-life-in-a-day-editor/.

69. Goodman, "Filmmaker."

70. Bhabha, *Location of Culture*, 208.

71. Bloch, "Nonsynchronism and Obligation to Dialectics," 22–38.

72. Bloch developed his theory of non-simultaneity as a reaction against orthodox Marxist theories of development.

73. *Life in a Day*, for instance, was advertised as a documentation of "what it was like to be alive on the 24th of July 2010."

74. Lampert, *Simultaneity and Delay*, 226.

75. A recent attempt to articulate a non-absolute theory of simultaneity comes from the Canadian philosopher Jay Lampert. In *Simultaneity and Delay: A Dialectical Theory of Staggered Time*, Lampert describes simultaneity in terms of its dialectic with delay. Inspired by Derrida's and Deleuze's rehabilitation of "delay," Lampert concludes: "total synchronization is impossible—it is delayed. Delay is not an epistemic aporia; it is the real structure of temporality. Simultaneity is always being actualized, but only in its delay-forms." Lampert, *Simultaneity and Delay*, 1. This emphasis on the ongoing "actualization" of simultaneity echoes Bloch in that it stresses the experimental potential of simultaneity. To apply Lampert's comment about arts to the realm of politics: "simultaneity and delay . . . are not parameters that limit what can or should be done but fields of experimentation with time as the sensible realm." Lampert, *Simultaneity and Delay*, 226.

76. Bloch, "Nonsynchronism and Obligation to Dialectics," 22.

77. See Rushkoff, *Present Shock*.

78. Greenhouse, "Time, Life and Society."

5. To-Gather in Space

1. Denis Wood, "Mapping," *This American Life*, NPR, episode 110, aired September, 4, 1998, http://www.thisamericanlife.org/radio-archives/episode/110/transcript.

2. This includes social media, where personal storytelling is part of social and content strategy.

3. For a useful introduction to the concept and history of story mapping, see Caquard and Cartwright, "Narrative Cartography."

4. "Mapping Sexual Violence," http://mapping-sexual-violence.appspot.com/.

5. Ramirez, "'Ushahidi' Technology Saves Lives"; Stephens and Richards, "Story Mapping and Sea Level Rise."

6. For a similar "real time" mapping project see Waag, "Amsterdam Real Time," https://waag.org/en/project/amsterdam-realtime. For more examples, see Lenart-Cheng, "Mapping Lives across Borders."

7. "Stories of Our City," Accessed January 28, 2021, https://www.storiesofourcity.org/.

8. Botkin, *Sidewalks of America*, 1.

9. White, *Here Is New York*, 22.

10. See also the long-standing column of the *New York Times*, "Metropolitan Diary" (https://www.nytimes.com/column/metropolitan-diary), and more recently the popular blog *City Room*, which have provided New Yorkers with a forum to share their "typical New York" stories. The film *Subway Stories: Tales from the Underground* (1997) was also a crowdsourced collection.

11. Lepore, "Joe Gould's Teeth." Gould thought of himself as the Walt Whitman of oral history, and he called his magnum opus "The Oral History of Our Time."

12. Milgram et al., "Psychological Map of New York City," 8, 89.

13. Milgram et al., "Psychological Map of New York City," 197. The first to use the idea of mental mapping was Kevin Lynch in *The Image of the City* (1960). This personalized approach to mapping is seeing its renaissance in today's "smart city" movement, which uses advanced crowdsourcing, gaming, and mapping technologies to create "sensory maps" and to quantify the livability and recognizability of cities. See Quercia et al., "Psychological Maps 2.0."

14. In *Poetics of Space*, Gaston Bachelard offered a phenomenological reading of how we familiarize spaces through poetic imagination. To quote Bachelard, "Space that has been seized upon by the imagination cannot remain indifferent space subject to the measures and estimates of the surveyor. It has been lived in, not in its positivity, but with all the partiality of the imagination" (Bachelard, *Poetics of Space*, xxxi-xxxii). This phenomenological approach was later extended to study the familiarization of urban spaces and the role that narratives play in "owning" space.

15. mapyourmemories, "Map Your Memories," Tumblr, https://mapyourmemories.tumblr.com/mappingmanhattan. The maps have also been published in book format, and Cooper has expanded the project to other cities as well, such as London and Istanbul. See Cooper, *Mapping Manhattan*.

16. Bachelard, *Poetics of Space*, xxxi–xxxii.

17. Tuan, *Space and Place*, 387.

18. Tuan, *Space and Place*, back cover. The idea of "place" is central to all collective story-maps. #places is also a popular hashtag for millions of pictures shared daily on social media, and it is common for story-sharing projects to invite people to write "love letters" to their favorite places. Tuan's dichotomy of place and space is based on other classic dichotomies such as subjectivity/objectivity, internal/external, and community/society; as such, it has been critiqued by both Marxist scholars, who called for a dialectical treatment of space and place, and by postmodern critics, who deconstructed it.

19. Crotty, "Story Mapping Challenge."

20. Barthes, "Semiology and the Urban." The city, according to Michel de Certeau, is that "most immoderate of human texts" (de Certeau, *Practice of Everyday Life*, 2), and this trope remains popular to this day. Semioticians read the city as a text to be read (Duncan, *City as Text*), with its own syntax, units, grammar, and vocabulary. The challenge is to lift the statement "the city is a discourse" out of its metaphoricity, which is why it is useful to combine urban semiotics with disciplines that highlight the material and social aspects of producing space.

21. The term "spatial turn" designates an increased interest in spatiality across all disciplines, starting in the 1960s. Up until then, due to the overemphasis on history and temporality, space was often treated as "dead" or "flat," as a neutral and inactive "thing" underlying social reality. To "enliven" space, scholars in the 1960s began to highlight the important role that space plays in shaping human relations. See Lefebvre's triad of perceived, conceived, and lived space in *Production of Space*, Soja's notion of thirdspace in *Thirdspace*, Foucault's concept of heterotopia in "Of Other Spaces," bell hooks' notion of margins as a "space of radical openness" in "Choosing the Margin," Bhabha's "hybridity" in *Location of Culture*, and Massey's concept of "lively space" in *For Space*.

22. Following the spatial turn, narrativity was increasingly associated with spatiality as scholars recognized the crucial role that storytelling and poetic imagination play in shaping our personal and collective relation to places. The first to draw attention to the spatial implications of our concepts of selfhood were feminist scholars who contrasted the private spaces of women's autobiographical narratives to the more public scenery of men's memoirs. This dualist model was soon superseded by arguments that pointed to the porosity of the private-public domains and to the importance of the interstitial spaces that characterize all forms of life writing. Today, autobiographical storytelling is often associated with spatial metaphors such as "personal topology," "safe spaces," "self-mapping," etc.

23. Newtown Creek Alliance, "Creek Speak," http://www.newtowncreekalliance.org/community-health/creek-speak/.

24. mapyourmemories, "Map Your Memories," Tumblr, https://mapyourmemories.tumblr.com/mappingmanhattan. "City of Memory," docubase, 2008, https://docubase.mit.edu/project/city-of-memory/. Emphasis added.

25. Cooper, *Mapping Manhattan*, 14. Emotions were also foregrounded when Cooper partnered with the city to display some of the story maps at LinkNYC kiosks throughout the city: "We know that all New Yorkers have *strong feelings about the boroughs they call home.* Becky Cooper put those thoughts and memories on paper and this new partnership allows us to expand their reach and bring them to the streets of NYC!" Emphasis added. "Map Your NYC Memories with LinkNYC," March 18, 2019, https://www1.nyc.gov/site/doitt/about/press-releases/map-your-nyc-memories-with-linknyc.page. Note the dynamic feedback mechanism whereby people create story maps which are then shared with other New Yorkers as they move through the city.

26. Stanton, "Humans of New York: About," Humans of New York, https://www.humansofnewyork.com/about.

27. Stanton, *Humans of New York,* introduction.

28. "Humans of New York: A Photographic Census," *Curious Fridays* (blog), June 8, 2012, https://curiousfridays.wordpress.com/2012/06/08/humans-of-new-york-a-photographic-census/. This 2012 version of the HONY map comes from the website

curiousfridays, which links back to this site: http://www.humansofnewyork.com/the-map/, but the original link no longer works. Stanton described this early version of the map as follows: "This map contains approximately 1,500 street portraits collected from the island of Manhattan. The portraits are separated into the neighborhoods from which they were gathered. I've also included casual, non-academic descriptions of these neighborhoods. These are not to be taken seriously. The big red dots denote 'Points of Interest' such as parks and museums. These are clickable. There are also nearly 50 stories of people I've met during my journey. These stories seem to be concentrated in the public parks. The map is constantly evolving, and new portraits will be added as they are collected. That's about it. Click away." https://curiousfridays.wordpress.com/2012/06/08/humans-of-new-york-a-photographic-census/#jp-carousel-5914. In later versions of the blog, the map was relegated to a secondary role. This was likely due to the structure of Facebook, which favors "timelines" and chronological searches over spatial arrangement. More recently, the global spread of HONY has again shifted this balance back towards spatiality, as seen in the blog's most recent structure, which arranges portraits into Stories, Countries, and Series.

29. "Watch people from all walks of life tell stories of life, love, and everything else in between." "Filmed over four years. Taken from 1200 interviews. New York City. One Story at a time." Humans of New York, Facebook, https://www.facebook.com/humansofnewyork/.

30. D'Addario, "Problem with Humans of New York."

31. City of Memory, "Map," http://www.cityofmemory.org/map/index.php.

32. "_City of Memory," _docubase, 2008, https://docubase.mit.edu/project/city-of-memory/. City of Memory distinguishes between two different types of stories based on their origin: "stories curated by City Lore" (a nonprofit organization dedicated to studying the cultural heritage of the city) are marked with orange, while "stories uploaded by users" are marked with blue dots on the map. City of Memory also offers curated "tours" which link several geographic points together to form an associative story, such as "Painting Brooklyn Stories" or "Haiti in New York." For instance, the tour called "Nuyorican Poet's Café" has the owner of the café give a "tour of the neighborhood, and the places that were part of the café's history," in addition to linking it to poem by Miguel Pinero, and inviting visitors to print the map of the tour which contains the addresses. Visitors can also sign up via the website for "customized walking tours based on the virtual excursion." http://www.cityofmemory.org:8080/media/pdf/pdf_1647_1.pdf.

33. Solnit and Jelly-Schapiro, *Nonstop Metropolis*, 1.

34. Popova, "Nonstop Metropolis." Emphasis added.

35. New York Public Library, "Community Oral History Project," https://wayback.archive-it.org/14173/20200910171016/http://oralhistory.nypl.org/. Since 2016, the collection has also been available in audio format through the program Voices of NYC, which showcases dozens of "the extraordinary stories that have been shared by New Yorkers." "Voices of NYC," New York Public Library, May 1, 2016, https://www.nypl.org/blog/2016/04/30/voices-of-nyc.

36. The others are either thematic or identity-based, such as the Latino Americans Memory Circles; the New York City Veterans project, which "record[s] the personal accounts of American war veterans in neighborhoods around the city"; or Visible Lives, which collects the stories of people living with disabilities.

37. The archive contains the unedited transcripts of all the interviews, and it is searchable using keywords. The library even organizes "transcription parties" for volunteers to incentivize the transcription process.

38. Little, "Real Humans of New York."

39. Rachel Dobson, "Humans of New York: A Big City Reclaims Its Community through Visual Storytelling," Resource Media, November 10, 2014, https://www.resource-media.org/humans-of-new-york-a-big-city-reclaims-its-community-through-visual-storytelling/.

40. Dobson, "Humans of New York." This article published on the Resource Media website presents HONY as an act of "reclaiming community": "A big city reclaims its community through visual storytelling." This is a good example of how the two arguments overlap, how story sharing is praised both for "developing" and for "restoring" a sense of community.

41. For more on urban social movements, grassroots organization, and the relationship between geography, capital and politics, see Harvey, Social Justice and the City.

42. Fusco, "Questioning the Frame."

43. D'Addario, "Problem With Humans of New York"; Humans of New York, "Are You Lonely?," https://www.humansofnewyork.com/post/91968870121/are-you-lonely-its-been-a-lifetime-of.

44. Lefebvre, *Production of Space*, 27–30. To further explain this three-dimensional processing of space, Lefebvre also used the triad of "perceived," "conceived," and "lived" space, which loosely corresponds to the above-mentioned triad in that "perceived space" is materialized, empirical space; "conceived space" is the idealized and ideological space that has been ordered and designed by those who conceptualize space; while "lived space" is the space of users who invest space with social dimensions.

45. Soja, *Thirdspace*, 79–80.

46. Queer geographers using GIS technologies were among the first to point to the "productive tensions" arising out of the confrontation between queer theory and the "norming fixity inherent in cartographic representation." See Brown and Knopp, "Queering the Map," 40.

47. "Voices of NYC," New York Public Library, May 1, 2016, https://www.nypl.org/blog/2016/04/30/voices-of-nyc. Similarly, Creek Speak's purpose is "to highlight and document the experiential knowledge of individuals." Newtown Creek Alliance, "Creek Speak," http://www.newtowncreekalliance.org/community-health/creek-speak/.

48. Newtown Creek Alliance, "Creek Speak."

49. Harley, "Deconstructing the Map."

50. Smith and Katz, "Grounding Metaphor," 69.

51. Brown and Knopp, "Queering the Map," 40.

52. "Humans of New York: A Photographic Census," *Curious Fridays* (blog), June 8, 2012, https://curiousfridays.wordpress.com/2012/06/08/humans-of-new-york-a-photographic-census/.

53. "Humans of New York: A Photographic Census."

54. "Abdou Karim Samb," New York Public Library, http://transcribe.oralhistory.nypl.org/transcripts/abdou-karim-samb-8qc7wy.

55. De Certeau, *Practice of Everyday Life*, 115.

56. De Certeau, *Practice of Everyday Life*, 120.

57. De Certeau, *Practice of Everyday Life*, 129.
58. De Certeau, *Practice of Everyday Life*, 120.
59. Kitchin and Dodge, "Rethinking Maps," cited in Kitchin, Gleeson, and Dodge, "Unfolding Mapping Practices," 481.
60. Schmidt and Xia, "Invisible Cities." For insightful analyses of the spatial self, social media, and public spaces, see Raz Schwartz.
61. Schmidt and Xia, "Invisible Cities." 1.
62. Schmidt and Xia, "Invisible Cities." 1.
63. "Revealing Social Networks in Cities: Invisible Cities," Schema Design, https://www.schemadesign.com/work/invisible-cities.
64. Schmidt and Xia, "Invisible Cities." 3.
65. Many of these dynamic collective story mapping projects are still in an experimental phase. For instance, another project with the same name, Invisible Cities, which is from Australia, describes itself as a "participatory art project exploring the relationships between people and place. It maps the memories held in sites around the city, and it explores the cities we each hold in our minds." Invisible Cities, "About Invisible Cities," http://invisiblecities.com.au/. Invisible Cities uses push notifications to unlock the embedded audio stories when users are at the site; however, the extent and spontaneity of these communal conversations is rather limited for now, since stories cannot be recorded automatically.
66. Map Your City, "A Map Where Explorers and Storytellers Meet," https://mapyour.city/.
67. There are, for instance, exciting new therapeutic and communicative strategies of self-mapping, such as the practice of "life-mapping" in which individuals create narrative maps of their lives to review past events and to plan for the future, or "body mapping," which uses people's visual representations of their bodies to tell their stories. However, as practitioners and scholars embrace phenomenology to play up the role that affect, embodiment, and experience have in neoliberal processes of subjectivation, we should keep in mind that the relationship between "mapping space" and "mapping ourselves" through narratives is never an either/or relation.
68. Doreen Massey warned already in the nineties that the unexamined use of spatial imagery risks again depoliticizing the concept of space. The unexamined use of spatial imagery has become even more common since the birth of the internet, social networks, and database technologies—all of which are spatial terms. I agree with Massey that the seeming dynamism of our new technologies and vocabularies betrays a disturbing comfort with the old tradition that imagines space as dead and flat.
69. Cooper and Priestnall, "Processual Intertextuality of Literary Cartographies," 253. The authors only apply their new concept to fictional works, but it is equally, if not more relevant to autobiographical narratives.
70. Mapping for Rights, "Participatory Mapping," https://www.mappingforrights.org/participatory-mapping/.

6. Stories and Statistics

1. Haggerty and Ericson, "Surveillant Assemblage."
2. McFarland, "Ethical Implications." See also Gordon, "Mining Commonsense Knowledge."

3. Gaiman qualifies his statement by adding, "but even that is a lie, for the people continue to suffer in numbers that themselves are numbing and meaningless." Gaiman, *American Gods*, 252.

4. Narrative Nation, "We're Shifting the Narrative of Health Disparities by Changing the Narrator," https://wewriteus.org/.

5. Narrative Nation, "Shifting the Narrative."

6. Narrative Nation, "Our Narrative Shifting Projects," https://wewriteus.org/the-irth-app. Designed as a "consumer application to capture and share experiences of bias," Irth encourages users to "Share Your Story. Find a hospital or doctor review from someone just like you. Be in the know!"

7. Booth, "Prosopography and Crowded Attention."

8. Stone, "Prosopography," 46, cited in Booth, "Prosopography and Crowded Attention," 89.

9. Verboven, Carlier, and Dumolyn, "A Short Manual," 37. Prosopography was revived in the 1970s, thanks to the popularity of microhistory, and more recently due to developments in computing and database technologies. For group analyses applied to autobiographical literature, see Popkin, "Coordinated Lives"; and Couser, "Making, Taking, and Faking Lives." Given the recent development of new text-mining methods in the digital humanities, prosopographies based on autobiographical narratives are likely to emerge.

10. Bruss paraphrases Virginia Woolf: "all one can do is to herd books into groups . . . and thus we get English literature into A B C; one, two, three; and lose all sense of what it's about." Bruss, *Autobiographical Acts*, 1.

11. Bruss, *Autobiographical Acts*, 1.

12. Georg Misch published *Geschichte der Autobiographie* (*The History of Autobiography*) in 1907.

13. Burr, *Autobiography*, 12.

14. Burr, *Autobiography*, 24.

15. Burr, *Autobiography*, 12.

16. Burr, *Autobiography*, 288.

17. Burr, *Autobiography*, 172.

18. Burr, *Autobiography*, 177.

19. Burr, *Autobiography*, 174.

20. Burr, *Autobiography*, 174.

21. Burr, *Autobiography*, 231.

22. Burr, *Autobiography*, 208.

23. Burr, *Autobiography*, 205.

24. Burr, *Autobiography*, 205.

25. Bates, *Inside Out*, 14. Bates explains his categories by pointing to the basic functions of life: "As regards the promised explanation as to why the particular kinds of persons who appear in the following chapters have been chosen, to the exclusion, of course, of others who may seem to have equal claims, it may be added that another idea also plays a part, the idea, namely, that human life consists mainly of four elements, Eating, Drinking, Sleeping and Prayer." Bates, *Inside Out*, 322.

26. Le Bon, *The Crowd*.

27. Burr, *Autobiography*, 174–75.

28. Online Etymology Dictionary, "Account," https://www.etymonline.com/word/account.

29. Rettberg, *Seeing Ourselves through Technology*, 10.

30. Medieval annals recorded the history of a community year by year, sometimes only listing the years. See White, *Content of the Form*, 8. Some entries included very short comments, such as "709. Hard winter. Duke Gottfried died. 710. Hard year and deficient in crops." White, *Content of the Form*, 6.

31. See his famous list of thirteen virtues in "Chapter 9: Plan for Attaining Moral Perfection," which he tracked daily throughout life, originally published in 1882. Benjamin Franklin, Autobiography of Benjamin Franklin, ed. Frank Woodworth Pine, Project Gutenberg, released December 28, 2006, ebook #20203, https://www.gutenberg.org/files/20203/20203-h/20203-h.htm#IX.

32. These examples come mostly from British literature, but the phenomenon is not limited to this tradition. See Marcus, *Auto/biographical Discourses*.

33. Wells, *Experiment in Autobiography*, 419.
34. Wells, *Experiment in Autobiography*, 670.
35. Wells, *Experiment in Autobiography*, 31.
36. Wells, *Experiment in Autobiography*, 37.
37. Wells, *Experiment in Autobiography*, 143.
38. Wells, *Experiment in Autobiography*, 133.
39. Wells, *Experiment in Autobiography*, 133.
40. Wells, *Experiment in Autobiography*, 467.
41. Wells, *Experiment in Autobiography*, 218. Emphasis added.
42. Wells, *Experiment in Autobiography*, 43.
43. Wells, *Experiment in Autobiography*, 47.
44. Wells, *Experiment in Autobiography*, 134–35.

45. Holst, "Wearable Technology." The definition of these terms is evolving, but most agree that lifelogging is distinct from self-tracking in that the former implies the specific practice of wearing cameras, sensors, and other computerized devices to automatically capture data over a certain period of time, whereas the latter covers a wider range of tracking practices. I use "self-tracking" as an umbrella term here. The question about how to interpret the connection between the number of people owning self-tracking devices or apps and the number of those who actually engage in self-tracking is also up for debate. Wolf and Ramirez, "How Many People Self-Track?" For lists of available apps, see the Quantified Self website and the website, Personal Informatics. For an extensive review of the variety of self-tracking devices and uses ,see Lupton, "Know Thyself," Quantified Self. For an insightful analysis of the history of Quantified Self and its relationship to diary-writing, see Rettberg, *Seeing Ourselves through Technology*.

46. Grant, "QS17 Preview." Emphasis added. Some Quantified Self apps were built specifically to emphasize the narrative component of self-tracking. For instance, the apps The Autobiographer, Narrative, and Ethnographer encourage users to chronicle everyday life, often by using a tiny camera to record everything that a self-tracker sees in a day, which then takes the form of a chronological story. Also, many self-trackers supplement their metric results with narrative reflection, either by constructing a story for audiences at Quantified Self gatherings, or through more traditional means, such as diary-writing.

47. Davis, "Qualified Self."
48. Boam and Webb, "Qualified Self." See also Humphreys, *Qualified Self*. Humphreys focuses more on the role of media in documenting daily life than on the distinction between quantitative and qualitative self-reflection.

49. Boam and Webb, "Qualified Self."

50. Chen et al., "Scribe," 3.

51. Wolf, "Are Self-Trackers Narcissists?"; Ames, Rose, and Anderson, "NPI-16."

52. Although single-subject research has a relatively long tradition, especially in fields such as behavioral analysis, special education, and counseling, it is often frowned upon by the scientific community for its lack of scientific rigor. See Gartenberg, cited in Carmichael, "Daniel Gartenberg." To respond to these charges, the Quantified Self community founded a journal: *N-of-1: The Journal of the Quantified Self.*

53. Craig William O'Brien, "I Am Not Running an n = 1 Study" (comment), Quantified Self, August 25, 2012, https://forum.quantifiedself.com/t/are-there-any-de-facto-standard-formats-for-common-auto-analytics-data/408/6. As Steven Jonas commented on a recent self-tracking experiment: "Would this work for you? Possibly not, but that's not the point. It is an excellent example of a person building a solution that is specifically designed for his personality, and also how meaning can be found in the unlikeliest of datasets." Jonas, "Abe Gong."

54. Solove, "Information-Age Privacy Concerns."

55. Wolf, "What Is the Quantified Self?"

56. Nafus and Sherman, "This One Does Not Go Up to 11."

57. Martijn de Groot argues that instead of adhering to a simplistic "me" versus "them" model, we should distinguish between four different modes of self-quantification: (1) the Quantified Self meaning "the gathering of personal data for and by you"; (2) the Quantified Us, meaning "when you start sharing your data online and other self-trackers share their data as well"; (3) the Quantified Other, which refers to the situation when "someone tells you 'Here you go, here is a sensor, I want you to go measure this so I can see how You are doing"; and (4) Citizen Science, where "citizens collect data for science." de Groot, "Quantified Self."

58. Carmichael, "Daniel Gartenberg," https://quantifiedself.com/blog/daniel-gartenberg-the-role-of-qs-in-scientific-discovery/. See, for instance, CureTogether, which is now part of 23andMe (https://www.23andme.com/?evr=epv). "CureTogether brings people together to track and compare their health data, to better understand their bodies and work toward cures." Crunchbase, "CureTogether," https://www.crunchbase.com/organization/curetogether.

59. Jordan and Pfarr, "Quantified Us."

60. Jordan and Pfarr, "Quantified Us." Note the ambiguity of the pronoun "we" in this passage.

61. Wells, *Experiment in Autobiography*, 242.

62. The etymology of the word "aggregate" (c. 1400) points to the Latin *aggretatus*, meaning "brought together" (literally "added to the flock"), while the intransitive meaning referring to the act of "coming together in a mass or group" did not arise until the nineteenth century. Online Etymology Dictionary, "aggregate," https://www.etymonline.com/word/aggregate.

63. Nietzsche uses the "creative etymology" of the German word *Mensch* (human being), attributing it to the Latin *mensurare* (measure), to argue that man is a "valuating animal" who tries to "calculate value." He writes: "Perhaps our word 'Mensch' (*manas*) still expresses just something of *this* self-pride: man denoted himself as the being who measures values, who values and measures, as the 'assessing' animal *par excellence*." Nietzsche, *Genealogy of Morals*, 45.

64. McFarland, "Ethical Implications of Data Aggregation."
65. Foucault, *Discipline and Punish*, 202.
66. Foucault, *Discipline and Punish*, 202.
67. Ban, "People Cannot Be Reduced."
68. D'Ignazio and Klein, *Data Feminism*, 17–18.
69. D'Ignazio and Klein, *Data Feminism*, 287n30.
70. Kleinreesink, *On Military Memoirs*, 60–61. The author herself published a military memoir.
71. Kleinreesink, *On Military Memoirs*, 125.
72. Kleinreesink, *On Military Memoirs*, 126.
73. Kleinreesink, *On Military Memoirs*, 282.
74. Kleinreesink, *On Military Memoirs*, 282.
75. The conclusion of the sentiment analysis seems particularly troubling as framed by this summary: "Remarkably, memoirs of soldiers who have served in Afghanistan often have a positive tone of voice. Merely 39 percent of the autobiographies has a plot that is characterised by d[i]sillusion," according to PhD research conducted by lieutenant colonel Esmeralda Kleinreesink. "Esmeralda Kleinreesink Wins Caforio Award for Dissertation on Experiences of Soldiers in Afghanistan," July 4, 2017. https://www.eur.nl/en/news/esmeralda-kleinreesink-wins-caforio-award-dissertation-experiences-soldiers-afghanistan.
76. D'Ignazio and Klein, *Data Feminism*, 160.
77. Igo traces the history of social surveys from the origins of statistics, when a "science of the state" was first designed to enhance effective and efficient governing, through nineteenth-century prescriptive trends which focused on deviancy, all the way to the twentieth century, when the birth of the social sciences brought on a whole new era in statistical sampling. In the process, the target audience was completely transformed. Whereas in earlier centuries, the findings of surveys and censuses were reserved for scientists and technocrats only, in the twentieth century the same people who were surveyed became the consumers of this information. While some protested against the "reduction" of their lives to numbers, others proudly embraced their new status as "average Americans." As Igo notes: "Being studied, and being privy to the results, is an understood and unexceptional feature of modern life. It is perhaps the principal way that we know ourselves to be part of a national community." Igo, *Averaged American*. 3. See also chapter 3 in this book about the target audience of memoir contests.
78. Igo, *Averaged American*, 285.
79. Wolf, "Data-Driven Life." Emphasis added.

Postscript

1. Covid-19 is "the first worldwide digitally witnessed pandemic, a test case for the making of global memory in the new media ecology." Erll, "Afterword," 867.
2. Crosby, *America's Forgotten Pandemic*.
3. Noah Y. Kim, "How the 1918 Pandemic Frayed Social Bonds," *Atlantic*, March 31, 2020, https://www.theatlantic.com/family/archive/2020/03/coronavirus-loneliness-and-mistrust-1918-flu-pandemic-quarantine/609163/.
4. Pandemic Journaling Project, "Home," April 8, 2020, https://pandemic-journaling-project.chip.uconn.edu/. In terms of access, a few Covid story archives were only

accessible to researchers or qualified users, while others provided instant access to "featured entries" or to the entire collection.

5. "Covid Diaries NYC," HBO, https://www.hbo.com/documentaries/covid-diaries-nyc.

6. "Film Discussion: #AfterLockdown: Very Short Stories About Enduring a Global Pandemic," https://worldwide.harvard.edu/event/film-discussion-afterlockdown-very-short-stories-about-enduring-global-pandemic.

7. "Pandemic Chronotope / The Firebird Fairy-Tale," http://firebirdtale.rocks/. As Fedorova explains, traditional fairytales represent the world's order, and in a pandemic people are desperately in need of shared narratives, so she "tailored" the Covid experiences people submitted to her website into magical elements and a single plot. For instance, the heroes have to use squirrels and birds to deliver packages to each other because of a dark, unknown force and they have to ride on horseback through the empty city to a healer, etc.

8. Covid-19 Memory Archival Project, "About the COVID-19 Memory Archival Project," April 27, 2020. https://storymaps.arcgis.com/stories/aa9bbd66da8c4c19bd75d08ce69b838f.

9. Carey, "Right Now Feels So Long."

10. WKYC Staff, "Many People Turning to Social Media." Emphasis added.

11. The philologically accurate etymology of the word "community" is *com-munis* ("together-obliged," referring to a joint ownership and responsibility).

12. Nierenberg, "Quarantine Diaries."

13. Süddeutsche Zeitung, "Wie geht es Uns?," https://projekte.sueddeutsche.de/artikel/politik/corona-krise-kollektives-tagebuch-e684784/.

14. Barbetta, "#Coronamaison, the Challenge."

15. Coronamaison, "#Coronamaison," https://coronamaison.fun/.

16. For instance, Facebook encouraged its businesses to use the Stories product to stay connected to their customers through the pandemic, arguing that "Stories' real-time, authentic nature can help humanize your brand, drive entertaining engagement and garner support for your business. See below for a few tips on how to use Stories during this challenging time." Facebook for Business, "How to Stay Connected Through Stories," April 23, 2020, https://www.facebook.com/business/news/how-to-stay-connected-through-stories. See also the intense debates about governments' access to personal data, including stories, during the pandemic.

17. Wang and Tsoi, "Fang Fang." There are many reasons for silences in story archives, including immigration status.

18. McBride, *Collective Dreams*, 116.

19. "One World: Together at Home" was the name of the concert series in which celebrities performed from the intimacy of their homes to support frontline healthcare workers.

20. See Jenkins, Ford, and Green, *Spreadable Media*. For a related phenomenon, see the "privacy paradox."

21. Dean, *Blog Theory*, 91–126.

22. Debord, *Society of the Spectacle*.

23. Dean, *Blog Theory*, 111.

24. Dean, *Blog Theory*, 111.

25. See also Butler, *Giving an Account of Oneself,* for a performative understanding of living in community.
26. Nancy, *Being Singular Plural,* 66.
27. Nancy, *Being Singular Plural,* 66.
28. See Husserl's transcendental intersubjectivity and solidarity.
29. Nancy, *Being Singular Plural,* 67.
30. Nancy, *Being Singular Plural,* 51.
31. Nancy, *Being Singular Plural,* 72.
32. Nancy, *Being Singular Plural,* 68.
33. For instance, when Rousseau described the scene of a village community gathering around a tree which it had planted as its own symbol, he was promoting the "good" kind of spectacle in which a community converges at the altar of its own togetherness.
34. Nancy, *Being Singular Plural,* 73.
35. Nancy, *Inoperative Community,* xxxviii.
36. Miami Theory Collective, *Community.* To simplify a bit, Western philosophical tradition has conceptualized community in two ways. The first, "organicist" view presupposes community as a common depth, as a shared origin from which subjects come into their social being (Hobbes). This organicist idea of community as oneness is reflected in the unofficial etymology of the word "community," explained as *com-unus* ("together-one"). The second view is rooted in the philologically more accurate etymology of the word "community" as *com-munis* ("together-obliged," referring to a joint ownership and responsibility). Community here is understood as an association, whose members come together freely to form a community (Rousseau).
37. Nancy, *Being Singular Plural,* 38.
38. Nancy, "The Confronted Community," 32.
39. I have used the expression "with-nessing" before in my coauthored article, Lenart-Cheng and Luca, "Memories in Dialogue." Trying to avoid the misleading connotations associated with the word "community," Nancy often used the terms "sharing" [*partage*] and "co-appearance" instead. The word "sharing" can of course still be misleading if we assume that sharing will result in the reconstitution of some previously existing unity. To avoid this impression, Nancy illustrates his peculiar notion of "sharing" with the following grammatically twisted expression: "you *shares* me" [*toi partage moi*] (Nancy, *Inoperative Community,* 29), that is, you and I are neither internally fused nor externally juxtaposed, but simply *co-ex-posed.*
40. Nancy, *Being Singular Plural,* 71.
41. Nancy, *Being Singular Plural,* 71.
42. This is how Roberto Esposito formulated this state of openness or co-exposure, echoing Nancy: "It is when every meaning that is already given, arranged in a frame of meaningful reference, goes missing that the meaning of the world as such is made visible, turned inside out, without enjoying a reference to any transcendental meaning. The community isn't anything else except the border and the point of transit between this immense devastation of meaning and the necessity that every singularity, every event, every fragment of existence makes sense in itself. Community refers to the singular and plural characteristic of an existence free from every meaning that is presumed, imposed, or postponed; of a world reduced to itself that is capable of simply being what it is: a planetary world without direction, without any cardinal points. In other words,

a nothing-other-than-world. It is this nothing held in common that is the world that joins us [*accomunarci*] in the condition of exposure to the most unyielding absence of meaning and simultaneously to that opening to a meaning that still remains unthought." Esposito, *Communitas*, 149.

43. Poletti, *Stories of the Self*, 58.

44. Smith and Schaffer, *Human Rights and Narrated Lives*.

45. Booth, "Prosopography and Crowded Attention," 97.

46. Booth, "Prosopography and Crowded Attention," 97.

47. Booth, "Prosopography and Crowded Attention," 88.

48. Iaconesi and Persico, "Algorithmic Autobiography." The authors ask: "What happens when non-human and algorithmic subjects/entities come into play, increasing the complexity of our interactions and influencing the process of construction and perception of the self?" Iaconesi and Persico are also the creators of Angel-F, the first fictional child artificial intelligence.

49. Iaconesi and Persico, "Writing an Autobiography."

50. Streaming Egos exhibit, Dusseldorf, 2016.

51. Iaconesi and Persico, "Algorithmic Autobiography."

52. Stephanie Dinkins, *Not the Only One,* https://www.stephaniedinkins.com/ntoo.html.

53. Stephanie Dinkins, "Not the Only One," https://www.stephaniedinkins.com/ntoo.html.

54. Dinkins, "HRI 2020 Keynote: Stephanie Dinkins—Community, Art and the Vernacular in Technological Ecosystems," ACM Special Interest Group on Computer-Human Interaction, April 6, 2020, https://www.youtube.com/watch?v=oVqL7FGMyTI. Passage referenced occurs at 6:40.

55. Stephanie Dinkins, "Not the Only One," https://www.stephaniedinkins.com/ntoo.html.

56. Stephanie Dinkins, "Not the Only One," https://www.stephaniedinkins.com/ntoo.html.

57. See also Dinkins's other project, Secret Garden, which is an interactive installation where listeners' movements trigger audio excerpts of personal stories, but the stories are not attached to images of specific storytellers; rather, "all the women wear all the stories." Dinkins encourages people to "listen congregationally." Dinkins, "Secret Garden: An Immersive Web Experience Created by Stephanie Dinkins," https://www.onx.studio/secret-garden.

BIBLIOGRAPHY

Abel, Theodore. *The Nazi Movement: Why Hitler Came to Power*. New York: Atherton Press, 1966.
Adzhubei, Aleksai, ed. *Den Mira*. Moscow: Izvestiia, 1961.
Allport, G. W., J. S. Bruner, and E. M. Jandorf. "Personality under Social Catastrophe: Ninety Life-Histories of the Nazi Revolution." *Journal of Personality* 10, no. 1 (September 1, 1941): 1–22.
Alsaleh, Asaad. *Voices of the Arab Spring: Personal Stories from the Arab Revolutions*. New York: Columbia University Press, 2015.
Ames, Daniel, Paul Rose, and Cameron Anderson. "The NPI-16 as a Short Measure of Narcissism." *Journal of Research in Personality* 40 (2006): 440–50.
Anderson, Benedict. *Imagined Communities: Reflections on the Origin and Spread of Nationalism*. Rev. and extended ed. London: Verso, 1991.
Andrejevic, Mark. "Watching Television without Pity: The Productivity of Online Fans." *Television & New Media* 9, no. 1 (January 1, 2008): 24–46.
Angelou, Maya. "Interview with Claudia Tate." In *Maya Angelou's "I Know Why the Caged Bird Sings": A Casebook*, edited by Joanne M. Braxton, 149–58. Oxford University Press, 1999.
Association des Maires Ruraux de France. "La parole aux citoyens." Doléances et propositions collectées par les maires ruraux de France. January 14, 2019. https://www.amrf.fr/wp-content/uploads/sites/46/2019/01/Synth%C3%A8se-Globale-V2.pdf.
Bachelard, Gaston. *The Poetics of Space*. Boston: Beacon Press, 1969.
Bamberg, Michael, and Alexandra Georgakopoulou. "Small Stories as a New Perspective in Narrative and Identity Analysis." *Text & Talk* 28, no. 3 (May 27, 2008): 377–96.
Ban Ki-moon. "People Cannot Be Reduced to Mere Numbers, Secretary-General Tells Commission on Population and Development, while Stressing Vital Need for Data Analysis." United Nations, April 11, 2016, https://www.un.org/press/en/2016/sgsm17661.doc.htm.

Barad, Karen. "Posthumanist Performativity: Toward an Understanding of How Matter Comes to Matter." *Signs* 28, no. 3 (2003): 801–31.
Barbetta, Cristina. "#Coronamaison, the Challenge: Drawing the House of Dreams for Quarantine." *Vita International,* March 24, 2020. http://www.vitainternational.media/en/article/2020/03/24/coronamaison-the-challenge-drawing-the-house-of-dreams-for-quarantine/769/.
Barnard, Frederick. *Herder's Social and Political Thought: From Enlightenment to Nationalism.* Oxford: Clarendon Press, 1965.
Barney, Darin, Gabriella Coleman, Christine Ross, Jonathan Sterne, and Tamar Tembeck, eds. *The Participatory Condition in the Digital Age.* Minneapolis: University of Minnesota Press, 2016.
Barthes, Roland. "Semiology and the Urban." In *The City and the Sign: An Introduction to Urban Semiotics,* edited by M. Gottdiener and Alexandros Lagopoulos, 87–98. New York: Columbia University Press, 1986.
Bates, Ernest Stuart. *Inside Out: An Introduction to Autobiography.* Sheridan House, 1937.
Bauman, Zygmunt. *Community: Seeking Safety in an Insecure World.* Malden, MA: Blackwell, 2001.
———. Foreword to *Individualization: Institutionalized Individualism and Its Social and Political Consequences,* by Ulrich Beck and Elisabeth Beck-Gernsheim, xiv–xix. Thousand Oaks: Sage, 2002.
———. *The Individualized Society.* Malden, MA: Polity Press, 2001.
———. "On Mass, Individuals, and Peg Communities." *Sociological Review* 49, no. 2 (October 1, 2001): 102–13.
Bennett, Nolan. *The Claims of Experience: Autobiography and American Democracy.* Oxford University Press, 2019.
Bergson, Henri. *Duration and Simultaneity, with Reference to Einstein's Theory.* Translated by Leon Jacobson. Indianapolis, IN: Bobbs-Merrill, 1965.
Berlant, Lauren. *The Female Complaint: The Unfinished Business of Sentimentality in American Culture.* Durham, NC: Duke University Press, 2008.
Berlant, Lauren, and Jay Prosser. "Life Writing and Intimate Publics: A Conversation with Lauren Berlant." *Biography* 1 (2011): 180–87.
Bessant, Kenneth C. *The Relational Fabric of Community.* New York: Palgrave Macmillan, 2018.
Bhabha, Homi K. *The Location of Culture.* New York: Routledge, 2004.
Bloch, Ernst. "Nonsynchronism and the Obligation to Its Dialectics." Translated by Mark Ritter. *New German Critique,* no. 11 (1977): 22–38.
Boam, Eric, and Jarrett Webb. "The Qualified Self: Going beyond Quantification." *DesignMind* (blog). May 2, 2014. https://web.archive.org/web/20150130064048/http://designmind.frogdesign.com/2014/05/qualified-self-going-beyond-quantification/.
Bohman, James F. "Formal Pragmatics and Social Criticism: The Philosophy of Language and the Critique of Ideology in Habermas's Theory of

Communicative Action." *Philosophy & Social Criticism* 11, no. 4 (October 1, 1986): 331–53.
Booth, Alison. "Prosopography and Crowded Attention." In *On Life-Writing*, edited by Zachary Leader. Oxford University Press, 2015.
Botkin, Benjamin Albert, ed. *Sidewalks of America: Folklore, Legends, Sagas, Traditions, Customs, Songs, Stories and Sayings of City Folk*. Indianapolis, IN: Bobbs-Merrill, 1954.
Boulby, Mark. *Karl Philipp Moritz: At the Fringe of Genius*. University of Toronto Press, 1979.
Boven, Martijn. "Review of Simultaneity and Delay." *Radical Philosophy* 176 (2012): 1–5.
Brand, Stewart, ed. *The Last Whole Earth Catalog: Access to Tools*. New York: Random House, 1971.
Bretonne, Rétif de la. *Monsieur Nicolas, ou le coeur humain dévoilé*. Edited by Jean-Jacques Pauvert. Vol. 1. Librairie de Tuileries, 1959.
Brown, Michael, and Larry Knopp. "Queering the Map: The Productive Tensions of Colliding Epistemologies." *Annals of the Association of American Geographers* 98, no. 1 (2008): 40–58.
Bruss, Elizabeth W. *Autobiographical Acts: The Changing Situation of a Literary Genre*. Baltimore, MD: Johns Hopkins University Press, 1976.
Burdick, Alan. *Why Time Flies: A Mostly Scientific Investigation*. New York: Simon & Schuster, 2017.
Burr, Anna Robeson Brown. *The Autobiography: A Critical and Comparative Study*. Boston: Houghton Mifflin, 1909.
Butler, Judith. *Giving an Account of Oneself: A Critique of Ethical Violence*. Uitgeverij Van Gorcum, 2003.
Campbell, Joseph Keim, Michael O'Rourke, and Harry Silverstein, eds. *Time and Identity*. Cambridge, MA: MIT Press, 2010.
Caquard, S., and W. Cartwright. "Narrative Cartography: From Mapping Stories to the Narrative of Maps and Mapping." *Cartographic Journal* 51, no. 2 (May 2014): 101–6.
Cardell, Kylie. *Dear World: Contemporary Uses of the Diary*. Madison: University of Wisconsin Press, 2014.
Cardell, Kylie, Kate Douglas, and Emma Maguire. "'Stories': Social Media and Ephemeral Narratives as Memoir." In *Mediating Memory: Tracing the Limits of Memoir*, edited by Bunty Avieson, Fiona Giles, and Sue Joseph, 157–72. New York: Routledge, 2017.
Carey, Benedict. "'Right Now Feels So Long and without Any End in Sight.'" *New York Times*, February 15, 2021, sec. Science. https://www.nytimes.com/2021/02/15/science/science-covid-mental-health.html.
Carmichael, Alexandra. "Daniel Gartenberg: The Role of QS in Scientific Discovery." *Quantified Self* (blog), August 10, 2012. http://quantifiedself.com/2012/08/daniel-gartenberg-the-role-of-qs-in-scientific-discovery/.

Chansky, Ricia A., ed. *Auto/Biography in the Americas: Relational Lives*. New York: Routledge, 2018.

Chansky, Ricia A., and Emily Hipchen, eds. *The Routledge Auto Biography Studies Reader*. New York: Routledge, 2015.

Chen, Yinqiu, Nina Dang, Ki Yeung, and Oscar Wong. "Scribe." Design Report, n.d. https://courses.cs.washington.edu/courses/cse440/15wi/projects/Scribe/Scribe_Testing_Designs.pdf.

Chernikova, Yulia. "27 September—A Day of the World | Уроки истории XX век." Translated by Ekaterina Kokorina. Уроки истории, January 10, 2012. https://urokiistorii.ru/articles/27-september-a-day-of-the-world.

Cochran, Sherman, Andrew C. K. Hsieh, and Janis Cochran, eds. *One Day in China, May 21, 1936*. New Haven, CT: Yale University Press, 1983.

Cohen, Jocelyn, and Daniel Soyer. *My Future Is in America: Autobiographies of Eastern European Jewish Immigrants*. New York University Press, 2008.

Coleman, Linda S. *Women's Life Writing: Finding Voice/Building Community*. Bowling Green, OH: Bowling Green State University Popular Press, 1997.

Cooper, Becky. *Mapping Manhattan: A Love (and Sometimes Hate) Story in Maps by 75 New Yorkers*. New York: Abrams, 2013.

Cooper, David, and Gary Priestnall. "The Processual Intertextuality of Literary Cartographies: Critical and Digital Practices." *Cartographic Journal* 48, no. 4 (November 2011): 250–62.

Couser, G. Thomas. "Making, Taking, and Faking Lives: The Ethics of Collaborative Life Writing." *Style* 32, no. 2 (1998): 334–50.

———. *Altered Egos: Authority in American Autobiography*. Oxford University Press, 1989.

Cox, James M. *Recovering Literature's Lost Ground: Essays in American Autobiography*. Baton Rouge: Louisiana State University Press, 1989.

Crosby, Alfred W. *America's Forgotten Pandemic: The Influenza of 1918*. 2nd ed. Cambridge: Cambridge University Press, 2003.

Crotty, Joey. "Story Mapping Challenge." Compassion Games International, December 28, 2015. https://www.compassiongames.org/ways-to-play/story-mapping-challenge/.

Culley, Amy. *British Women's Life Writing, 1760–1840: Friendship, Community, and Collaboration*. New York: Palgrave Macmillan, 2014.

Cyca, Michelle. "Snapchat, Instagram Stories, or Facebook Stories? What's the Difference?" *Hootsuite* (blog), March 28, 2018. Accessed May 26, 2021. https://blog.hootsuite.com/snapchat-instagram-facebook-stories/.

D'Addario, Daniel. "The Problem with Humans of New York." *Gawker*. August 13, 2014. http://gawker.com/the-problem-with-humans-of-new-york-1617812880.

Davies, Martin L. "Karl Philipp Moritz's *Erfahrungsseelenkunde*: Its Social and Intellectual Origins." *Literature Criticism from 1400 to 1800*. Oxford University Press, 1985.

Davis, Jenny. "The Qualified Self." Cyborgology, March 13, 2013. https://thesocietypages.org/cyborgology/2013/03/13/the-qualified-self/.
Day, Graham. *Community and Everyday Life*. London: Routledge, 2006.
Dean, Jodi. *Blog Theory: Feedback and Capture in the Circuits of Drive*. Malden, MA: Polity Press, 2010.
———. *Publicity's Secret: How Technoculture Capitalizes on Democracy*. Ithaca, NY: Cornell University Press, 2002.
de Certeau, Michel. *The Practice of Everyday Life*. Berkeley: University of California Press, 1984.
Debord, Guy. *Society of the Spectacle*. Detroit, MI: Black & Red, 2002.
Delanty, Gerard. *Community*. 2nd ed. New York: Routledge, 2010.
Derrida, Jacques. "Declarations of Independence." *New Political Science* 7, no. 1 (1986): 7–15.
———. *Politics of Friendship*. New York: Verso: 1997.
———. *Rogues: Two Essays on Reason*. Translated by Pascale-Anne Brault and Michael Naas. Redwood City, CA: Stanford University Press, 2005.
Dessalles, Jean-Louis. *Why We Talk: The Evolutionary Origins of Language*. Oxford University Press, 2007.
Devisch, Ignaas. *Jean-Luc Nancy and the Question of Community*. New York: Bloomsbury Academic, 2013.
D'Ignazio, Catherine, and Lauren F. Klein. *Data Feminism*. Cambridge, MA: MIT Press, 2020.
Dilthey, Wilhelm. *Gesammelte Schriften*. Edited by Karlfried Gründer, and Frithjof Rodi. Leipzig: Teubner, 1921.
Dodes, Rachel. "'Life in a Day' Director Aims to Elevate YouTube Videos into Art." *Wall Street Journal*, July 22, 2011, sec. Speakeasy. https://www.wsj.com/articles/BL-SEB-66274.
Duncan, James S. *The City as Text: The Politics of Landscape Interpretation in the Kandyan Kingdom*. Cambridge University Press, 2005.
Eakin, Paul John. *How Our Lives Become Stories: Making Selves*. Ithaca, NY: Cornell University Press, 1999.
———. *Writing Life Writing: Narrative, History, Autobiography*. New York: Routledge, 2020.
Egan, Susanna. *Mirror Talk: Genres of Crisis in Contemporary Autobiography*. Chapel Hill: University of North Carolina Press, 1999.
Eggers, Dave. *The Circle*. New York: Knopf Doubleday Publishing Group, 2013.
Eisenstein, Sergei. *Film Form: Essays in Film Theory*. Edited by Jay Leyda. Boston: Houghton Mifflin Harcourt, 2014.
Elborough, Travis. *Our History of the 20th Century: As Told in Diaries, Journals and Letters*. London: Michael O'Mara, 2017.
Erll, Astrid. "Afterword: Memory Worlds in Times of Corona." *Memory Studies* 13, no. 5 (October 1, 2020): 861–74.

Esposito, Roberto. *Communitas: The Origin and Destiny of Community.* Redwood City, CA: Stanford University Press, 2010.
Fabian, Johannes. *Time and the Other: How Anthropology Makes Its Object.* New York: Columbia University Press, 2002.
Farrar, Max. *The Struggle for "Community" in a British Multi-Ethnic Inner-City Area.* Lewiston, NY: Edwin Mellen, 2002.
Federal Writers' Project and Regional Staff. *These Are Our Lives.* Chapel Hill: University of North Carolina Press Books, 2016.
Fernandes, Sujatha. *Curated Stories : The Uses and Misuses of Storytelling.* Oxford University Press, 2017.
Fiegerman, Seth. "Facebook Acquires Storytelling Site Storylane in Talent Grab." Mashable. March 8, 2013. https://mashable.com/2013/03/08/facebook-acquires-storylane/.
———. "Storylane Prompts You to Share Your Life Story, One Question at a Time." Mashable. October 12, 2012. https://mashable.com/2012/10/12/storylane-prompts-you-to-share-your-life-story-one-question-at-a-time/.
Fink, Eugen. *Zur ontologischen Frühgeschichte von Raum, Zeit, Bewegung* (The early ontological history of space, time and movement). M. Nijhoff, 1957.
Förstl, H., M. Angermeyer, and R. Howard. "Karl Philipp Moritz' Journal of Empirical Psychology (1783–1793): An Analysis of 124 Case Reports." *Psychological Medicine* 21, no. 2 (May 1991): 299–304.
Foucault, Michel. *Discipline and Punish: The Birth of the Prison.* New York: Pantheon Books, 1977.
———. "Of Other Spaces." Translated by Jay Miskowiec. *Diacritics* 16, no. 1 (1986): 22–27. Originally published in *Architecture /Mouvement/ Continuité* (March 1967).
Frank, Arthur W. *Letting Stories Breathe.* University of Chicago Press, 2010.
Frank, Jacob. "'Steller Stories' Wants to Bring Longform Storytelling to Social Media." *Popular Science* (blog). Accessed May 30, 2021. https://www.popsci.com/steller-stories-brings-longform-storytelling-to-social-media/.
Franklin, Benjamin. *Autobiography of Benjamin Franklin.* Edited by Frank Woodworth Pine. Project Gutenberg, December 28, 2006. https://www.gutenberg.org/files/20203/20203-h/20203-h.htm#IX.
Freund, Alexander. "Under Storytelling's Spell? Oral History in a Neoliberal Age." *Oral History Review* 42, no. 1 (April 1, 2015): 96–132.
Fuchs, Christian. *Social Media: A Critical Introduction.* Thousand Oaks, CA: Sage, 2013.
Fusco, Coco. "Questioning the Frame." *In These Times,* December 16, 2004. https://inthesetimes.com/article/questioning-the-frame.
Gailus, Andreas. "A Case of Individuality: Karl Philipp Moritz and the Magazine for Empirical Psychology." *New German Critique,* no. 79 (2000): 67–105.
Gaiman, Neil. *American Gods.* New York: Harper Collins, 2001.

Garcia, Sandra E. "The Woman Who Created #MeToo Long before Hashtags." *New York Times*, January 20, 2018, https://www.nytimes.com/2017/10/20/us/me-too-movement-tarana-burke.html.
Gide, André. *Œuvres complètes*. Vol. X. Paris: Gallimard, 1936.
Gilmore, Leigh. *Tainted Witness: Why We Doubt What Women Say about Their Lives*. New York: Columbia University Press, 2017.
Goodman, Abbey. "Filmmaker, YouTube Capture 'Life in a Day.'" CNN Entertainment, July 27, 2011.
Goodman, Kay. "Autobiographie und deutsche Nation: Goethe und Herder." In *Goethe im Kontext: Kunst und Humanität, Naturwissenschaft und Politik von der Aufklärung bis zur Restauration: Ein Symposium* (1984): 260–83.
Goodmann, Katherine R. "Weibliche Autobiographien." In *Frauen Literatur Geschichte: Schreibende Frauen vom Mittelalter bis zur Gegenwart*, edited by Hiltrud Gnüg and Renate Möhrmann, 166–76. Stuttgart: J. B. Metzler, 1999.
Gordon, A. "Mining Commonsense Knowledge from Personal Stories in Internet Weblogs," Proceedings of the First Workshop on Automated Knowledge Base Construction, Grenoble, France, May 17–19, 2010, 8.
Gorky, Maxim, and Mikhail Koltsov, eds. *Den Mira*. Moscow: Zhurgaz, 1937.
Gottschall, Jonathan. *The Storytelling Animal: How Stories Make Us Human*. Boston: Mariner Books, 2013.
Grant, Azure. "QS17 Preview: Counting Scars." *Quantified Self* (blog), May 27, 2017. https://quantifiedself.com/blog/qs17-preview-counting-scars/.
Gray, Richard. "The World's Knowledge Is Being Buried in a Salt Mine." BBC, October 18, 2016. https://www.bbc.com/future/article/20161018-the-worlds-knowledge-is-being-buried-in-a-salt-mine.
Greenhouse, Carol J. "Time, Life and Society." In *A Moment's Notice: Time Politics across Cultures*, 19–48. Cornell University Press, 1996.
Groot, Martijn de. "Quantified Self, Quantified Us, Quantified Other." *Quantified Self Institute* (blog), January 15, 2014. https://qsinstitute.com/quantified-self-quantified-us-quantified-other/.
Gullestad, Marianne. "The Intimacy of Anonymity: Reflections on a Norwegian Life Story Competition." *Oral History* 23, no. 2 (1995): 51–59.
Ha, Anthony. "Storylane Combats Social Media Glibness with w Sharing Platform for In-Depth Stories and Opinions." *TechCrunch* (blog), November 12, 2012. https://social.techcrunch.com/2012/10/12/storylane-launch/.
Habermas, Jurgen. "Further Reflections on the Public Sphere." In *The Political Economy of the Media. Volume 2*, edited by Peter Golding and Graham Murdock, 151–91. Elgar Reference Collection, 1997.
———. *The Structural Transformation of the Public Sphere: An Inquiry into a Category of Bourgeois Society*. Translated by Thomas Burger and Frederick Lawrence. Cambridge, MA: MIT Press, 1991.

Haggerty, Kevin D., and Richard V. Ericson. "The Surveillant Assemblage." *British Journal of Sociology* 51 (2000): 605–22.

Hallberg, Peter. "The Nature of Collective Individuals: J. G. Herder's Concept of Community." *History of European Ideas* 25, no. 6 (November 1, 1999): 291–304.

Haraway, Donna. "Situated Knowledges: The Science Question in Feminism and the Privilege of Partial Perspective." *Feminist Studies* 14, no. 3 (1988): 575–99.

Harley, J. B. "Deconstructing the Map." *Passages* 26, no. 2 (1992): 1–20.

Harootunian, Harry D. *History's Disquiet: Modernity, Cultural Practice, and the Question of Everyday Life.* New York: Columbia University Press, 2000.

Harris, Jonathan. "Back to Life." Cowbird. http://cowbird.com/story/259443/Back_To_Life/.

Harrisson, Tom. "The Future of Sociology." *Pilot Papers* 2, no. 1 (1947): 10–25.

Harrisson, Tom, Humphrey Jennings, and Charles Madge. "Anthropology at Home." *New Statesman and Nation* 30 (1937).

Harvey, David. *Social Justice and the City.* Athens, GA: University of Georgia Press, 2010.

Hayles, Katherine. *How We Think: Digital Media and Contemporary Technogenesis.* University of Chicago Press, 2012.

Hecklinger, John. "Globalgiving's Storytelling Project." *Global Goodness* (blog), December 13, 2012. https://blog.globalgiving.org/2010/12/13/globalgivings-storytelling-project/.

Herder, Johann Gottfried. *Herders sämmtliche Werke.* Edited by Jakob Balde, Bernhard Suphan, Carl Christian Redlich, Otto Hoffmann, and Reinhold Steig. 33 Vols. Berlin: Weidmann, 1877.

Hesse-Biber, Sharlene. "Qualitative Approaches to Mixed Methods Practice." *Qualitative Inquiry* 16, no. 6 (July 2010): 455–68.

[Hillers, Marta]. *Eine Frau in Berlin. Tagebuchaufzeichnungen vom 20. April bis 22. Juni 1945.* Frankfurt: Eichborn, 2003.

Holmes, Ryan. "4 Tips on How to Succeed with Stories." *Fast Company* (blog), October 22, 2018. https://www.fastcompany.com/90252767/4-tips-on-how-to-succeed-with-stories.

Holst, Arne. "Wearable Technology—Statistics & Facts." *Statista*, March 9, 2020. https://www.statista.com/topics/1556/wearable-technology/.

hooks, bell. "Choosing the Margin as a Space of Radical Openness." *Framework: The Journal of Cinema and Media*, no. 36 (1989): 15–23.

Humphreys, Lee. *The Qualified Self: Social Media and the Accounting of Everyday Life.* Cambridge, MA: MIT Press, 2018.

Iaconesi, Salvatore and Oriana Persico. "Writing an Autobiography: From Authorship to Curatorship. That Is, the Narrative and Processual Nature of the Self." *Art is Open Source* (blog). February 16, 2016. https://www.artisopensource.net/2016/02/16/algorithmic-autobiography-the-uncertain-boundaries-of-the-i-and-the-self-in-the-age-of-hyperconnectivity/.

Igo, Sarah Elizabeth. *The Averaged American: Surveys, Citizens, and the Making of a Mass Public*. Cambridge, MA: Harvard University Press, 2007.

Isay, Dave, and Robin Sparkman. "Letter from Leadership." StoryCorps Annual Report, 2019, https://storycorpsorg-staging.s3.amazonaws.com/uploads/StoryCorps_Annual-Report-2019-1.pdf.

James, Felicity, and Julian North. *Writing Lives Together: Romantic and Victorian Auto/Biography*. New York: Routledge, 2017.

Jammer, Max. *Concepts of Simultaneity: From Antiquity to Einstein and Beyond*. Baltimore, MD: Johns Hopkins University Press, 2006.

Jasper, James M. *Protest: A Cultural Introduction to Social Movements*. Malden, MA: Polity Press, 2014.

Jeffery, Simon. "Ushahidi: Crowdmapping Collective that Exposed Kenyan Election Killings." *Guardian*, April 7, 2011. http://www.theguardian.com/news/blog/2011/apr/07/ushahidi-crowdmap-kenya-violence-hague.

Jenkins, Henry, Sam Ford, and Joshua Green. *Spreadable Media: Creating Value and Meaning in a Networked Culture*. New York University Press, 2013.

Jennings, Humphrey, and Charles Madge. *May the Twelfth: Mass Observation Day Survey*. London: Faber & Faber, 2009.

Jimenez, Ray. "Is Your Organization Losing Its Brain? Collecting Stories to Transfer Knowledge." *Vignettes Learning*(blog), 2017. http://archive.constantcontact.com/fs130/1011065179978/archive/1120493392728.html.

John, Nicholas A. *The Age of Sharing*. Malden, MA: Polity, 2016. http://search.ebscohost.com/login.aspx?direct=true&db=edsebk&AN=1441144&site=eds-live.

Jonas, Steven. "Abe Gong: Changing Sleep Habits with Unforgettable Reminders." *Quantified Self* (blog), May 10, 2016. https://quantifiedself.com/blog/abe-gong-hacking-sleep-habits-unforgettable-reminders/.

Jordan, Matthew and Nikki Pfarr. "The Quantified Us." *Medium* (blog). December 11, 2014. https://medium.com/artefact-stories/the-quantified-us-d7291a6d9968

Kaplan, Danny. "The Architecture of Collective Intimacy: Masonic Friendships as a Model for Collective Attachments." *American Anthropologist* 116, no. 1 (2014): 81–93.

———. "Public Intimacy in Social Media: The Mass Audience as a Third Party." *Media, Culture & Society* 43, no. 4 (February 11, 2021): 595–612.

Keren, Michael. *Politics and Literature at the Turn of the Millennium*. University of Calgary Press, 2015.

Kitchin, Rob, and Martin Dodge. "Rethinking Maps." *Progress in Human Geography* 31, no. 3 (June 1, 2007): 331–44.

Kitchin, Rob, J. Gleeson, and M. Dodge. "Unfolding Mapping Practices: A New Epistemology for Cartography." *Transactions of the Institute of British Geographers* 38, no. 3 (July 2013): 480–96.

Klein, Hilary. *Compañeras: Zapatista Women's Stories*. New York: Seven Stories Press, 2015.

Kleinreesink, L. H. E. (Esmeralda). *On Military Memoirs: A Quantitative Comparison of International Afghanistan War Autobiographies, 2001–2010.* Leiden: Brill, 2016.

Köhnen, Ralph. "Selbstschrift mit Beobachter: Karl Philipp Moritz und die Menschenwissenschaften.'" In *Selbstoptimierung*, 111–30. Peter Lang AG, 2018.

Kozlowska, Hanna. "Facebook Is Pinning Its Future on the Idea It Stole from Snapchat." *Quartz*, February 1, 2018, https://qz.com/1196002/facebook-is-pinning-its-future-on-stories-the-idea-it-stole-from-snapchat/.

Kurtz, Cynthia. "About Participatory Narrative Inquiry." Working with Stories. https://www.workingwithstories.org/aboutpni.html.

———. "Participatory Narrative Inquiry: An Introduction with Examples," March 2016, https://cfkurtz.com/Kurtz_PNI_March2016.pdf.

La Vopa, Anthony J. "Herder's *Publikum*: Language, Print, and Sociability in Eighteenth-Century Germany." *Eighteenth-Century Studies* 29, no. 1 (1995): 5–24.

Lambert, Joe. *Digital Storytelling: Capturing Lives, Creating Community.* 4th ed. New York: Routledge, 2013.

Lampert, Jay. *Simultaneity and Delay: A Dialectical Theory of Staggered Time.* New York: Bloomsbury, 2012.

Landwehr, Peter M., and Kathleen M. Carley. "Social Media in Disaster Relief." In *Data Mining and Knowledge Discovery for Big Data: Methodologies, Challenge and Opportunities*, 225–57. Edited by Wesley W. Chu. Berlin: Springer, 2014.

Latour, Bruno. "The Search for Political Heteronomy: New Ledgers of Complaints." Translated by Stephen Muecke. *Esprit*, March 2019, 1–8.

Laughlin, Charles A. *Chinese Reportage: The Aesthetics of Historical Experience.* Durham, NC: Duke University Press, 2002.

Le Bon, Gustave. *The Crowd, a Study of the Popular Mind.* 1930. New York: Macmillan, 2022.

Lebow, Katherine. "Autobiography as Complaint: Polish Social Memoir between the World Wars." *Laboratorium: Russian Review of Social Research* 6, no. 3 (September 16, 2014): 13–26.

Lefebvre, Henri. *The Production of Space.* Cambridge, MA: Blackwell, 1991.

Lejeune, Philippe. *L'autobiographie en France.* 2nd ed. Paris: Armand Colin, 1998.

Lenart-Cheng, Helga. "Mapping Lives across Borders." *A/B: Auto/Biography Studies* 32, no. 3 (January 1, 2017): 654–59.

———. "Personal Stories in Migration Museums and Our Notions of Hospitality: A Case Study from France's National Museum of the History of Immigration." *European Journal of Cultural Studies* (2021): 1–18.

———. "Wilhelm Dilthey's Views on Autobiography." *Life Writing* 15, no. 3 (September 1, 2018): 353–68.

Lenart-Cheng, Helga, and Ioana Luca. "Memories in Dialogue: Transnational Stories About Socialist Childhoods." In *Childhood and Schooling in (Post)*

Socialist Societies: Memories of Everyday Life. Edited by Iveta Silova, Nelli Piattoeva, and Zsuzsa Millei. New York: Palgrave MacMillan, 2017. 19–40.

Lepore, Jill. "Joe Gould's Teeth." *New Yorker*, July 20, 2015. https://www.newyorker.com/magazine/2015/07/27/joe-goulds-teeth.

Liebersohn, Harry, and Dorothee Schneider. "'My Life in Germany before and after January 30, 1933': A Guide to a Manuscript Collection at Houghton Library, Harvard University." *Transactions of the American Philosophical Society* 91, no. 3 (2001): 1–130.

Lindgren, Simon. *Digital Media and Society*. Thousand Oaks, CA: Sage, 2017.

Lingel, Jessica. *Digital Countercultures and the Struggle for Community*. Cambridge, MA: MIT Press, 2017.

Little, Myles. "The Real Humans of New York: Jerome Liebling Remembered." *TIME*, May 6, 2015. https://time.com/3823955/the-real-humans-of-new-york-jerome-liebling-remembered/.

Lockshin, Vanessa. "How to Measure the Effectiveness of Stories." *The Storytelling Non-Profit* (blog), August 4, 2014. https://www.thestorytellingnonprofit.com/blog/how-to-measure-the-effectiveness-of-stories/.

Lorentzen, Nick. "Deafblind." The Human Library Organization, October 20, 2018. https://humanlibrary.org/books/deafblind/.

Luca, Ioana. "Secret Police Files, Tangled Life Narratives: The 1.5 Generation of Communist Surveillance." *Biography* 38, no. 3 (June 22, 2015): 363–94.

Madge, Charles. "The Birth of Mass-Observation." *Times Literary Supplement*, 1976, 1395.

Madge, C. M., and T. H. Harrisson, eds. *First Year's Work 1937–38 by Mass-Observation*. London: Lindsay Drummond, 1938.

Maguire, Emma. *Girls, Autobiography, Media: Gender and Self-Mediation in Digital Economies*. New York: Palgrave Macmillan, 2018.

Maguire, Jack. *The Power of Personal Storytelling: Spinning Tales to Connect with Others*. New York: Putnam, 1998.

Maier, Christopher. "Creating Community through Storytelling." *National Storytelling Network* (blog), 2008. https://storynet.org/creating-community-through-storytelling/.

Manovich, Lev. *The Language of New Media*. Cambridge, MA: MIT Press, 2002.

Manuel, Frank Edward. Introduction to *Reflections on the Philosophy of the History of Mankind* by Johann Gottfried Herder. Translated by T. O. Churchill. University of Chicago Press, 1968.

Marcus, Laura. *Auto/biographical Discourses: Criticism, Theory, Practice*. Manchester University Press, 1998.

Mass Observation. *May the Twelfth: Mass Observation Day Survey*. Main Edition. London: Faber & Faber, 2012.

Massey, Doreen. *For Space*. Thousand Oaks, CA: Sage, 2005.

McBride, Keally D. *Collective Dreams: Political Imagination and Community*. University Park, PA: Penn State University Press, 2006.

McFarland, Michael. "Ethical Implications of Data Aggregation." June 1, 2012. https://www.scu.edu/ethics/focus-areas/internet-ethics/resources/ethical-implications-of-data-aggregation/.

McHugh, Kathleen, and Catherine Komisaruk. "Something Other than Autobiography: Collaborative Life-Narratives in the Americas—An Introduction." *Biography* 31, no. 3 (2008): vii–xii.

McNeill, Laurie, and John David Zuern. "Online Lives 2.0: Introduction." *Biography* 38, no. 2 (2015): v–xlvi.

Meijers, Anthonie. "Collective Speech Acts." *Intentional Acts and Institutional Facts* (January 1, 200): 93–110.

Menchú, Rigoberta. *I, Rigoberta Menchú: An Indian Woman in Guatemala*. 2nd ed. Edited by Elisabeth Burgos-Debray. Translated by Ann Wright. New York: Verso, 2009.

Miami Theory Collective (Oxford, Ohio), ed. *Community at Loose Ends*. Minneapolis: University of Minnesota Press, 1991.

Milgram, Stanley, Judith Greenwald, Suzanne Kessler, Wendy McKenna, and Judith Waters. "A Psychological Map of New York City: Cities Possess Psychological Dimensions that Can Be Mapped through New Cartographic Techniques." *American Scientist* (March-April 1972)194–200.

Miller, Nancy K. *Getting Personal: Feminist Occasions and Other Autobiographical Acts*. Vols. 1–10. New York: Routledge, 1991.

Miranda, Joseph. *Against the Romance of Community*. Minneapolis: University of Minnesota Press, 2002.

Montaigne, Michel de. *The Complete Essays*. Edited by Michael Andrew Screech. New York: Penguin Classics, 1987.

Moretti, Franco. *Distant Reading*. New York: Verso, 2013.

Moritz, Karl Philipp. *Karl Philipp Moritz: Die Schriften in dreißig Bänden*. Edited by Petra Nettelbeck and Uwe Nettelbeck. 10 vols. Nördlingen: Franz Greno, 1986.

———. *Reisen eines Deutschen in England im Jahr 1782*. Insel, Frankfurt, 2000

———. *Reisen eines Deutschen in England im Jahre 1782*. Edited by Horst Günther. 3 vols. Frankfurt am Main, 1981.

———. "Vorschlag zu einem Magazin einer Erfahrungsseelenkunde." *Deutsches Museum* 1 (1782): 485–503.

Moritz, Karl Philipp, Salomon Maimon, and Karl Friedrich Pockels, eds. *Gnothi Seauton; oder, Magazin zur Erfahrungsseelenkunde als ein Lesebuch für Gelehrte und Ungelehrte*. Edited by Alfredo Guzzoni and Anke Bennholdt-Thomsen. 10 vols. Reprinted with afterword by Guzzoni and Bennholdt-Thomsen. Lindau: Antiqua-Verlag, 1978. First published 1782–93 by Mylius.

Morrison, Aimée. "Autobiography in Real Time: A Genre Analysis of Personal Mommy Blogging." *Cyberpsychology: Journal of Psychosocial Research on Cyberspace* 4, no. 2 (December 1, 2010).

Müller, Lothar. *Die kranke Seele und das Licht der Erkenntnis: Karl Philipp Moritz' Anton Reiser*. Frankfurt am Main: Athenäum, 1987.

Nafus, Dawn, and Jamie Sherman. "This One Does Not Go Up to 11: The Quantified Self Movement as an Alternative Big Data Practice." *International Journal of Communication* 8 (2014): 11.
Nakamura, Lisa. "Feeling Good about Feeling Bad: Virtuous Virtual Reality and the Automation of Racial Empathy." *Journal of Visual Culture* 19, no. 1 (April 1, 2020): 47–64.
Nancy, Jean-Luc. *Being Singular Plural*. Redwood City, CA: Stanford University Press, 2000.
———. "The Confronted Community." *Postcolonial Studies* 6, no. 1 (2003): 23–36.
———. *The Inoperative Community*. Edited by Peter Conner. Translated by Peter Connor, Lisa Garbus, Michael Holland, and Simona Sawhney. Minneapolis: University of Minnesota Press, 1991.
Nichols, Joshua Ben David. *The End(s) of Community: History, Sovereignty, and the Question of Law*. Waterloo, ON: Wilfrid Laurier University Press, 2013.
Nierenberg, Amelia. "The Quarantine Diaries." *New York Times*, March 30, 2020, sec. Style. Accessed June 2, 2021. https://www.nytimes.com/2020/03/30/style/coronavirus-diaries-social-history.html.
Nietzsche, Friedrich. *The Genealogy of Morals*. Mineola, NY: Dover, 2003.
Niglas, Katrin. "Combining Quantitative and Qualitative Approaches," October 5, 2000. http://www.leeds.ac.uk/educol/documents/00001544.htm
Niles, John D. *Homo Narrans: The Poetics and Anthropology of Oral Literature*. Philadelphia, PA: University of Pennsylvania Press, 2010.
Nübel, Birgit. "Menschliche Selbstbilder als Seelen- und Gesellschaftsinkarnat : Herder in zivilisationstheoretischer Perspektive," 2004. http://publikationen.ub.uni-frankfurt.de/frontdoor/index/index/docId/10256.
Nussbaum, Felicity. *The Autobiographical Subject: Gender and Ideology in Eighteenth-Century England*. Baltimore, MD: Johns Hopkins University Press, 1989.
Ohlheiser, Abby. "The Woman behind 'Me Too' Knew the Power of the Phrase when She Created It—10 Years Ago." *Washington Post*, October 19, 2017. https://www.washingtonpost.com/news/the-intersect/wp/2017/10/19/the-woman-behind-me-too-knew-the-power-of-the-phrase-when-she-created-it-10-years-ago/.
Orlando, Monica. "Double Voicing and Personhood in Collaborative Life Writing about Autism: The Transformative Narrative of Carly's Voice." *Journal of Medical Humanities* 39, no. 2 (2018): 217–31.
Papacharissi, Zizi, ed. *A Networked Self: Identity, Community, and Culture on Social Network Sites*. New York: Routledge, 2011.
Park, Andrea. "#MeToo Reaches 85 Countries with 1.7M Tweets." *CBS News*, October 24, 2017. https://www.cbsnews.com/news/metoo-reaches-85-countries-with-1-7-million-tweets/.

Partridge, Tim. "Life in a Day." *Official Google Blog* (blog). July 6, 2010. https://googleblog.blogspot.com/2010/07/life-in-day.html.

Persico, Chrissy. "This Is My Story: An Oral History Project in Grand Central Terminal Chronicles the Lives of Ordinary New Yorkers." *New York Daily News*, February 22, 2004. https://www.nydailynews.com/story-oral-history-project-grand-central-terminal-chronicles-lives-ordinary-new-yorkers-article-1.631571.

Pflum, Mary. "A Year Ago, Alyssa Milano Started a Conversation about #MeToo. These Women Replied." NBC News, October 15, 2018. https://www.nbcnews.com/news/us-news/year-ago-alyssa-milano-started-conversation-about-metoo-these-women-n920246.

Poletti, Anna. "Intimate Economies: 'Postsecret' and the Affect of Confession." *Biography* 34, No. 1 (2011): 25–36.

Poletti, Anna. *Stories of the Self: Life Writing after the Book*. New York University Press, 2020.

Poletti, Anna, and Julie Rak, eds. *Identity Technologies: Constructing the Self Online*. University of Wisconsin Press, 2014.

Polletta, Francesca. *It Was Like a Fever: Storytelling in Protest and Politics*. University of Chicago Press, 2009.

Popkin, Jeremy D. "Coordinated Lives: Between Autobiography and Scholarship." *Biography* 24, no. 4 (2001): 781–805.

Popova, Maria. "Nonstop Metropolis: An Atlas of Maps Reclaiming New York's Untold Stories and Unseen Populations." *Brain Pickings* (blog), October 19, 2016. https://www.brainpickings.org/2016/10/19/nonstop-metropolis-atlas-new-york-rebecca-solnit/.

Preston, Jennifer. "Pull Up a Mouse and Stay a While." *Media Decoder Blog* (blog), February 19, 2012. https://mediadecoder.blogs.nytimes.com/2012/02/19/pull-up-a-mouse-and-stay-a-while/.

Quercia, Daniele, Joao Paulo Pesce, Virgilio Almeida, and Jon Crowcroft. "Psychological Maps 2.0: A Web Engagement Enterprise Starting in London." In *Proceedings of the 22nd International Conference on World Wide Web*, 1065–76. Association for Computing Machinery, 2013.

Rak, Julie. *Boom!: Manufacturing Memoir for the Popular Market*. Illustrated edition. Waterloo, ON: Wilfrid Laurier University Press, 2013.

Ramirez, Jessica. "'Ushahidi' Technology Saves Lives in Haiti and Chile." *Newsweek*, March 3, 2010. https://www.newsweek.com/ushahidi-technology-saves-lives-haiti-and-chile-210262.

Reilly, Jill, and Eddie Wrenn. "Just One Day in the World: Extraordinary Collection of 100,000 Images—All Taken on May 15th—Which Will Be Buried in a Copper Mine for Future Generations." Daily Mail Online, October 16, 2012. https://www.dailymail.co.uk/news/article-2217896/Just-day-world-Extraordinary-collection-100-000-images-taken-May-15th-buried-copper-future-generations.html.

Rettberg, Jill Walker. *Seeing Ourselves through Technology: How We Use Selfies, Blogs and Wearable Devices to See and Shape Ourselves.* New York: Palgrave Macmillan, 2014.
Ricœur, Paul. *Time and Narrative.* University of Chicago Press, 1984.
Rothfeld, Lindsay. "Crowd-Sourced Storytelling: How Innovators Are Opening Up the Creative Process." Mashable, August 21, 2015. https://mashable.com/2015/08/21/innovative-crowd-sourced-storytelling/.
Rousseau, Jean-Jacques. *Reveries of the Solitary Walker.* New York: Penguin Classics, 1979.
Ruddick, Kyle. "One Day on Earth." *New York Times,* June 1, 2012. https://www.nytimes.com/2012/06/01/movies/one-day-on-earth-directed-by-kyle-ruddick.html?_r=0.
Rushkoff, Douglas. *Present Shock: When Everything Happens Now.* Reprint edition. New York: Current, 2014.
Scheffel, Michael, Antonius Weixler, and Lukas Werner. "Time." The Living Handbook of Narratology, November 20, 2013. http://www.lhn.uni-hamburg.de/node/106.html.
Schmidt, Christian Marc, and Liangjie Xia. "Invisible Cities: Representing Social Networks in an Urban Context." *Parsons Journal for Information Mapping* 3, no. 1 (2011).
Schubart, Christian Friedrich Daniel, and Ludwig Albrecht Schubart. *Schubarts Leben und Gesinnungen: Von ihm selbst, im Kerker aufgesetzt.* Norderstedt: Hansebooks, 2020.
Scott, David. *Gilbert Simondon's Psychic and Collective Individuation: A Critical Introduction and Guide: A Critical Introduction and Guide.* Edinburgh University Press, 2014.
Sennett, Richard. *The Fall of Public Man.* New York: W. W. Norton, 2017.
Sung-chiao Shen. "One Day in China or China in One Day: Everyday Life Narrative and the Imagination of Nationhood in 1930s China." Institute of Modern History, Academia Sinica. *New History Journal,* 2012.
Sheridan, Dorothy, Brian V. Street, and David Bloome. *Writing Ourselves: Mass-Observation and Literacy Practices.* Cresskill, NJ: Hampton Press, 2000.
Shiller, Robert J. *Narrative Economics: How Stories Go Viral and Drive Major Economic Events.* Princeton, NJ: Princeton University Press, 2019.
Simanowski, Roberto. *Facebook Society: Losing Ourselves in Sharing Ourselves.* Translated by Susan H. Gillespie. New York: Columbia University Press, 2018.
Smith, Neil, and Cindi Katz. "Grounding Metaphor: Towards a Spatialized Politics." In *Place and the Politics of Identity.* 66–81, New York: Routledge, 1993.
Smith, Sidonie, and Julia Watson. *Reading Autobiography: A Guide for Interpreting Life Narratives.* Minneapolis: University of Minnesota Press, 2010.
Smith, Sidonie, and Kay Schaffer. *Human Rights and Narrated Lives: The Ethics of Recognition.* New York: Palgrave Macmillan, 2004.

Soja, Edward W. *Thirdspace: Journeys to Los Angeles and Other Real-and-Imagined Places.* Cambridge, MA: Blackwell, 1996.

Solnit, Rebecca, and Joshua Jelly-Schapiro, eds. *Nonstop Metropolis: A New York City Atlas.* Oakland, CA: University of California Press, 2016

Solove, Daniel J. "Information-Age Privacy Concerns Are More Kafkaesque Than Orwellian." *Chronicle of Higher Education,* December 10, 2004. https://www.chronicle.com/article/information-age-privacy-concerns-are-more-kafkaesque-than-orwellian/.

Soyer, Daniel. "Documenting Immigrant Lives at an Immigrant Institution: Yivo's Autobiography Contest of 1942." *Jewish Social Studies* 5, no. 3 (1999): 218–43.

Stampler, Laura. "Snapchat Just Unveiled a New Feature." *Time,* June 17, 2014. https://time.com/2890073/snapchat-new-feature/.

Stanton, Brandon. *Humans of New York : Stories.* New York: St. Martin's Press, 2015.

Stephens, Sonia, and Daniel Richards. "Story Mapping and Sea Level Rise: Listening to Global Risks at Street Level." *Communication Design Quarterly* 8 (February 1, 2020). http://sigdoc.acm.org/wp-content/uploads/2020/02/CDQ19005_Stephens_Richards.pdf.

Stone, Lawrence. "Prosopography." *Daedalus* 100, no. 1 (1971): 46–79.

Strawson, Galen. "Against Narrativity." *Ratio* 17, no. 4 (2004): 428–52.

Thomas, William I., and Florian Znaniecki. "Introduction." In *The Polish Peasant in Europe and America,* Vol. III. Boston: Gorham Press, 1919.

Thompson, Paul. *The Voice of the Past: Oral History.* 3rd ed. Oxford University Press, 2000.

Tönnies, Ferdinant. *Community and Society (Gemeinschaft und Gesellschaft).* East Lansing, MI: Michigan State University Press, 1957.

Tuan, Yi-Fu. *Space and Place: The Perspective of Experience.* Minneapolis: University of Minnesota Press, 1977.

Valle, Firuzeh Shokooh. "Silence Speaks: Multimedia Storytelling in Republic of Congo." *Global Voices* (blog), February 26, 2010. https://globalvoices.org/2010/02/26/silence-speaks-multi-media-storytelling-in-republic-of-congo/.

Van Dijck, José. *The Culture of Connectivity: A Critical History of Social Media.* Oxford University Press, 2013.

Van Dijck, José, and David Nieborg. "Wikinomics and Its Discontents: A Critical Analysis of Web 2.0 Business Manifestos." *New Media & Society* 11, no. 5 (August 1, 2009): 855–74.

Verboven, Koenraad, Carlier, Myriam, and Jan Dumolyn. "A Short Manual to the Art of Prosopography," in *Prosopography Approaches and Applications: A Handbook,* 35. Unit for Prosopographical Research, Linacre College, 2007.

Walsh, Bill. "Filmmaker Claudia Stack Turns Her Lens on Sharecroppers." *Wilmington Star News,* October 23, 2016. https://www.starnewsonline.com/entertainment/20161023/filmmaker-claudia-stack-turns-her-lens-on-sharecroppers.

Wang, Fan and Grace Tsoi. "Fang Fang: Author Vilified for Wuhan Diary Speaks Out a Year On." *BBC News,* January 19, 2021, sec. Asia. https://www.bbc.com/news/world-asia-54987675.
Warkentin, Raija. "Writing Competitions as a New Research Method." *International Journal of Qualitative Methods* 1, no. 4 (December 1, 2002): 10–25.
Webber, Jeremy H. A., Rebecca Johnson, and Hester Lessard. *Storied Communities: Narratives of Contact and Arrival in Constituting Political Community.* Vancouver: University of British Columbia Press, 2011.
Weinman, Joe. *Digital Disciplines: Attaining Market Leadership via the Cloud, Big Data, Social, Mobile, and the Internet of Things.* Hoboken, NJ: John Wiley & Sons, 2015.
———. "How Customer Intimacy Is Evolving to Collective Intimacy, Thanks to Big Data." *Forbes,* June 4, 2013. https://www.forbes.com/sites/joeweinman/2013/06/04/how-customer-intimacy-is-evolving-to-collective-intimacy-thanks-to-big-data/.
Weinreich, M. *Der YIVO in a Yor Fun Umkum: Barikht-Rede Gehaltn Oyf Der Efenung Fun Der 17ter Yorbukh Konferents Fun YIVO.* New York: Yidisher Visnshaftlekher Institut, 1943.
Weintraub, Karl Joachim. *The Value of the Individual: Self and Circumstance in Autobiography.* University of Chicago Press, 1978.
Weller, Chris. "Libraries of the Future Are Going to Change in Some Unexpected Ways." Business Insider, August 24, 2016. http://www.businessinsider.com/libraries-of-the-future-2016-8.
Wells, H. G. *Experiment in Autobiography: Discoveries and Conclusions of a Very Ordinary Brain (since 1866).* New York: Macmillan, 1934.
Wende, E., Gregory King, and G. Schwabe. "Exploring Storytelling as a Knowledge Transfer Technique in Offshore Outsourcing." Paper presented at ICIS (International Conference on Information Systems), 2014. https://www.researchgate.net/publication/270790796_Exploring_Storytelling_as_a_Knowledge_Transfer_Technique_in_Offshore_Outsourcing.
White, Elwyn Brooks. *Here Is New York.* New York Review of Books / Little Bookroom, 1999.
White, Hayden V. *The Content of the Form: Narrative Discourse and Historical Representation.* Baltimore, MD: Johns Hopkins University Press, 1987.
Whitlock, Gillian. "In the Second Person: Narrative Transactions in Stolen Generations Testimony." *Biography* 24, No. 1 (2001): 197–214.
———. *Soft Weapons.* University of Chicago Press, 2006.
Whitrow, G. J. *The Natural Philosophy of Time.* 2nd ed. Oxford University Press, 1980.
Whitton, Brian J. "Herder's Critique of the Enlightenment: Cultural Community versus Cosmopolitan Rationalism." *History and Theory* 27, no. 2 (1988): 146–68.
Wittel, Andreas. "Toward a Network Sociality." *Theory, Culture & Society* 18, no. 6 (December 1, 2001): 51–76.

WKYC Staff. "Many People Turning to Social Media to Document Daily Quarantine Life." WKYC Studios, March 25, 2020. https://www.wkyc.com/article/life/social-media-quarantine-life-coronavirus/95-43cc3f57-2e05-4ba8-9af9-e3a34b9678c7.

Wolf, Christa. *One Day a Year, 1960–2000.* New York: Europa Editions, 2007.

Wolf, Gary. "Are Self-Trackers Narcissists?" *Quantified Self* (blog), February 17, 2009. https://quantifiedself.com/blog/are-self-trackers-narcissists/.

———. "The Data-Driven Life." *New York Times*, April 28, 2010. https://www.nytimes.com/2010/05/02/magazine/02self-measurement-t.html.

———. "What Is The Quantified Self?" *Quantified Self* (blog), March 4, 2011. https://quantifiedself.com/blog/what-is-the-quantified-self/.

Wolf, Gary and Ernesto Ramirez. "How Many People Self-Track?" *Quantified Self* (blog), January 30, 2013. https://quantifiedself.com/blog/how-many-people-self-track/.

Wolfe, Thomas C. *Governing Soviet Journalism: The Press and the Socialist Person after Stalin.* Bloomington: Indiana University Press, 2005.

Zak, Paul J. "How Stories Change the Brain." *Greater Good*, December 17, 2013. https://greatergood.berkeley.edu/article/item/how_stories_change_brain.

———. "Why Your Brain Loves Good Storytelling." *Harvard Business Review*, October 28, 2014. https://hbr.org/2014/10/why-your-brain-loves-good-storytelling.

Zaretsky, Robert. "The Old Regime and the Yellow Revolution." *Foreign Policy*, January 15, 2019. https://foreignpolicy.com/2019/01/15/the-yellow-revolution-france-macron/.

Zuboff, Shoshana. *The Age of Surveillance Capitalism: The Fight for a Human Future at the Frontier of Power.* New York: Public Affairs: 2019.

Zuern, John. "Online Lives: Introduction." *Biography* 26, no. 1 (2003): v–xxv.

INDEX

Page numbers in italics indicate illustrations.

Abel, Theodore: background of, 176n23; compared to Allport et al.'s contest, 176n40, 177n44; Hoover Institution as home of Abel's collection, 176n26; limited impact of stories in contest, 79; memoir contest conducted by, 61–62, 64–67, 177n45; *Nazi Movement*, 176n26, 176n29; *Why Hitler Came into Power: An Answer Based on the Original Life Stories of Six Hundred of His Followers*, 62, 67. *See also* memoir contests
abolitionists' use of former slaves' autobiographies, 175n77
activism: "by us for us approach," 127, 142; community and, 4; personal stories' roles in, 10, 18, 54; social media and, 4; story maps, use of, 104
#afterlockdown, 150
agency, 20, 35, 140, 142, 143, 154
Age of Maps, 103
Age of Memoirs, 103
Age of Reason. *See* Enlightenment
"age of sharing," 5–6, 28
aggregation: advantages of, 130, 146; complicity with self-aggregation, 142, 145, 162; definition and etymology of, 125, 140, 192n62; double face of, 140–42, 153; emerging patterns revealed through, 26; Facebook's Community Voices and, 30–31, 169n87; means of, 8, 11, 20–21; mobile phone recordings to provide witness, 24; new insights serving purposes other than those intended, 32; Snapchat and, 30; social network analysis (SNA) of, 19; soft resistance to, 138
AI. *See* artificial intelligence technologies
algorithms: experiments with algorithmic autobiography, 158–62; extreme collective narration and, 11–12, 20, 22, 159; use of, 54, 125–26, 144–45, 167n47
Allex, Vaughn, 13
Allport, Gordon Willard, et al.: compared to Abel's contest criteria, 176n40, 177n44; memoir contest conducted by, 62–67; "Personality under Social Catastrophe: Ninety Life-Histories of the Nazi Revolution" (with Fay and Hartshorne), 64, 67, 176n33; positivist perspective of, 66, 79. *See also* memoir contests
Ancient Greeks and Romans: archetype of good spectacle, 156–57; "know thyself" maxim of, 135
Anderson, Benedict, *Imagined Communities*, 91–92, 95, 100
Angelou, Maya, *I Know Why the Caged Bird Sings*, 15
anonymity: authors of autobiographies, 16; memoir contest entrants, 63, 72, 177n44, 178n68; others in same nation engaged in simultaneous activity, 92
anthropology, 178n62
Arab Spring, 4

216 / INDEX

Archive of Immigrant Voices, 178–79n73
archives: convergent with and distinguished from libraries, 71; of Covid-19 pandemic stories, 193–94n4; design of, 11; "lived experience" in context of story archives, 73; of StoryCorps, 13, 24, 55, 175n3. *See also* Mass Observation Archive
Arendt, Hannah, 171n114
Aristotle, 182n37
artificial intelligence (AI) technologies, 101–2, 136–37, 160–62
assembled stories, 3–6; ability to transform communities, 11; books as collections of stories, 9; as case studies to examine community concept, 7–8; increasing community cohesion through, 4–5, 50, 52; time and space ritualized in, 36–37. *See also* collections of autobiographical stories; one-day diaries; story mapping
Augustine, Saint, 90
authoritarian implications: of reduction of people to data, 126; of story mapping, 116
authorship: machine-human collaborative program (Ghostwriter), 159–60; social media complicating question of, 20, 158–59. *See also* ghostwriting
autobiographies and memoirs, 6; aggregations and classification of, 4, 131; AI-generated, 160–62; anonymous authors of, 16; as antithesis of "raw data," 143; Augustine as early memoirist, 90; biographies vs., 20–21; co-emergence of writers with social media, 21, 31, 158–62; collaborative form of, 17, 53, 166n18; to counter data bias and reduction of people to data, 126, 128, 142; criticism of representativeness of, 16; deindividualization by autobiographers, 132; ego media and, 17; emergence in nineteenth century, 15; Enlightenment ideals and, 8, 38; expanding to collections of personal stories, 22; field of study of, 163–64n9; of former slaves, 175n77; Foucault's subjectivation and, 141; generalizing to measure life with view on statistical whole, 134; genres of, 17, 129–30; graphic memoirs, 17; interrogating context, limitations, and validity of, 144; as literary form joined with democracy as most congruent to unique, autonomous self, 171n1; Moritz's views on value of each life, 43–44; from my story to our story, 14–17; national unity and, 48–49; Native American, 17; network autobiography's shortcomings, 31; online imperative to produce appealing products, 35; from our story to our stories, 17–21; pathological memoirists, 131; quantifying in, 128; relationality in, 16–17; representative readings of, 15–16; Romantic poets focusing on selfhood of, 15; situatedness and positionality in, 16; of soldier-authors, 143–44, 193n75; spatial turn and, 109, 186nn21–22; statistics applied to, 129, 132–34; terminology for, 163n9; twentieth century's collectivist approach to, 15. *See also* collections of autobiographical stories; libraries of human experience; memoir contests; personal stories
autonomy: of authors, 17, 38; of readers, 52

Bachelard, Gaston, 107, 185n14
Ban Ki-moon, 142
Barad, Karen, 21
Barthes, Roland, 109
Bartholomeus, Ellis, 135
Bates, E. Stuart, 131, 190n25
Bauman, Zygmunt, 5–6, 31–32, 164n18, 170n90
belonging. *See* sense of belonging
Be Nourished (website), 179n73
Bergson, Henri, 91, 95–96, 182n45, 183n58, 184n65
Berlant, Lauren, 22, 166–67n44
Bhabha, Homi, 100
big data, 6; collective intimacy and, 22; distant reading practices associated with, 7; false binary with small data, 128, 141; negatives of, 78–79; personal stories as part, 19–20; sharing encouraged by, 10; soft resistance to, 138
biograms, 62, 177n45
biographies: vs. autobiographies, 20–21; historical use of anthologies of, 128–32
Bloch, Ernst, 100–101, 184n72, 184n75
blogs, 17–18
body mapping, 189n67
body positivity movement, 179n73
body story, 179n73
bonding. *See* social engagement of storytelling

books: autobiographical self-expression in, 17; human libraries and, 75–77; limitations of access to, 9; as method to circulate stories, 8–9. *See also* eighteenth-century story collections; print culture
Booth, Alison, 20, 159
Born in Slavery: Slave Narratives from the Federal Writers' Project, 1936–1938 (oral history), 59
Botkin, Benjamin A., 105
bottom-up approaches. *See* top-down vs. bottom-up approaches
brain: neurochemical oxytocin, effect of release in, 25; storytelling's effect on, 25, 167–68n57; Wells's assessment of his own brain, 133
Brasch, Thomas, 182n31
Bretonne, Rétif de la, 15
Brian, Christopher, 83
Britain: *Britain in a Day* (November 12, 2011), 81; mass observations on abdication of Edward VIII, 69–71; *May the Twelfth* anthology (one-day diary of May 12, 1937), 88, 181n30
Bruss, Elizabeth, 129, 190n10
Burke, Tarana, 1–2, 9
Burr, Anna Robeson, *The Autobiography: A Critical and Comparative Study*, 129–32

cahiers de doléances (notebooks of complaints), role in lead-up to French Revolution, 49–51, 174n63, 174n65
Calvino, Italo, *Invisible Cities*, 107
Canevacci, Massimo, 160
capitalism: communicative capitalism, 33–35; community's relationship with, 6, 10; consumer capitalism, 154; domination of, 113; platform capitalism, 53; surveillance capitalism, 32
Cardano, Gerolamo, 132
Carmichael, Alexandra, 138–39
cartography. *See* mapping and cartography; story mapping
Cerezo, Briana, Humans of Portland (story map), 112
Charles (British prince), wedding day to Princess Diana, 69
Chernikova, Yulia, 182n33
China's Covid-19 lockdown diary of Fang Fang, 153

China's *One Day in China* (May 21, 1936), 84, 86–89, 181n26; compared to earlier Soviet project, 87; as "field of experimentation," 101; inspiring local clones, 88; validity of truths and observations equally applicable to other days, 182n35
chronopolitics, 90
circularity of knowledge production, 24–25, 145–46
cities: narrative definition of, 105; personal stories' transgressive potential of urban spaces, 118–19; smart city movement, 185n13; storybooths in, 13; storytelling about, 105; as texts to be read, 186n20. *See also* New York City; story mapping
citizen cartography, 116
Citizen Science, 138–39, 139, 192n57
City of Memory (story map), 110, 111, 187n32
Civil Rights Movement (US), 177n45
coincidence, simultaneity based on, 91–95, 100
Coleman, Linda S., 53
collaborative writing: AI-based, 160–62; of autobiographies, 17, 53, 166n18; of Covid-19 pandemic stories, 150
collections of autobiographical stories: collective intimacy and, 23, 151; Covid-19 pandemic and, 150; emergent public sphere and, 51; Herder's view of, 39–40, 45–50; as models on how to handle data, 142; Moritz's view of, 39–45; on New York City, 106; Plutarch as early example of, 128–29; statistical aggregates, creation of, 145. *See also* autobiographies and memoirs; memoir contests
collective amnesia of 1918 flu pandemic, 149
collective intimacy, 21–37, 53; big data and, 22; collections of personal stories and, 23, 151; collective story-maps and, 112; community development and, 24, 27; complementary practices, 34–37; creation by story sharing, 22; critique of, 31–34; distinguished from personalization, 23; Facebook and, 31; intimacy as cultural imaginary and as political force, 22; marketing and exploitation for profit, 22–23, 33–34, 38, 113; priorities of, 31, 39, 73; relational knowledge in, 24–25; sense of belonging and, 23, 24–28, 38, 73; in social media, 28–31; "with-nessing" and, 158

collective sharing of stories: as alternative to data mining, 142; bonding through, 5; collective intimacy created through, 26; competing motives between databases and stories, 36; of Covid-19 pandemic, 150; discovery of new connections through, 5; increase in, 2; no optimal strategy for, 35; purpose to get word out, 31; time and space in terms of, 11; ways of achieving, 4, 10, 164n11. *See also* story sharing
collective speech acts, role in political imagination, 51
Columbia University's sociology department, 61–62
common good: contributing to large databases for, 141; instrumentalization of, 145; personal stories as part of, 42; virtual reality as genre for, 77
communicative capitalism, 33–35
communicative rationality, 52
communism, 88
communitarianism: conflict between corporate domination and, 170n96; corporate adoption of ethos of, 33; vs. individualism, 6, 10, 28
community: "age of sharing" changing nature of, 28; benefits of community-based storytelling, 25; capitalism's relationship with, 6, 10; city reclaiming sense of community, 188n40; collective intimacy's benefits for, 24, 27; corporations' use for commodification, 11, 154; creation of, as reason for sharing, 3; criticism of spawned communities, 31–32; development of field of community studies, 164n24; digital media creating without personal encounter, 21; eighteenth-century recognition of bonds from sharing personal stories, 39, 171n2; ethnic community of immigrant Jewish Americans, 68; etymology of, 151, 194n11, 195n36; Facebook's desire for "Building Global Community," 29; Franklin's interest in, 42; global community considered as asset of story libraries, 79; humanity as, dystopia of, 141, 153; illusions created by story sharing, 113; Miranda's concept of, 10–11; Nancy's concept of, 10–11, 157, 195n39; one-day diaries and community-building, 99; openness and, 11, 24, 170, 195–96n42; as polarizing concept in academia, 7; Romantic narrative of, 10; shared sense of time and, 82; story mapping as way to cultivate, 105, 112; story-sharing platforms as opposite of community-building, 32; surrogate relationship with identity, 164n18; "us" and "them" dichotomy in, 7, 11–12, 165n27; Western society's focus on, 6–7. *See also* collective sharing of stories; sense of belonging
community-based mapping, 123
Community Oral History Project (New York Public Library), 112; "A People's History of Harlem," 117
community voices, 30–31, 169n86
complicity: aggregation with self-aggregation, 142, 145; posting personal stories in context of surveillance capitalism, 32
Confucius, 41
connectedness: connectivity vs., 33; contemporary story libraries drawing on power to connect and create solidarity, 72–73; discovery of new connections through collective sharing of stories, 5; emotional manipulation of, 113; print culture's simultaneous isolation and connection, 174n75. *See also* solidarity
consumerism, 154
contemporary story libraries, 72–75; drawing on power to connect and create solidarity, 72–73; feelings and social emotional learning in, 74, 76, 78; futurists on libraries of the future, 75; meaning of "experience" vs. "lived experience" in, 73–75; *A Mile in My Shoes* (traveling exhibit), 74–75
Cooper, Becky, 103, 105, 107, 109, 185n15, 186n25, 189n69
Cooper, David, 123
Coronamaison (visual collection), 152–53, 152
corporations: archives of employees' stories, 56; autobiographical stories used by, 18; community-building used by, 11. *See also* marketing
Couser, G. Thomas, 166n18, 171n1
Covid-19 pandemic, 149–54; *Covid Diaries NYC* (film), 150; global memory of, 193n1; lived experience of, 74; mood survey in, 151–52; negative side of sharing

stories in, 153; Pandemic Journaling Project, 150; sharing of story archives, 193–94n4; sharing stories of isolation in, 157; story sharing's value in light of, 14
Cowbird (story library), 23, 55–56, 73
Creek Speak (story map), 109–10, 115, 188n47
critical media theorists, 34
critical perspective, 10–12
crowd-mapping, online, 24
crowd psychology, 131
crowdsourcing, 4; benefits of, 37, 145; closing of feedback loop by, 9, 145; community and, 6; of diaries from a single day, 11, 81–86, 89; documentary function of, 24; of eighteenth century, 39, 44–45, 50; of story libraries, 78–79; story sharing encouraged by, 10
Culley, Amy, 53
CureTogether, 192n58

D'Addario, Daniel, 113
daily life: daily reflection rituals and, 82; rhythm of life based on a single day, 82; story sharing in, 9, 165n30. *See also* everyday people/life; one-day diaries
Darwin, Charles, 133
data bias, 125–28; no such thing as "uncooked" data, 143–44
datafication, 8, 36, 139–42, 145, 162
data justice, 125, 142
data mining: collective storytelling as offering distinct alternative to, 142; difficulty of isolating self-knowledge of individual, 137; function creep of, 125–26; of story data, 127–28; techniques used for personal stories, 19
data positivism, 78
data profiling, 126–27
dataveillance, 137, 141
Davis, Jenny, 135
Day in the Life of London, A, photo series, 82
Day, A, project (May 15, 2012), 81–82
Dean, Jodi, *Blog Theory,* 33–34, 155–56, 171n100
Debord, Guy, 155
de Certeau, Michel, 186n20; "Spatial Stories," 118–19
de Groot, Martijn, 138–39, 192n57
Deleuze, Gilles, 184n75

democratizing culture, 27–28, 37, 38; "by us for us approach" and, 127; cartography and, 116; collection of stories and, 52–53; constant negotiation in, 51; of Covid-19 pandemic story sites, 150; delusions and dangers of sharing stories in, 153; reflexive democracy, 155
Den Mira (Soviet Union, September 27, 1935), 81, 85–89, 92–93, 101, 182n31, 182n33
Derrida, Jacques, 7, 174n71, 184n75
development agencies, use of personal stories by, 3
Devisch, Ignaas, 165n27
Diana (British princess), wedding day to Prince Charles, 69
diaries, 17, 81–102; of Covid-19 pandemic, 150–51; evolution of genre of, 132; Florentine account books as diaries in fourteenth century, 132; Japanese diaries of eighth century, 132; *Our History of the 20th Century: As Told in Diaries, Journals and Letters* (MOA, Britain), 70–71; self-optimization's history and, 42. *See also* one-day diaries
digital divide's effect on one-day diaries, 99
digital humanities, 7, 20, 128, 143, 190n9
digital positivism, 79
D'Ignazio, Catherine, *Data Feminism* (with Klein), 142
Dilthey, Wilhelm, 58
Dinkins, Stephanie: *Not the Only One (N'TOO),* 160–62, *161;* Secret Garden, 196n57
disability studies, 17
diversity: heightened sense of, from one-day diaries, 84, 98–99; *Stories of Our City* (story map) showing common humanity, 105
domestic abuse. *See* sexual violence and misconduct
double voicing, 23, 166n18

Eakin, Paul John, *How Our Lives Become Stories,* 16
economic decisions based on storytelling, 154
Edward VIII (British king), 69
Egan, Susanna, *Mirror Talk,* 16
Eggers, Dave, *The Circle,* 141
ego media, 17

eighteenth-century story collections, 38–54; Enlightenment building of, 38–43; Habermas on public sphere and formation of public opinion, 51; Herder and, 45–50, 51; Moritz and, 39–45, 51; political expression and spectacle of public forum, 50–54; time periods chosen for study, 8–9, 165n29. *See also* Herder, Johann Gottfried; Moritz, Karl Philipp

Einstein, Albert, 73–74, 91, 100, 182–83n45, 183–84n65

Eisenstein, Sergei, 94

Ellis Island Oral History Collection, 56

empathy, 73–78, 112

Empathy Museum, 179n80

empowerment, 28, 72–73, 74

England. *See* Britain

Enlightenment, 38–43; ethos of progress in, 41–42; Herder and, 47; historical perspective of, 8, 38–39; passive notion of space in, 115; self-observation as imperative of, 41

environmentalists' use of story maps, 104

Esposito, Roberto, 195n42

essentialism, 11, 34

ethicists: on datafication of human life, 140; on inequalities resulting from data mining, 125–26

ethnic studies, 17

European Research Group on Military and Society, 144

everyday people/life: Covid-19 pandemic diaries of, 151; Cowbird stories of, 73; *Den Mira* day-in-life diary of, 85; in Nazi Germany, memoir contest aimed to investigate, 60–67; social history and, 71; *Stories of Our City* collecting real stories of, 105; StoryCorps stories of, 13. *See also* daily life; Mass Observation Archive; memoir contests; one-day diaries

exclusion, 7, 12; challenges to justification for, 145–46; narratives' ability to normalize, 35–36

experience: collections of autobiographies with variety of human experience, 39, 54; contemporary story libraries and, 73; experiential knowledge of story maps, 109; meaning of "experience" vs. "lived experience," 73–75; no such thing as "pure" experiences, 77; Wells's generalizing from his autobiography to general experience, 134

Experience Project (story-sharing platform, 2007–16), 73, 178n72

Fabian, Johannes, 90

Facebook: collective intimacy and, 31; Community Voices (renamed from Facebook Stories), 30–31, 169n87, 194n16; ghostwriting on, 20, 159–60; lack of positive collective purposes on, 29; #metoo posts, 1–2; mission statement, 169n81; sellable data as result of connectivity on, 33; shift from "town square" to "living room," 170–71n99; Storylane's acquisition by, 18–19; story sharing on, 2, 28–30; Timeline, 20, 159. *See also* Zuckerberg, Mark

Fang Fang's diary of Covid-19 lockdown in China, 153

fantasy of comprehensiveness, 78–79, 115

Farah, Abdi, 26

Fay, Sidney Bradshaw, 62–67. *See also* Allport, Gordon Willard, et al.

Fedorova, Maria, 150, 194n7

feedback mechanism, 9, 136, 146

feminism, 16, 186n22

Fernandes, Sujatha, *Curated Stories: Uses and Misuses of Storytelling*, 32

Fink, Eugen, 97–98, 184n65

Finnish Literature Society, 60

First Congress of Soviet Writers (1935), 85

Fitzgerald, F. Scott, *My Lost City*, 106

Flickr, 120

Florentine account books as early diaries, 132

Forbes magazine on collective intimacy vs. personalization, 23

Ford, Sam, 35

Foucault, Michel, 43–45, 141, 186n21

Foursquare, 121

Franklin, Benjamin, *Autobiography*, 38, 42, 132–33, 173n50, 191n31

French Revolution, 38, 49–51

Freund, Alexander, 32

Fusco, Coco, 113

futurists on libraries of the future, 75

Gailus, Andreas, 44

Gaiman, Neil, *American Gods*, 126, 190n3

genealogical industry's preservation of memories of "personal historians," 57
geographic information system (GIS) mapping, 114
geopolitics, 90
George VI (British king), 88
geospatial analysis, 121
geotagging, 103–4, 119
Germany: compared to life-writing tradition of France or Britain, 48–49, 173n57; cultural relativism in, 47; in eighteenth century, 38; fragmentation and underdevelopment in late eighteenth century in, 47; Herder on national unity of, 48. *See also* Nazi Germany
Gheller, Jonathan, 18–19
GhostWriter (machine-human collaborative program), 159–60
ghostwriting, 17; Facebook or Twitter posts as ghosted memoirs, 20, 159–60
Gide, André, 15, 182n31
GIS (geographic information system) mapping, 114
Gitelman, Lisa, 21; *"Raw Data" Is an Oxymoron*, 143
Global North, bias toward, 9, 101, 106, 153–54
God's role in "sharing out" time, 90
Google Earth, 122
Google Maps, 109
Gorky, Maxim, 85–87, 89, 181n30. See also *Den Mira*
Gould, Joe (Professor Seagull), 106, 110, 185n11
Green, Joshua, 35
Green, Matt, hand-drawn story map of Manhattan, *108*
Greenhouse, Carol, 90, 97, 102
Griggs, E. H., *Great Autobiographies: Types and Problems of Manhood and Womanhood*, 131

Habermas, Jürgen, 45, 51–52, 174n76
Habitat Map, 109
Haitian storytelling ("crick-crack"), 4
Hallberg, Peter, 48
Hamill, Pete, *Downtown: My Manhattan*, 106
Haraway, Donna, 44
Harris, Jonathan, 55, 56

Harrisson, Tom, 69–70
Hartshorne, Edward Yarnall, 62–67. *See also* Allport, Gordon Willard, et al.
Harvard University's memoir contest, 62–64
Hayles, Katherine, 36
health technology industry, 138, 192n58
Herder, Johann Gottfried, 39–40, 45–50; on autobiographies' role, 45–46, 48, 55, 172n33, 173n50; background of, 45; choice as case study, 39; on collective individuality, 47–48, 173n46; on democratic potential of collections of autobiographies, 46, 173n49; Franklin and, 173n50; on German nationalism and unity, 48–49, 151, 173n59; on Germany's undeveloped life-writing tradition, 173n57; limits on collections due to era of, 54; on nation-state as environment of storytellers, 52; reluctance to deduce individual from the general, 47; on scope of history, 47
heterogenous non-simultaneity, 101
Hill, Amy, 27
Hitler and Nazism in Germany. *See* Nazi Germany
homogenous simultaneity, 95–96, 100
Humanity House (The Hague), 75
Human Library (story library), 75–78
Humans of New York (HONY, story map), 2, 110–13, 115–17, 186–87n28, 188n40
Humphreys, Lee, 191n48
Hungarian Revolution (1956), Memory Project, 56
Husserl, Edmund, 74
Huxley, T. H., 133
hybrid approach. *See* mixed methods research

Iaconesi, Salvatore, "Algorithmic Autobiography: The Uncertain Boundaries of the 'I' and the 'Self' in the Age of Hyperconnectivity" (with Persico), 159, 196n48
identity: autobiographical authors and, 15–16; new media of the self and, 21; personal identity, 170n91; relationality and, 16–17; relationship between time and social identity, 90, 182n40; rise of identity politics, 15; surrogate relationship with community, 164n18

ideographic approach (research paradigm), 58, 65
Igo, Sarah E., *The Averaged American*, 146, 193n77
imagination, 51, 52; political imagination, 154; spatial imagination, 109, 122
immediacy of the present, 98
immigration: Archive of Immigrant Voices, 178–79n73; effect of categorizing immigrants into separate groups, 145; Ellis Island Oral History Collection, 56; empowerment of immigrant women on The Moth, 74; Humanity House (The Hague), virtual meeting with refugees at, 75; Jewish migrants entering memoir contests, 64, 67–68; Migration Trail (interactive site), 105; 1947 Partition Archive, 104; personal stories of first Polish immigrants to US (*The Polish Peasant in Europe and America*), 59, 176n23; Polish immigrants to US, 59
inclusivity: challenges to justification for, 145; of Covid-19 pandemic story sites, 150; fantasy of comprehensiveness of story libraries, 78–79, 153; narratives' ability to normalize, 36; neutral repository of knowledge and, 80; statistical databases, limitations of, 147; statistics, need to count everyone in, 142; of story mapping, 112; unified public as fantasy and, 51; of YIVO memoir contest, 68–69
individualism vs. communitarianism, 6, 10, 28
individualizing vs. generalizing approaches, 58
infographics, 128
Instagram: autobiographical self-expression on, 17; Instagram Stories, popularity of, 19; story map (Invisible Cities) showing emergence of, 120; story sharing on, 2, 30
instant sharing, 101
internet: participatory culture of, 155; personal stories disseminated via, 18; rise of, 8; storytelling startups on, 18. *See also* social media
Internet of Things (IoT), 140, 160
intimacy as cultural imaginary and as political force, 22
intimate publics, 22, 167n44. *See also* collective intimacy
Invisible Cities (Australia), 189n65

Invisible Cities (story map), 120–21, *120–21*
Irth (mobile app for maternal care stories), 127, 139, 142, 190n6
Isay, David, 13
#IStayHome, 150

Jacobs, Harriet, 175n77
Jang, Lucia, 26
Japanese diaries of eighth century, role of, 132
Jenkins, Henry, 35
Jennings, Humphrey, 69, 181n19
Jewish migrants entering memoir contests, 64, 67–68
Jonas, Steven, 192n53
journaling, 132, 136, 150
Journal of Personality, 64
Justice Project (StoryCorps), 13

Kant, Immanuel, 52
Kaplan, Danny, 170n88
Kazin, Alfred, *A Walker in the City*, 106
Kenya, post-election violence in (2007), 24
Khrushchev, Nikita, 182n33
Kinsey Reports, 146
Kitchin, Rob, 119
Klein, Lauren F., *Data Feminism* (with D'Ignazio), 142
Kleinreesink, Esmeralda: *On Military Memoirs: A Quantitative Comparison of International Afghanistan War Autobiographies, 2001–2010*, 143–44, 193n75
knowledge production, 11; circular, 24–25, 145–46; collections of autobiographies with variety of human experience, 39, 54; in collective intimacy, 24–25; criticism of story sharing as, 32; eighteenth-century effort to collect, classify, and publish all human knowledge, 39; eighteenth-century writings on people as "describable, analysable objects," 43; emotional knowledge, 74; experiential knowledge of story maps, 109; memoir contests and, 59; participatory aspects of, 25; "self-knowledge through numbers," 136; situatedness in, 44; story libraries and, 57, 73, 78–79; transformative potential of, 71
Köhnen, Ralph, 42
Koltsov, Mikhail, 85
Kunze, Martin, 56

INDEX / 223

Lampert, Jay, 184n75
Latin American tradition of testimonio, 165n29
Latour, Bruno, 38, 50–51
Le Bon, Gustave, *The Crowd: A Study of the Popular Mind (Psychologie des Foules)*, 131
Lebow, Katherine, 59–60
Lefebvre, Henri, 113–14, 122, 186n21, 188n44
libraries of human experience, 55–80; contemporary story libraries, 72–75; Cowbird's history, 55–56; critique of human libraries, 75–80; empathy and, 73–78; fantasy of comprehensiveness and, 78–79; first story libraries, 59; Human Library (story library), 75–78; narratives' ability to mediate experience, loss of, 76–77; Nazi Germany, collecting firsthand knowledge about, 60–67; oral history and memoir contests, 58–60; YIVO and MOA, 67–72, 177n49. *See also* memoir contests; Nazi Germany
life-casting, 101–2
Life in a Day (YouTube documentary, 2010), 83–84, 93–97, 183n59; 2020 sequel, 180n7; asynchronous music used in, 94; community-building effect of, 83; connectedness of humanity depicted in, 99; as "field of experimentation," 101; online archive, 183n61; repetitive actions aligned and underscoring shared nature, 97; simultaneously occurring events as fantasy in, 93–95; starting with image of moon, 96; virtual stops of artificial simultaneities in, 96
life writing, use of terminology for, 163n9. *See also* autobiographies and memoirs
"lived experience": in context of story archives, 73; dogmatism of, 77, 79; Human Library and, 76; of marginalized communities, 74; meaning of "experience" vs., 73–75; readers transformed by encounter with, 74
live story-sharing events, 2, 4
Louis IX (French king), 174n63
Louis XVI (French king), 49–51
Love, Rose, 26
Love This Place! (story map), 107–9
Lynch, Kevin, 185n13

Macdonald, Kevin, 83–84, 94, 99, 183n49, 184n68

machine learning, 136, 145, 159. *See also* artificial intelligence technologies
Macron, Emmanuel, 174n65
Madge, Charles, 69, 178n62
Maier, Christopher, 1
Manovich, Lev, 36
Manuel, Frank E., 47
Mao Dun, 87, 93, 181n30, 182n35
mapping and cartography, 103–5, 114, 115–16; "always-of-the-moment" maps, 119; citizen cartography, 116; literary cartographers and intertextuality, 122–24; modern maps as static, 118; open-source mapping, 116; original purpose to show itineraries of travel, 118; participatory mapping, 123–24; queer theory and cartographic representation, 188n46; transformation due to technological development, 119. *See also* story mapping
Mapping for Rights (website), 123–24
Mapping Sexual Violence, 104
Map Your City (commercial story mapping), 121–22
Map Your Memories (story map), 107, 109–10, 185n15
marginalized communities: autobiographical stories and, 15, 18; Human Library's representation of, 77–78; lived experience of, 74; in story mapping, 111–12
marketing: collective intimacy and, 22–23, 33–34, 38, 113; target marketing based on story maps, 116–17, 121–22
Marxism, 100–101, 184n72, 185n18
mashing technology, 82
Massey, Doreen, 189n68
Mass Observation Archive (MOA, Britain), 69–71, 178n62; on abdication of Edward VIII (British king), 69–71; choice of term "observers" and "observation," 70; compared to memoir contests about Nazi Germany, 70; *Mass Observation—Meet Yourself at the Doctor's*, 70; *Mass Observation—Meet Yourself on Sunday*, 70; *May the Twelfth*, 88; mirror-like function of publications, 71; *Our History of the 20th Century: As Told in Diaries, Journals and Letters*, 70–71; publication of materials to distribute to British people, 70–71; on wedding of Prince Charles and Princess Diana, 69–71; World War II role of (home front espionage), 70

mass science based on public observations, 88
May the Twelfth anthology (one-day diary of May 12, 1937 in Britain), 88, 181n30
McBride, Keally D., 154
McFarland, Michael, 126
McNeill, Laurie, 164n10
"me decades," 5
Memoir (magazine), memoir contest for #MeToo essays, 72–73
memoir contests, 4, 57, 59–67, 176n22; Abel's Nazi Germany contest, 61–62, 177n45; Allport et al.'s Nazi Germany contest, 62–67, 176n33, 176n36, 176n40; anonymity of entrants, 63, 72, 177n44; biograms (autobiographical sketches) in, 62, 177n45; contemporary contests, 72–73, 178n67; documentary evidence and, 66; lack of distribution to contributing community of contestants, 67; *Memoir* (magazine), #MeToo essay contest, 72–73; mixed (hybrid) methods research used in, 65–67, 69–70, 178n62; Polish method, 59–61, 68, 178n69; positive ethos of, 66; qualitative analysis used in, 65; quantitative analysis used in, 65, 79; scholarly nature of research, 67; scientific value of individual life stories in, 66, 68; uneducated respondents in, 65; in US, 61; YIVO contest for Jewish immigrants, 68–69
memoirs. *See* autobiographies and memoirs
memories and memory: collective memory and "with-ness," 157–58; genealogical industry's preservation of memories of "personal historians," 57; mediated memories of algorithmic autobiography, 159–60; story mapping of collective memory of a city, 120; story mapping's recovery of repressed and forgotten memories of the city, 111–12
Memory of Mankind (time capsule), 56
Memory Project (Hungarian Revolution of 1956), 56
Menchú, Rigoberta, 15
mental health: benefits of story sharing for, 14; lived experience storytelling of platforms for, 74
mental mapping, 106–11, 114, 185n13
Me Too movement: collective power of assembled personal stories, 4, 139; gender categories in, 145; memoir contest for #MeToo essays, 72–73; #metoo hashtag, 1–2, 4, 9, 163n3
Michelet, Jules, 179n84
Middle Ages, anthologies and annals of, 129, 191n30
Middletown Studies, 146
migrants. *See* immigration
Migration Trail (interactive site with maps and storytelling), 105
Milano, Alyssa, 1–2
Mile in My Shoes, A (traveling exhibit), 74–75
Milgram, Stanley, 106–7, 116
military service: European Research Group on Military and Society, 144; Kleinreesink's study of Afghanistan War autobiographies, 143–44, 193n75; Military Voices (StoryCorps), 13
Mill, John Stuart, 133
Miller, Nancy, *Getting Personal*, 16
Miranda, Joseph, *Against the Romance of Community*, 10–11
mirror metaphors, 40–45, 50, 55, 67, 71
mixed (hybrid) methods research, 65–67, 69–70, 143, 178n62
MOA. *See* Mass Observation Archive
modern society, rise of, 39
montage, definition and use of, 93–95
Montaigne, Michel de, *Essays*, 15
Moritz, Karl Philipp, 39–45; *Anton Reiser*, 40; background of, 40; choice as case study, 39; collected reports of pathological behaviors published by, 40–41; common mirror for humankind, creation of, 40–45, 50, 55, 67; crowdsourcing and, 44–45, 50; Foucault and, 44–45; *Gnothi Sauton; oder, Magazin zur Erfahrungsseelenkunde*, 40–45, 171–72n4; limits of journal circulation due to era of, 54; nation-state as environment of storytellers for, 52; proposal of library containing personal stories as scientific knowledge, 55; reading public as contributors to journal, 45; self-observations published without moralizing or systematizing, 43–44, 172n24; sense of unity created by, 151; on situated knowledges, 44
Mosco, Vincent, 79
Moth, The (story-sharing platform), 2, 26–27, 74, 168n64

Mullen, Thomas, 149–50
Müller, Johann Georg (ed.), *Memoirs of Remarkable Men*, 46
MySpace, 1, 9

Nafus, Dawn, 125, 138
Nakamura, Lisa, 77–78
Nancy, Jean-Luc, 7, 10–11, 156–58, 195n39
narcissism, 3, 134, 136
Narrative Nation (health equity advocates using multi-media), 126–27
narratives: ability to mediate experience, 76–77; open-ended nature of, 146; relationship with judgment, 35; relationship with spatiality, 186n22; symbiotic relationship with databases, 36; "tour" narrative to describe space, 118–19; transgressive potential of, 118–19. *See also* self-narratives
nation-state: Anderson's use of simultaneity across time for, 91–92; Bhabha's criticism of Anderson's interpretation, 100; as environment of Moritz's storytellers, 52
Native American autobiographies, 17
Nazi Germany, collecting firsthand knowledge about, 60–67; Abel's memoir contest (Columbia University), 61–62, 176n26, 176n29, 176n36, 177nn43–44; Allport et al.'s memoir contest (Harvard University), 62–67, 176n33, 176n36, 176n40. *See also* memoir contests
Neff, Gina, 125
neologisms created for storifying and job classifications of story tellers, 2
network autobiography's shortcomings, 31
network sociality, 21–22, 170n96
neutrality: of data, false assumptions about, 127, 142; of memoir contests of twentieth century, 66; not applicable to time, 90; problematic nature of, 37, 80; rejected by contemporary story libraries, 73; of space, 186n21, 189n68; story maps' presumption of, 115
"New Communalists" of 1960s Bay Area counterculture, 33
newspapers, simultaneous morning reading as shared ritual, 92
New York City, 109–18; choice as case study, 106; City of Memory (story map), 110, 111, 187n32; collections of autobiographical stories on, 106; Community Oral History Project, 112, 117; Humans of New York (HONY, story map), 2, 110–13, 115–17, 186–87n28, 188n40; LinkNYC kiosks, 186n25; Map Your Memories (story map), 107, *108*, 109–10, 185n15; memoirs of, 106; Milgram's experiment in asking New Yorkers to draw neighborhood sketches, 106–7; Newtown Creek in project Creek Speak, 109–10, 115, 188n47; as one of most mapped cities in the world, 105; Voices of NYC (audio program), 187n35
New York Public Library (NYPL): Community Oral History Project, 112, 117, 187n36; Voices of NYC (audio program), 187n35
New York Times: on one-day global diaries, 81, 99; publishing of "typical New York" stories by New Yorkers, 185n10
Nietzsche, Friedrich, 140–41, 192n63
9/11 terrorist attacks (September 11, 2001): September 11 Digital Archive, 56; September 11th Initiative (StoryCorps), 13
1947 Partition Archive, 104
nomothetic approach (research paradigm), 58, 65
nonprofit sector's use of personal stories, 2, 18–19
Northup, Solomon, 175n77
Norway, memoir contests in, 60
Nussbaum, Felicity, 16, 53

Occupy movements, 4
one-day diaries: in 1930s, 8, 84–89, 92, 101; analogy to simultaneous morning reading of newspapers as shared ritual, 92; based on synchronization, 92; *Britain in a Day* (November 12, 2011), 81; community-building and, 99; competing temporalities of, 100; crowdsourcing of, 11, 81–83, 99; *A Day in the Life of London* photo series, 82; A Day project (May 15, 2012), 81–82; *Den Mira* (Soviet Union, September 27, 1935), 85–89, 92–93, 101, 182n31, 182n33; digital divide's effect on, 99; diversity, heightened sense of, 84, 98–99; one day in the life of us, 81–83; one day in the world (1935), 84–86; One Day on Earth project (October 10, 2010, November 11, 2011, and December 12, 2012), 81; personal investment of

one-day diaries (*continued*)
participants, 95; personal ownership of time by participants, 96; purposeful choice of random day for, 85–86, 88–89, 92, 96, 182n35; ritualization of simultaneity in, 91–92; as spectacles of togetherness, 82, 151–53; time in the making, 99–102; "true representation" and, 99; in twenty-first century, 8, 82–84, 93; *24 Hours in the Life of Los Angeles* (photo series), 82; universal Here and Now presumed by, 98, 184n65. *See also* China; *Life in a Day* (YouTube documentary); simultaneity

open-source mapping, 116

oral history, 4, 58–60, 175n15; 1930s projects of, 59; of cities, 105; defined, 58; devaluation of, 175n15; maps enhanced by, 103, 104, 110; methods used in, 59

ordinary people. *See* everyday people

Orlando, Monica, 166n18

"other," the, 17, 90

pandemic. *See* Covid-19 pandemic; Spanish flu (1918)

Pandemic Journaling Project, 150

parallel editing, 93–94, 183n55

parallel time flows, 95–97

participatory culture of internet and social media, 155

participatory democracy, 4, 5, 24, 27–28

participatory mapping, 123–24

participatory narrative inquiry (PNI), 25, 167n54

participatory research, 25

peg communities, 32, 170n90

Persico, Oriana, "Algorithmic Autobiography: The Uncertain Boundaries of the 'I' and the 'Self' in the Age of Hyperconnectivity" (with Iaconesi), 159, 196n48

Personal Informatics (website), 135

personalized communities: as alternative to binary of individualism vs. communitarianism, 6, 28; creation of, 5; distinguished from individualized society, 5; enabling personal as means to communal, 28

personal stories: advantages of, 142–47; as big data, 19; collective aspects of, 6; of Covid-19 pandemic, 149–51; definition of, 2; emotional appeal of, 19–20; rapid growth of platforms for, 18; statistics becoming people through, 126; terminology for, 163n9. *See also* autobiographies and memoirs; Covid-19 pandemic; memoir contests; story mapping; *specific platforms and programs*

Personal Story (website), 57

Pinero, Miguel, 187n32

#places (photo sharing on social media), 185n18

platform capitalism, 53

Plutarch, *Parallel Lives*, 128–29

PNI (participatory narrative inquiry), 25, 167n54

Poland: immigration to US, 59; memoir contests, 59, 177n49

Poletti, Anna, *Stories of the Self*, 21, 167n45

political engagement of storytelling, 1–2, 4; aggregation of witnesses' voices and, 24; collective intimacy and, 28; collective speech acts' role in political imagination, 51, 52; community and, 6, 50; distortion as result of, 32; Enlightenment and, 8, 38–43; Herder's interest in, 39; Louis XVI seeking *cahiers de doléances* (notebooks of complaints), 49–51. *See also* activism; democratizing culture

positive ethos, 4, 29, 58, 66, 75, 78; digital positivism, 79

Priestnall, Gary, 123, 189n69

print culture: of eighteenth century, 174n75; emergence of, 51–52; isolation and connection at same time in, 174n75; Moritz and Herder's shared view on public exchange allowed via, 52. *See also* books

Prisoner, The (television series), 126

privacy, 35, 106, 126, 128, 137, 161

profiling, 126–27

prosopography, 129, 190n9

psychology and psychiatry: crowd psychology, 131; Moritz's *Gnothi Sauton's* contribution to, 40–41, 45; Moritz's goal to create censor-free space on, 44; professionalization linked to Enlightenment values of classification, 43

"public," change in meaning of, 51

public intimacy, 22, 170n88

public opinion, 51, 174n63, 174n75

Qualified Self, 134–41; privacy issues, 137; self-management for person's best interest, 141
Qualified Us, 138–41
qualitative analysis, 65, 74
Quantified Other, 138–39, *139*, 143, 192n57
Quantified Self (apps and websites), 134–41, *139*, 191n46; criticism of, 143; meaning of, 192n57; motto of "self-knowledge through numbers," 136; privacy issues, 137; self-management for person's best interest, 141
Quantified Us, 138–41, *139*, 151, 192n57
quantitative analysis, 65, 79, 128
#QuarantineLife, 150
queer theory and cartographic representation, 188n46
Quetelet, Adolphe, 129–30, 133

Ranke, Leopold von, 66
"raw data" fallacy, 143–44, 162
readers/audiences: autonomy of, 52; equal concern for experience of, 76; tracing steps of book characters in real world, 103; transformed by encounter with lived experiences of storytellers, 74
reading: distant reading vs. close reading, 7–8; representative reading of autobiographies, 15–16; solitary reading of books, 9
realist illusion of space, 113–15
reciprocity, 3, 9, 14, 109
recognizability, 116–17, 185n13
reflexive communication, 155
relationality, 6; in autobiographies, 16–17; digital networks and, 19–21; relative simultaneity, 95, 100; representational vs. relational views of data, 180n99
renegotiating borders of inclusion and exclusion, 7, 12
representativeness: autobiographies and, 15–16; representational vs. relational views of data, 180n99; statistical, 133
Rettberg, Jill Walker, 132
ritualization shown in assembled stories, 36–37, 82, 91–92, 151
Rodchenko, Alexander, *A Day in the Life of the World* (photo series), 82
Romanticism, 10, 15
Rousseau, Jean-Jacques, 15, 41, 195n33; *Confessions*, 38
Rukeyser, Muriel, ix

Samb, Abdou Karim, 117
Scandinavia, memoir contests in, 60
Schmidt, Christian Marc, 120–21, *120–21*
Schubart, Friedrich Daniel, 46
Scribe (journaling app), 136
Seals Allers, Kimberly, 126–27
Seattle Times, Her Story: Our Story (story library), 78
selfie maps, 4
selfies, 17
self-narratives: Enlightenment's publications of self-observation, 41; episodic, 2. *See also* autobiographies and memoirs; personal stories
self-optimization and societal optimization of Enlightenment, 41–42
self-quantification, 134–36; distinguishing between four different modes of, 138, *139*, 192n57. *See also* Citizen Science; Quantified Other; Quantified Self; Quantified Us
self-reflection: AI-assisted practices of, 136, 160–62; collective, 138; narrative required for, 90; purpose of, 71; social media and, 31, 155; spectacle of autobiographical stories and, 155; statistical data from, 129, 132; story mapping and, 121
self-tracking trends, 134–39, 141, 147, 191n45, 192n53
Sennett, Richard, 170n90
SenseMaker, 169n87
sense of belonging: to anonymous community, 92; autobiographies' spatial turn and, 109; collective intimacy and, 23, 24–28, 38, 73; collective story sharing creating, 32, 54; in Covid-19 pandemic, 151; emotional manipulation of connectedness and, 113; Herder creating for German citizens, 45–50; of immigrant Jewish Americans, 68; #metoo tweets and posts as illustration of, 1–2; as politically charged concept, 7, 153; relational knowledge and, 24–28; sharing the same day with our contemporaries and, 82; in statistical categories, 146; story maps creating, 112; story sharing creating, 3–4
sense of unity: autobiographies' role in creating, 48–49, 151; in Covid-19 pandemic, 151, 153; spectacles of public forums and, 50–54; synchronization of acts and, 93; in worldwide "Now," 98

228 / INDEX

September 11 Digital Archive, 56
September 11th Initiative (StoryCorps), 13
September 27th one-day diaries, 85–89, 182n31, 182n33. See also Den Mira; Soviet one-day diaries
Seven Families, Seven Journeys (India, story map), 104
sexual violence and misconduct: benefits of sharing stories by victims, 3, 9; Mapping Sexual Violence, 104; memoir contest related to, 72–73. See also Me Too movement
Seybold, David Christoph (ed.), *Autobiographies of Famous Men*, 46
sharing of stories. See collective sharing of stories; story sharing; *specific social media and projects*
Sherman, Jamie, 138
Shiller, Robert, *Narrative Economics: How Stories Go Viral and Drive Major Economic Events*, 154, 167n56
Short Manual to the Art of Prosopography, A (Verboven, Carlier, and Dumolyn), 129
Silence Speaks (digital storytelling project), 27
Simanowksi, Roberto, *Facebook Society: Losing Ourselves in Sharing Ourselves*, 31, 170n91
simultaneity, 84, 89–99; based on coincidence, 91–95, 100; based on parallel time flows, 95–97; Bergson's view of, 91, 95–96; cinematographic use of parallel editing and montage to create, 93–95; derivation of term, 89, 182n37; described in terms of delay, 184n75; "double time," creation of, 100; Einstein's definition of, 91, 100; as "field of experimentation," 101; heterogenous non-simultaneity, 101; homogenous, 95–96, 100; immediacy of the present, 98; new technologies' potential to create, 101–2; perfect simultaneity, misconstruction of, 101–2; relative simultaneity, 95, 100; social function of, 89–91; totalizing sense of, 97–99; universal simultaneity, concept of, 98; utopian promise of, 100
single-subject research, 160, 192n52
situatedness: in autobiographical writing, 16; in knowledge, 44, 76
slavery: autobiographies of former slaves, 175n77; *Born in Slavery: Slave Narratives from the Federal Writers' Project, 1936–1938* (oral history), 59
small data, 78; false binary with big data, 128, 141; ghostwriting software using, 161
small stories, 2, 20, 51, 166n28
smart city movement, 185n13
Smith, Sidonie, *Reading Autobiography* (with Watson), 17, 21
Smithsonian Folklife Festival, 111
Snapchat, 169n86; My Story, 30; Our Story, 30; Snap Map, 30; story sharing on, 2
social Darwinism, 133
social emotional learning, 74, 76, 78
social engagement of storytelling, 2, 4; bonding, 5, 39, 110, 121, 171n2; Enlightenment and, 8, 38–43; Herder's interest in, 39; social media's use for, 19. See also activism
social history, rise of, 71
socialism, 88–89, 139
social justice, 18, 27, 32, 58, 72, 73, 158–59, 178n69
social media: activists' use of, 4; advantages over prior eras' platforms, 9, 165n30; as case study for assembled stories, 8; co-emergence of storytellers with, 21, 31, 158–62; collective intimacy in, 28–31; community and, 6; as crowd-sourced life-writing project, 20; evolution of, 3; participatory culture of, 155; performative aspect of stories on, 2–3; self-reflection and, 31; small stories as suited to, 20; story map (Invisible Cities) showing emergence of, 120–21; story products on, 19; story sharing's popularity on, 2, 9, 14, 19. See also *specific platforms*
social media companies, 32–33, 151
social network analysis (SNA), 19
social reality, 46, 65–66, 162, 186n21
social unrest, examples from eras of, 8
Society for Utopian Studies, 134
Socrates, 41
soft power, 141
soft resistance, 138
Soja, Edward, 114, 186n21
solidarity, 27, 49, 72, 101, 112, 145, 151
Solnit, Rebecca, 111; *Nonstop Metropolis: A New York City Atlas*, 187n33
Soviet one-day diaries: 1935, 84–89; as "field of experimentation," 101; September 27, 1960, 88. See also Den Mira

INDEX / 229

Soyer, Daniel, 68
space. *See* time and space
Spanish flu (1918), compared with Covid-19 pandemic, 149–51
spatial turn, 109, 186n21
spectacles of togetherness: Ancient Greek and Roman archetypes, 156–57; dangers of entrapment in, 155–57; one-day diaries and, 82, 151–53; of public forums, 50–54, 156; in Rousseau, 195n33
Spencer, Herbert, 133
Stack, Claudia, 74
Stanton, Brandon, 110–11, 115–17, 187n28
statistics, 125–47; advantages of complicity of story data with, 142–47; aggregation in, 125, 130; autobiographical storytelling and, 126, 128, 129; average man as statistical concept, 133; complementary to personal stories, 128; data bias, 125–28, 143–44; data-driven storytelling and, 128; double face of aggregation, 140–42, 153; false opposition with stories, 127, 142; historical examples of early memoirists, 128–32; historical examples of memoirists quantifying and generalizing their own experience, 132–34; inclusion/exclusion of social statistics, 146; inclusion of counting everyone, 142; infographics and, 128; nineteenth-century rise of, 129, 133; original purpose of, 126; prosopography, 129, 190n9; Qualified Self and, 135–40; Quantified Self and, 134–40; "raw data" fallacy, 143–44, 162; representativeness of, 133; totality of statistical categories, 53
Steller Stories (story-sharing platform), 18, 166n21
stereotypes: contemporary story libraries challenging, 77; story maps reinforcing, 117
Stories of Our City (story map), 105
storification of culture, 2–4, 30–31
Storify (story-sharing platform), 18, 166n23
StoryCenter (Berkeley, California), 25
story collections, 4. *See also* aggregation; collections of autobiographical stories; eighteenth-century story collections; libraries of human experience; memoir contests; one-day diaries; story mapping
StoryCorps: archives of, 13, 24, 55, 175n3; autobiographies from conversation between two people as model for, 17; criticism of, 32; depoliticizing public discourse by normalizing all Americans, 32; feature of "StoryCorps communities," 27, 168n70; founding of, 13; lived experience interviews on, 74; mission of, 3, 23–24, 55; story sharing on, 2, 13, 175n3; success of, 14, 165n2
Storylane (story-sharing platform), 18–19, 23
story libraries. *See* libraries of human experience
story mapping, 4, 103–24; alternative epistemologies of, 111–12, 113; authoritarian implications of, 116; body mapping, 189n67; cartographic conventions used by, 114; collective maps, rise of, 104–5; criticism of, 113–16; documentary function of, 115; environmentalists' use of, 104; fantasy of completeness and, 115; future of, 119, 123–24; Matt Green, hand-drawn story map of Manhattan, *108*; increased interest in and uses of, 104–5; intertexuality of, 122–23; life-mapping, 189n67; maintaining tension of conflicting epistemologies, 122–24; Map Your City (commercial venture), 121–22; marginalized places and voices included in, 111–12; mediation between map usage and communal sense-making, 123; mental mapping as basis of, 106–11; new generation of dynamic story maps, 120–21; New York traditions, 105–6; participatory mapping, 123–24; proximity of geographers and storytellers in, 122; recovery of repressed and forgotten memories of the city, 111–12; segregated stories created by recognizability, 116–17; from a single city, 11; solidifying collective bonds via, 121; technological developments enhancing, 119; transgressive stories and maps, 118–22. *See also* New York City
story sharing: distinguished from storytelling, 14; mental health benefits of, 14; negatives of data-centric inquiry and, 79, 153; potential of, 34, 145; power of stories to connect people, 72; reciprocal nature of, 3, 9, 14; as staging of co-appearance, 158. *See also* collective sharing of stories
storytelling apps, 18–19

storytelling/storytellers: author's father as, ix; benefits of, 3, 167–68n57; distrust of, ix; economic decisions based on, 154; political theory as, 171n14; purpose to get story out, 31; revolution in, 2; shift to story sharing, 14; strangers sharing stories, ix. *See also specific types of stories and delivery mechanisms*
strategic storytelling, 18, 31
subjectivization, 141
Süddeutsche Zeitung (German newspaper), mood survey in, 151–52
surveillance capitalism, 32
survey technologies, 146, 151–52, 193n77
Sweden: A Day project buried in for future historians, 82; memoir contests in, 60
synchronicity, 94, 183n54

Tacitus, 173n42
TechCrunch, 18, 30
Thomas, William I., 59
Thompson, Paul, 175n15
time and space: assembled stories ritualizing, 36–37; dangers of recreating old categories of, 11, 122; "double time," creation of, 100; homogenous time, 95–96, 100; immediacy of the present, 98; intersection of, 103, 104–5; invention of portable mechanical clock, 90, 96; neutrality of space, 186n21, 189n68; new technologies reviving tradition of space as dead and neutral, 189n68; personal and collective ownership of space, 111, 185n14; personal ownership of time by collective diary participants, 96; personal sense of time as more natural than standardized time, 97; personal stories' transgressive potential of urban spaces, 118–19; public time as official time, 91; realist illusion of space, 113–15; reciprocity of space speaking to people and vice versa, 109; relationship between time and social identity, 90, 182n40; shared sense of time and community-building, 82, 84; social production of space, 113–14; space vs. place, 107; temporal lag creating artificial single day for diary of a given day, 93; time as most commonly used English noun, 90; transparency of space as illusion, 113–14. *See also* one-day diaries; simultaneity

time capsules, 56, 92–93, 183n49
togetherness. *See* community; sense of unity; spectacles of togetherness
Tönnies, Ferdinand, 171n2
top-down vs. bottom-up approaches, 34, 36, 122, 140, 145, 154
transformation: assembled stories' ability to transform communities, 11; by encounter with lived experiences of storytellers, 74, 76; knowledge production's transformative potential, 71; transformative storytelling, 18
Transformative Stories, 27–28
transparency, 21, 51–53; of data used in AI-based autobiographical story, 161; of space, 113–14
Tuan, Yi-Fu, *Space and Place: The Perspective of Experience*, 107, 185n18
Tumblr, 113
Turkle, Sherry, 13
24 Hours in the Life of Los Angeles (photo series), 82
Twitter: #Coronamaison, 152–53, *152*; ghostwriting on, 20, 159–60; #metoo stories, 1–2, 4, 9; story map (Invisible Cities) showing emergence of, 120; story sharing on, 2

unity. *See* one-day diaries; sense of unity; spectacles of togetherness
universality and universal knowledge, 53, 77; Cowbird and, 73; idea of universal time, 97; *Life in a Day* recognizing universally shared temporal condition, 84; Moritz and Herder on, 52; universal simultaneity, concept of, 98–99, 102, 183n65
Ushahidi (online crowd-map), 24, 104
US Holocaust Memorial Museum, 178n73

Van Dijck, José, *The Culture of Connectivity*, 32–33, 170n96
Virtual Empathy Museum, 179n80
virtual knowledge communities formed through user-generated content, 25
virtual reality (VR) technologies, 77–78, 101–2
virtual sociality, 21
visual storytelling, 2, 19, 20, 81–82, 104–6. *See also* story mapping
Voices of NYC (audio program), 187n35

Walker, Joe, 83–84, 99, 183n49, 184n68
Watson, Julia, *Reading Autobiography* (with Smith), 17, 21
Web 2.0, 25, 104
Webb, Beatrice, 133
Weinman, Joe, 167n47
Weinstein, Harvey, 1
Wells, H. G., *Experiment in Autobiography: Discoveries and Conclusions of a Very Ordinary Brain (Since 1866)*, 133–34, 139
Western culture, 6–7, 9, 38, 101, 165n29; *Den Mira* to show decay of, 85
West Side Stories (West Oakland, California, story map), 104
White, E. B., 106
Whitrow, Gerard James, 89–90
Whole Earth Catalog, 33, 149
wholeness, 11, 83, 99
"with-nessing," 157–62, 195n39
Wittgenstein, Ludwig, 183n58
Wolf, Christa, 182n31
Wolf, Gary, 137–38, 147
women: collaborative life writing and, 53, 166n18; computer-generated composite of women co-authors, 161, *161*; of eighteenth century, 53; feminist view on women's autobiographies, 16, 186n22; Her Story: Our Story (story library of *Seattle Times*), 78; women's culture as shared intimacy, 22
Wood, Denis, 103
World War II, home front espionage of MOA in Britain, 70
"Write Your Life" (Norwegian memoir contest), 60

Xia, Liangjie, 120–21, *120–21*

Yiddish Scientific Institute (YIVO) memoir contest of Jewish immigrants (1942), 67–72, 177n49; compared to Abel's and Allport et al.'s contests, 68; social therapeutic function of collective story sharing in, 68
YouTube. See *Life in a Day* (documentary, 2010)

Zak, Paul J., 25–26, 167–68n57
Zaretsky, Robert, 50
Znaniecki, Florian, 59–60, 61, 68, 176n23, 176n36
Zuckerberg, Mark, 6, 28–30; "Building Global Community" (open letter), 29–31; mission statement for Facebook by, 169n81; shift from "town square" to "living room," 170–71n99. *See also* Facebook
Zuern, John, 164n10

Cultural Frames, Framing Culture

Robert Higney
Institutional Character: Collectivity, Agency, and the Modernist Novel

Cristina Rodriguez
Walk the Barrio: The Streets of Twenty-First-Century Transnational Latinx Literature

Lauren S. Cardon
Fashioning Character: Style, Performance, and Identity in Contemporary American Literature

Daniel Worden
Neoliberal Nonfictions: The Documentary Aesthetic from Joan Didion to Jay-Z

Len Gutkin
Dandyism: Forming Fiction from Modernism to the Present

Marian Eide
Terrible Beauty: The Violent Aesthetic and Twentieth-Century Literature

Mary Paniccia Carden
Women Writers of the Beat Era: Autobiography and Intertextuality

Josh Toth
Stranger America: A Narrative Ethics of Exclusion

Lauren S. Cardon
Fashion and Fiction: Self-Transformation in Twentieth-Century American Literature

Ann Brigham
American Road Narratives: Reimagining Mobility in Literature and Film

Jinny Huh
The Arresting Eye: Race and the Anxiety of Detection

James J. Donahue
Failed Frontiersmen: White Men and Myth in the Post-Sixties American Historical Romance

Eric Aronoff
Composing Cultures: Modernism, American Literary Studies, and the Problem of Culture

Samuel Chase Coale
Quirks of the Quantum: Postmodernism and Contemporary American Fiction

Stephanie Harzewski
Chick Lit and Postfeminism

Stephanie L. Hawkins
American Iconographic: "National Geographic," Global Culture, and the Visual Imagination

Rachel Hall
Wanted: The Outlaw in American Visual Culture

Jon Robert Adams
Male Armor: The Soldier-Hero in Contemporary American Culture

Debra Walker King
African Americans and the Culture of Pain

Naomi Mandel
Against the Unspeakable: Complicity, the Holocaust, and Slavery in America

Ellen Tremper
I'm No Angel: The Blonde in Fiction and Film

Robin Blaetz
Visions of the Maid: Joan of Arc in American Film and Culture

Margot Norris
Writing War in the Twentieth Century

Raphael Sassower and Louis Cicotello
The Golden Avant-Garde: Idolatry, Commercialism, and Art

Nancy Martha West
Kodak and the Lens of Nostalgia

www.ingramcontent.com/pod-product-compliance
Lightning Source LLC
Chambersburg PA
CBHW031809220426
43662CB00007B/578